D1738371

MASS MEDIA IN 2025

Recent Titles in
Contributions to the Study of Mass Media and Communications

MASS MEDIA IN 2025

Industries, Organizations, People, and Nations

Edited by Erwin K. Thomas
and Brown H. Carpenter

P
96
.F67
M37
2001
West

Contributions to the Study of Mass Media and Communications, Number 62

GREENWOOD PRESS
Westport, Connecticut • London

Library of Congress Cataloging-in-Publication Data

Mass media in 2025 : industries, organizations, people, and nations / edited by
 Erwin K. Thomas and Brown H. Carpenter.
  p.   cm. — (Contributions to the study of mass media and communications, ISSN
  0732–4456 ; no. 62)
  Includes bibliographical references and index.
  ISBN 0–313–31398–9 (alk. paper)
  1. Mass media—Forecasting.   I. Thomas, Erwin Kenneth.   II. Carpenter, Brown H.
 III. Series.
 P96.F67 M37   2001
 302.23′01′12—dc21   2001016055

British Library Cataloguing in Publication Data is available.

Library of Congress Catalog Card Number: 2001016055
ISBN: 0–313–31398–9
ISSN: 0732–4456

First published in 2001

Greenwood Press, 88 Post Road West, Westport, CT 06881
An imprint of Greenwood Publishing Group, Inc.
www.greenwood.com

Printed in the United States of America

The paper used in this book complies with the
Permanent Paper Standard issued by the National
Information Standards Organization (Z39.48–1984).

10   9   8   7   6   5   4   3   2   1

Contents

Acknowledgments

We express our appreciation to the contributors: Paula Briggs, Carolyn M. Byerly, O. Patricia Cambridge, Steven J. Dick, Julie K. Henderson, Curtis R. Holsopple, Robert M. Knight, Michael Lescelius, Michael A. Longinow, Randy E. Miller, Bala A. Musa, Emeka J. Okoli, Leara D. Rhodes, Randall Scott Sumpter, George Thottam, and Edward Turner.

In addition, we are grateful for the support of our wives, Mary Barta Thomas and Linda H. Carpenter. Finally, we thank our acquisitions editor, Pamela St. Clair.

Introduction

Erwin K. Thomas and Brown H. Carpenter

It is difficult to think of human communication without considering technology. The development of the printing press in the late fifteenth century was the first step in the creation of what today is regarded as "mass media." Four hundred years later, the camera, telegraph, and telephone brought printed newspapers up to date, making current events a national, or even a worldwide, experience. At another level, people could use this new technology to record their own histories in photo albums or talk directly to friends and relatives across town or far away by simply asking the phone operator for a connection.

Communicating became even easier in the twentieth century, as technology accelerated. Radio, motion pictures, and television created a national popular culture, some would even say a "global village." The term "media" emerged in the 1920s as advertising jargon. Later, the word encompassed the entire news-gathering apparatus of print and television journalism. Today, "media" often refers to the entire communication field.

If communication development can be compared to a roller coaster, the centuries between the first printing press and the telegraph seem like a long, slow climb. The next 100 years or so are filled with fast-paced loops and dips, spinning around the onslaught of television, transistor radios, compact discs, cell phones, and satellites. By the 1990s, our roller coaster rockets into a mind-boggling, fiber-optic spiral at mega- and giga-speeds. Inventions and trends flash by so rapidly, they defy rational analysis.

Computers. Cyberspace. E-mail. World Wide Web. Internet. These terms sound like a science fiction vocabulary from the 1960s. Even a computer not so long ago was a super calculator inhabiting the Pentagon and college math departments. But today, as the twenty-first century begins, computer technology has surged at such a dizzying pace that one company, the software giant Microsoft, faces a government-enforced split-up into two separate corporations. Another, America Online, is swallowing media goliath Time–Warner, itself a recent amalgamation of media mergers.

In the 1980s, Microsoft and America Online were hardly household trademarks. But those and other innovative high-tech companies, including, perhaps, a few that haven't yet been established, stand poised to dominate the mass media during the twenty-first century's first quarter. In fact, computer technology figures in most of the projections put forth in this book.

Modern journalism made a giant step when the telegraph enabled newspaper reporters to dispatch their stories quickly to their editors. They packed many facts in the opening paragraphs to overcome the frequent breakdowns in the communication systems, a nuisance that hasn't been cured by modern computers. But tomorrow's newspaper reader might scan the headlines electronically on a portable receiving device or receive a more traditional paper through a home printer. The news will be up-to-the-minute fresh—perhaps, on the electronic product, changing as it is being read.

Furthermore, sophisticated tracking satellites could permit the public to view unfolding news events unfiltered. In any case, reporters, armed with tiny laptops, cell phones, and digital cameras, can transmit their stories and photos instantaneously to their supervisors, who work for a media company that supplies both visual and printed versions of the news. Despite all this electronic magic, the news media will remain more dependent than ever on a steady source of electricity. Readers in 2025 may customize their daily papers to reflect their individual reading tastes, favorite sports teams, and stock portfolios.

Magazines, on the other hand, seem destined to become "a refuge from data overload." Technology will allow them to become more glittery; they will use Web sites and television shows as adjuncts (*National Geographic* has long been active in the latter field). But these periodicals seem likely to survive as a hand-held, foldable source of information and entertainment, much as they are today.

The same can be said for books. Books are too ingrained in the human experience to disappear anytime soon. Technology will affect them: Books can already be downloaded from the Internet. Most personal computers are equipped with dictionaries. Many of us purchase books on-line. All true, but the book's familiarity and independence from outside power sources likely ensures its survival.

As for television, what television? That picture-frame-size screen on the wall in 2025 functions as a communication center, containing the TV, stereo, computer, radio, telephone, and security system controls. Television lineups may not be all that innovative over the next twenty-five years. The major technological improvements over the past couple of decades have led to repetitious all-news formats, a saturation of sports, reruns of older shows, and endless "safe," predictable programming. Nothing on the horizon indicates this will change remarkably.

One result may be the disappearance of cable television as it is known today. Cable companies are expanding and merging into telephony, Internet access, and entertainment formats; in other words, all the services offered by that aforementioned communication center. Former telephone companies are already providing competition in this field. Telecommunication satellites, once on the cutting edge of technology, are already losing out to fiber optics, which offers cheaper, faster delivery of communication signals. Satellites will remain the medium of choice for providing distance-insensitive communication to mobile receivers, which could revive the fortunes of radio.

Radio, a medium that refuses to become extinct, should benefit from the clarity of sound produced by digital technology. Low-power FM transmitters might give voice to eclectic musicians and spark more politically charged debates. Satellites could create national and international radio stations, particularly geared to automobiles equipped with adaptors. Webcasting offers a chance for radio to cooperate with the Internet, allowing the downloading of music and other programs.

Music recordings have improved light years over the old 78 rpms that dominated the field until the 1950s. No major technological innovation is on the horizon for improving the quality of sound, but the issue of royalties for performers must be resolved because today's equipment can easily duplicate professional recordings without copyright payment to the producers.

If media delivery experiences a techno-bedazzling future, what about the substance of the delivered information? The end product is not so technically dependent. Business practices, sociological trends, and politics will all play a role.

As the twentieth century closed, political reporting became enveloped in frivolity. Issues were displaced by an obsession with rooting out the minor sins and malapropisms of candidates. Will this continue? Does the public really want "dumbed-down" political journalism? Are reporters, increasingly working in a noncompetitive environment, reluctant to deal with substantial concerns?

Women have made major gains in the media industry, at least in the Western industrialized nations, and feminist issues are regularly featured in newscasts. But the progress will remain threatened by an industry dominated by white males.

Since Gutenberg's printed Bible, the keepers of Western religions have used technology to preserve the faith. Ironically, new inventions have been quite effective at disseminating the word as originally transcribed in ancient, venerable texts, such as the Bible, Torah, and Koran. Christian evangelists, in particular, quickly grasped the power of radio and television. They have likewise embraced the World Wide Web without hesitation. This insight, or inspiration, should continue.

The field of public relations thrives amidst controversy and communication outlets. Points of view need to be aired. The big issue facing this industry is an accreditation process for its practitioners, something that appears headed for resolution within a few years.

Developing nations will be especially challenged by the technological explosion. Many are lagging behind the West. Failure to keep up means the media will continue to reflect the biases of the industrialized world. Also, the gap between rich and poor people could widen as Third World countries are omitted from the information revolution. The developed nations face the task of making the techno-boom fruitful and applicable to all levels of society. In any case, major changes appear to be on the way.

1

Books

Randall Scott Sumpter

Family-owned houses dominated book publishing in the United States in the last decade of the nineteenth century. These ventures published about 5,500 new titles annually, and their stock-in-trade was the hardcover, slightly sensa-tional $1.50 fiction. At the time, one critic warned, "Everything printable is printed. Nothing is so low that it cannot be stooped to; nothing too remote and abstruse to be reached after" (Brooks, 1890, p. 570). A hundred years later, the industry is dominated by conglomerates that annually produce nearly 70,000 titles, many as mass-market paperbacks and others as hardbound vol-umes that cost more than $30 each.

Latter-day critics say this phenomenal growth obscures problems for the book in the future. Some believe that consolidation of the industry, which provided the capital for business growth, and mass marketing of a few vol-umes will contribute to the indirect censorship of books. Troublesome changes in illiteracy and aliteracy rates indicate that fewer people may read books in the twenty-first century. Others fear the evolution of the inexpensive personal computer will mean the end for the traditional ink-on-paper volume.

This chapter briefly reviews the history of the book over the past 100 years and industry and readership trends at the end of the twentieth century. Those trends and the book's history are used as guideposts for evaluating predic-tions about the book's future that are presented in the chapter's final sections.

THE BOOK'S PAST 100 YEARS

Market forces and technology contributed to the rapid evolution of book-making, bookselling, and book buying in the nineteenth century. At the beginning of the century, book publishing was still a cottage industry. Scriptoriums had made the last major change in the book's format several hundred years earlier, when monks began producing book codices rather than book rolls. The pairing of Gutenberg's movable type with the hand-operated, sheet-fed press had marked the last watershed in production technology. At the end of the nineteenth century, family book houses dominated the acquisition of manuscripts and promotion of finished books.

Others handled production tasks, which had become completely mechanized, and book retail sales. These technological and organizational developments that made it possible to mass produce cheap books occurred at a fortuitous time. Other factors had produced a mass audience. Between 1900 and 1910, the U.S. population grew from 76 million to 92 million, and the illiteracy rate declined from about 11 percent to 8 percent for Americans fourteen or older (Snyder, 1993; U.S. Bureau of the Census, 1998). This was a substantial improvement over the 20-percent illiteracy rate estimated for the population in 1870. A strong demand for books, particularly works of fiction, matched this growth in population, decline in illiteracy, and production efficiencies that made $1.50 the standard price for a hardcover volume during the 1900s:

Novels were devoured as much as read, and the public appetite appeared to be insatiable. Advertising budgets reflected this phenomenon: Most houses used about 70 percent of them for fiction. At the peak of this craze, novels . . . enjoyed hardcover sales in the hundreds of thousands for each title. (Tebbel, 1975–1981, p. 170)

Historians have offered several explanations for this demand for fiction, which lasted until World War I. Lehmann-Haupt (1951) speculated readers' tastes indirectly reflected the international copyright agreement of 1891. The copyright accord made it possible for American authors to compete on favorable economic terms with their British counterparts for readers in the United States. This development attracted new talent, which, according to Lehmann-Haupt, attracted new readers. Tebbel (1975–1981) also cited contemporary accounts that Americans read fiction to escape from the chaotic pace of life at the turn of the century and from forces that disrupted the social order.

In 1910, these factors produced a book-publishing record of 13,470 new titles that endured into the 1950s. The 1910 record is an estimate (Tebbel, 1975–1981). Accurate statistics on the book industry are difficult to obtain before the mid-1970s. The U.S. Census of Manufactures and *Publishers Weekly*, which began an annual report on the U.S. industry in 1881, compiled some statistics. These sources often disagreed about the definition of a book, sometimes counting pamphlets, sometimes not, and it is unclear whether they counted duplicate works, new editions, and imports in the new title total. Tebbel's careful evaluation of these two sources in the statistical appendices to his four-volume history of American book publishing is probably the most reliable. He noted that when *Publishers Weekly* adopted an international book classification system in 1911, the new title count for that year dropped to 11,123. This lower total still was a multidecade record.

THE INTERWAR YEARS

Popular fiction could still be purchased for $1.50 per volume in 1918, but the Great War, the Depression, and World War II limited new titles. Between 1915 and 1945, the American book industry published an average of slightly less than 9,000 new titles annually (Tebbel, 1975–1981). Fiction and children's books were the largest annual categories for the thirty-year period, accounting for about 1,502 and 713 new titles, respectively. Science-related works averaged 441 new titles per year. The number of houses publishing five or more volumes each year grew from 150 in 1923 to 274 in 1942. These publishers were concentrated in New York, Chicago, and Boston. Their dollar volume grew by three and a half times between 1914 and 1945; their output was prodigious, climbing from 175.16 million books and pamphlets in 1914 to half a billion volumes in 1945.

Tebbel (1975–1981) believed that four factors supported this strong book market: First was a growing and increasingly literate population. Between 1915 and 1945, the U.S. population grew from 100.5 million to 139.9 million, and the illiteracy rate dropped from between 7.7 percent and 6 percent to less than 3 percent (Snyder, 1993; U.S. Bureau of the Census, 1998). Second, the number of educational institutions and their enrollments increased. Third, urbanization brought book buyers closer to booksellers. Fourth, quota and literacy requirements for immigrants added indirectly to the urban market for books. Reading tastes also slanted more to nonfiction. This benefited publishers, who generally charged higher prices for nonfiction books, which had a longer shelf life than fiction. Other changes added new readers. More newspapers began book-review sections that treated books as news, and more popular books were converted into movies. Book houses added children's departments headed by women editors. Finally, publishers began selling small-format editions, like Pocket Books, that were cheaper than the $3 that hardcover novels began fetching in the 1920s. These inexpensive editions added "a new class of buyers . . . who could afford quarters for books but not necessarily dollars" (Tebbel, 1987, p. 296).

MERGERS AND BABY BOOMERS

The book-publishing industry resumed its strong growth after World War II and now produces nearly 70,000 new titles per year (Perman, 1998). The demographic bulge known as the "baby boom" and legislation like the GI Bill that opened higher-education opportunities to more people also contributed to more and different growth. For example, textbook sales doubled between 1945 and 1958 to $280 million, while the population grew by about 25 percent to 175 million.

In the decade between 1978 and 1988, book sales grew from $5.7 billion to $13.2 billion, and the average hardcover book price rose from $18.95 to $31 (Baker, 1990). Mass-produced audio books, another format, also became popular (Tangorra, 1990; Tebbel, 1987). Short-term forecasts are for more growth beyond the turn of the twentieth century. The predicted volumes of printed material and sales are huge. The Book Industry Study Group (1998) estimated publishers' net dollar sales, excluding revenue from standardized tests, would be $23.56 billion in 2000, compared with an estimated $16.33 billion in 1992. Adult and juvenile trade books, including mass-market paperbacks, would account for 25 percent of the net sales, compared with 28 percent in 1992. Professional books for business, law, medicine, and the sciences would account for 20.8 percent, about 2 percent higher than in 1992. College and public school texts could account for about 14 percent each. The industry study group estimated that publishers sold 2.192 billion books in 1992 and would sell 2.361 billion in 2000. In that year, 827.7 million would be trade or general-interest books; 178.7 million would be professional; 276.6 million would be for public schools, and 184.4 million for colleges and universities.

To finance its continuous growth in the last half of the twentieth century, the publishing industry tapped new capital markets and production efficiencies made possible by computers. The family-owned book houses disappeared as publishers sought new cash through public stock offerings and two distinct waves of mergers, the first among publishers and the second involving conglomerates. Between 1958 and 1970, publishing houses were involved in 307 mergers; however, 224 of these combinations were deals made among publishers (Tebbel, 1975–1981). More recent acquisitions involved companies not previously in the book-publishing business. For instance, twelve major paperback publishers were acquired in the 1970s by larger corporations, only three of which had previously been involved in publishing (Tebbel, 1987). The surviving corporations control huge chunks of the book-publishing industry. Bertelsmann AG's 1998 acquisition of Random House for $1.4 billion is an example of the end result. The combined company is double the size of its nearest competitor, Simon & Schuster, and has a 23-percent share in the $7-billion American trade-book market (Perman, 1998).

Computers and digital technology began penetrating the book-publishing industry in the late 1970s. The advent of inexpensive personal computers and public access to the Internet and affiliated World Wide Web sites in the 1980s and 1990s also changed the way that books are published, promoted, and sold. As early as 1983, two-thirds of the manuscripts received from authors were prepared on word processors, and many of these manuscripts were accompanied by floppy disks (Goodrum & Dalrymple, 1987).

A decade later, articles in trade magazines explained to authors how to use the Internet to publish and to sell cheap digital volumes, known as "e-books," directly to buyers (Haynes, 1994). Several companies, like Softlock Inc. and Floppy-back Publishing, also entered the market for distributing this new book format from their computer network servers. Internet bookstores like Amazon. com also changed how traditional ink-on-paper books were promoted and sold. At the end of the 1990s, one securities firm estimated that 600 on-line booksellers were in business, and book industry executives projected that e-commerce with these stores would account for 10 percent of the $25-billion book market in 2003 (Millot, 1998).

PROBLEMS AND SOLUTIONS

Besides phenomenal growth, three trends dominated what the Library of Congress (1984) called the "Culture of the Book" at the end of the twentieth century: indirect censorship of content caused by publishing-house mergers and the costly promotion and mass marketing of a handful of books, stagnating literacy rates, and the new digital technologies that might doom traditional ink-on-paper book. Experts disagreed on whether the trends represented insurmountable problems or incorporated their own solutions.

Illiteracy, Aliteracy

In the twenty-first century, the future of traditional as well as e-books may be in the hands of a public unwilling or unable to read. Illiteracy rates, gauged on extremely fundamental measures of reading and writing ability, declined from 20 percent in 1870 for Americans fourteen or older to less than 1 percent in 1979 (Snyder, 1993). The level at the end of the nineteenth century was about 11 percent. These percentages, however, do not adequately account for the proportion of society that is functionally illiterate and aliterate, or those who can but do not read.

Book Industry Study Group surveys in 1978 and 1983 found that only half the American public could be called book readers, defined as individuals who had read one or more books in the past six months (Library of Congress, 1984). In the mid-1980s, about 23 million adults were classed as functionally illiterate, and their numbers were growing by about 10 percent per year. Another 44 percent of the population was classified as aliterate. This aliteracy rate was fairly stable ("Reading between the Videos," 1992).

Others evaluating the illiteracy and aliteracy problems are more optimistic about the future. Tests of young adults' prose, document, and quantitative literacy in 1985 and 1992 found that literacy had declined somewhat, perhaps reflecting the influx of immigrants who were learning English as a second language and differences in the rules used in the two surveys for counting nonrespondents (Kirsch, Jungeblut, Jenkins, & Kolstad, 1993). Department of Education researchers did not believe the difference in literacy rates between the 1985 and 1992 surveys warranted concern. Experts contributing to the Library of Congress (1984) study also did not find compelling evidence that competition from television had contributed to aliteracy. They matched predictions from the 1970s that television would signal the demise of the book with current publishing statistics to support their point.

Bessie (1987), for example, reported that book publishers produced 11,000 titles in the United States in 1950, compared with 53,000 in 1983. He concluded that the number of titles produced depended upon many factors, such as the economy, the amount of money available to educational institutions and libraries, the number of publishers, and the impact of technology. The study also hypothesized that book consumers had found more efficient ways to use their leisure time. This leisure time "elasticity" accommodated both television and books (Library of Congress, 1984; Cole, 1987).

Homogenizing Content

Others fear that industry consolidation and the current emphasis on mass marketing a few potential bestsellers are homogenizing the content of books (Moran, 1997; Lorimer, 1993; Bagdikian, 1992). Ownership by large conglomerates causes "contraceptive" self-censorship, "by making certain houses unwilling to publish controversial books, particularly if they are embarrassing to the parent company. . . . Large conglomerates are increasingly wary of publishing books which may cause public offense or involve them in costly legal action" (Moran, 1997, p. 450).

More than 40 percent of the books sold in America are retailed by chain stores (Baker, 1990). Their buying decisions influence publishers to place more emphasis on "blockbuster" best-sellers because unsold books are returned to the publishers. This synergy diminishes the publication of new and experimental literature and squeezes out mid-list authors (Curtis, 1998; Tebbel, 1987). Mid-list authors are those whose books sell less than 15,000 copies or who earn less than a $25,000 advance (Moran, 1997), or whose sales do not improve with each new book (Bard, 1998). Consolidation of the industry could also limit the marketplace of ideas found in educational texts. Six conglomerates controlled the textbook publishing industry in the 1980s (Tebbel, 1987).

Book publishing, according to Bard, has become like Hollywood. Publicity, which is essential to success, often begins with high-priced auctions for the paperback rights to a book. Media attention to these auctions began in the 1970s when James Michener's *The Drifters* earned the first $1-million paperback advance, followed shortly thereafter by Bantam's payment of $2 million for the rights to E. L. Doctorow's *Ragtime*. Print orders of 900,000 copies for mass-market titles have become routine.

A favorable mention of a book by a daytime talk-show host can sell more than a million copies. The eventual outcome for trade-book publishing could be "a book published by Random, chosen by Oprah, critically acclaimed by all and penned by a first-time author named Danielle King Grisham" (Maryles, 1998, p. 43). International politics can also cause censorship (Baker, 1990). Two major U.S. booksellers temporarily banned *The Satanic Verses* after Iranian religious authorities passed a death sentence on the book's author, Salman Rushdie.

Some argue that these trends only appear harmful or may disappear in the near future. While the largest publishers in the industry continue to consolidate, small firms are being added at an annual rate of 2.5 percent (Bessie, 1987). The trend toward mass production and consumption of fewer books also may prevent higher illiteracy rates by preserving at least one market for books: "Better to have readers who buy only mass market books, it is said, than to have the total number of readers reduced to a mere trickle, as some fear, with books going the way of the horse-drawn carriage" (Tebbel, 1987, p. 463).

Computer and communication technologies that have made virtual bookstores possible also may add book readers in remote domestic and foreign locations and among the computer literate (Book Industry Study Group, 1998).

An "Electronic" Cottage Industry

E-commerce—along with the Internet, inexpensive personal computers, and digital technologies—may solve the problems of content homogenization in the twenty-first century. Book publishing could become an "electronic" cottage industry, much like its nineteenth-century counterpart, by offering inexpensive but unique products to individual customers. Computers already are "dis-intermediating" some publisher–buyer transactions and are making publishing on demand of customized products for one reader possible (Curtis, 1998). Dis-intermediation permits

The book consumer to sit down in a bookstore kiosk, insert his credit card, order any book of his choice, and in minutes download a bound copy, printed from text stored in a vast memory bank. If this seems visionary, it is in fact already happening, especially in the college market where it is cheaper for students to acquire texts through "custom publishing" than to buy them in traditional form in traditional stores. (Curtis, 1998, p. 19)

Whether e-books and e-commerce remain free of more direct forms of censorship remains to be seen. Early indications are that the information superhighway may be susceptible to both indirect contraceptive and direct regulatory censorship (Foerstel, 1998, pp. 42–52). The federal Communications Decency Act of 1996, for example, prohibited Internet users from exchanging information about obtaining or performing abortions and prohibited dissemination of material defined as indecent. The U.S. Supreme Court later ruled the law unconstitutional, but as the decade ended, federal courts were grappling with another measure, the Child On-Line Protection Act, which is designed to shield children from Internet pornography.

FUTURE OF THE BOOK

Like any forecast, making reasonable predictions about the future of the book in the next twenty-five years requires as much art as science. Weak predictions often share four attributes (Coates & Jarratt, 1992): (1) They extrapolate from existing trends that either disappear or change direction, (2) they incorporate unexamined assumptions about the future, (3) they are made by forecasters who have limited experience, and (4) they represent a basic failure of the forecaster's imagination. Forecasts can incorporate other pitfalls. Current "futurists" often uncritically accept science and technology "as the dominant if not primary drivers of change" (Coates & Jarratt, 1992, p. 20). Predictions often have a middle- or upper-class bias because members of those social strata frequently make the forecasts that are saved and consulted (Center, 1990). While some of the future can be inferred from present conditions and technologies, the soundest forecasts usually balance these things against demographics and economics, utility value, and opportunism on the part of people. With these caveats in mind, it is possible to make some conditional projections about the future of the book or to sort through those already made.

Specialists who contributed to the Library of Congress's (1994) *Books in Our Future* study speculated that the traditional ink-on-paper book will remain a force in the twenty-first century for several reasons: Books are omnipresent, constitute the chief depositories of our knowledge, and represent a huge financial investment on the part of society. At the time the study was issued, the Library of Congress alone held 18 million printed volumes and added about 1,000 more each day.

The study concluded that "the proverbial convenience, accessibility, and individuality of the book are unrivaled now or by any technology in sight. The book is independent of outside power sources, and offers unique opportunities for freedom of choice" (Library of Congress, 1984, p. 5). For these reasons, the printed book will likely remain in demand until the last baby boomer quits reading sometime near the middle of the twenty-first century. Eventually, however, the future of the book will be in the hands of children who are preliterate now or who will not be born until the first decades of the twenty-first century. These readers will be socialized to a new book "culture" of e-books and virtual bookstores and libraries. They may phase out ink-on-paper volumes, according to Richard Curtis (1998), former president of the Association of Authors Representatives, because,

> By the start of the 21st century, thanks to computers, Nintendos, and Gameboys, a generation of children completely at ease with electronically delivered literature will make handheld electronic books the device of choice for reading. The awesome memory capacity of CDs, storing scores of volumes of miniature discs [*sic*], may make bookstores and libraries obsolete. Thanks to the multimedia and interactive features of the new breed of computers, tomorrow's electronic books will entertain readers with audio and video displays that make traditional books look as crude as cuneiform writing on stone tablets. (p. 7)

While appealing, Curtis's (1998) prediction is based on the broad assumption that the availability of cheap, improved personal computers will be universal. This is not currently true (Glyn-Jones, 1998). However, his prediction is made on a sounder basis than some of those made 100 years ago when forecasters predicted there would be no trees left in the United States by the 1920s (Center, 1990). If that prediction had been accurate, questions about the book's future would have been moot for most of the twentieth century.

REFERENCES

Bagdikian, B. H. (1992). *The media monopoly* (4th ed.). Boston: Beacon Press.

Baker, J. F. (1990, January 5). The '80s: Reaching new heights. *Publishers Weekly*, 19–20.

Bard, M. (1998, January). Book publishing: The state of the industry 1998. *Writer's Digest*, 36–40.

Bessie, S. M. (1987). The book in the future: A publisher's perspective. In J. Y. Cole (Ed.), *Books in our future: Perspectives and proposals* (pp. 220–230). Washington, DC: U.S. Government Printing Office.

Book Industry Study Group. (1998). *Book industry trends: Covering the years 1992–2002*. New York: Book Industry Study Group.

Brooks, N. (1890, July). The newspaper of the future. *Forum*, 569–579.

Center, J. (1990). Where America was a century ago: History as a guide to the future. *The Futurist, 24* (1), 22–28.

Coates, J. F., & Jarratt, J. (1992). Exploring the future: A 200-year record of expanding competence. In J. F. Coates & J. Jarratt (Special Eds.), The future: Trends into the twenty-first century. *The Annals of the American Academy of Political and Social Sciences*, 12–24.

Cole, J. Y. (Ed.). (1987). *Books in our future: Perspectives and proposals*. Washington, DC: U.S. Government Printing Office.

Curtis, R. (1998). *This business of publishing: An insider's view of current trends and tactics*. New York: Allworth Press.

Foerstel, H. N. (1998). *Banned in the media: A reference guide to censorship in the press, motion pictures, broadcasting, and the Internet*. Westport, CT: Greenwood Press.

Glyn-Jones, F. (1998). Preparing for the twenty-first century: Into the technological storm. *The Political Quarterly, 69*, 277–287.

Goodrum, C. A., & Dalrymple, H. (1987). The computer and the book. In J. Y. Cole (Ed.), *Books in our future: Perspectives and proposals* (pp. 151–178). Washington, DC: U.S. Government Printing Office.

Haynes, C. (1994, November). Paperless publishing: The future is now. *Writer's Digest*, 43–49.

Kirsch, I. S., Jungeblut, A., Jenkins, L., & Kolstad, A. (1993). Adult literacy in America: A first look at the results of the National Adult Literacy Survey. *1992 National Adult Literacy Survey* [On-line]. Available: http://nces.ed.gov/nadlits/naal92/trends.html#illit.

Lehmann-Haupt, H. (1951). *The book in America: A history of the making and selling of books in the United States* (2d ed.). New York: R. R. Bowker.

Library of Congress. (1984). *Books in our future*. Washington, DC: Joint Committee on the Library, Congress of the United States.

Lorimer, R. (1993). The socioeconomy of scholarly and cultural book publishing. *Media, Culture and Society, 15*, 203–216.

Maryles, D. (1998, January 5). The big got bigger and better. *Publishers Weekly*, 40–43.

Millot, J. (1998). Issue of the year: On-line bookselling. In Book Industry Study Group, *Book industry trends: Covering the years 1992–2002* (pp. 1-1–1-5). New York: Book Industry Study Group.

Moran, J. (1997). The role of multimedia conglomerates in American trade book publishing. *Media, Culture and Society, 19*, 441–455.

Perman, S. (1998, April 6). The book on Bertelsmann. *Time*, 54–56.

Reading between the videos. (1992, February 29). *The Economist*, 29.

Snyder, T. (Ed.). (1993). 120 years of American education: A statistical portrait. *1992 National Adult Literacy Survey* [On-line]. Available: http://nces.ed.gov/nadlits/naal92/trends.html#illit.

Tangorra, J. (1990, January 5). Getting the word out. *Publishers Weekly*, 52–53.

Tebbel, J. (1975–1981). *A history of book publishing in the United States* (Vols. 2–4). New York: R. R. Bowker.

Tebbel, J. (1987). *Between covers: The rise and transformation of book publishing in America*. New York: Oxford University Press.

U.S. Bureau of the Census. (1998, April 2). *Historical national population estimates: July 1, 1900 to July 1, 1997*. [On-line]. Available: http://www.census.gov:80/population/estimates/nation/popclockest.txt.

2

Cable

George Thottam

Cable television began as a device for improving the reception of over-the-air broadcast signals in communities that were hemmed in by barriers such as mountains and skyscrapers. Cable has become a major force in broadcasting today. Half a century ago, the first generation of cable operators erected antennas on hilltops, ran cables downhill into homes, and charged a monthly fee. Gradually, they began delivering programming from faraway stations. The second generation wired whole cities and created a wired nation, while making enormous profits.

Today, broadcast television reaches most of its audience through cable. In fact, cable has become the biggest threat to its one-time master, broadcast television, in programming and advertising. The proliferation of cable channels covering specific areas, such as science, history, art, food, sports, and leisure, has fragmented the mass audience of broadcast television.

According to the 2000 year-end review of the National Cable Television Association (NCTA), cable television is a $42.1-billion industry in the United States, reaching 69 million of the 96.7 million households that have television sets. That amounts to approximately seven out of ten TV homes. Of all American TV homes, 96.7 percent are within the range of the 133,705 cable systems operating in 34,000 communities; the number of cable networks has increased from 79 in 1990 to 224 in 2000 (NCTA, 2001).

The Telecommunications Act of 1996 has opened new avenues for cable, including telephony and data transmission in the United States. Cable is also becoming a major competitor in the Internet market. Internationally, cable is the major component of the communication explosion. It is a big part of the media systems in the former Soviet Bloc countries and in Asia. In many countries, the government monopoly of television has crumbled with the penetration of cable. Through the use of microwave and satellite technology, cable is able to reach places broadcast television will not reach for a long time. Suddenly, cable television has brought the world to the rural huts and urban slums of the developing nations.

CABLE TECHNOLOGY

The basic technology used in traditional coaxial cable is known as "tree and branch" architecture (Willis & Aldridge, 1992, pp. 112–113). It consists of the headend, the trunk cable, the feeder cable, the drop cable, and the converter box. In a cable system, unlike in broadcast television, signals are sent along wires rather than through the air. The headend is the point at which the cable operator receives signals from different sources. The headend picks up broadcast signals using traditional antennas and dishes. Signals from distant television stations reach the headend by microwave. Some cable systems produce original programming. These signals are also fed to the headend.

The headend amplifies signals and sends them through the trunk, which consists of coaxial cable. From the trunk, the signals travel through feeder lines and branch off into neighborhoods. Along the way, amplifiers and equalizers are placed into the coaxial cable network to enhance the signal level for delivery over long distances. Then a drop cable is run from the feeder cable into the subscriber's home and television set. The drop is connected to a converter box if the television set is not cable ready. Pay channels and services are scrambled at the point where the drop line is attached to the feeder. The converter box unscrambles signals for paying customers. A cable system can have thousands of miles of fiber and coaxial cable, hundreds of amplifiers, and thousands of distribution amplifiers (Parsons & Friedman, 1998, p. 100).

Gradually, fiber optics became a better alternative to the copper cables of the coaxial system. Fiber-optic technology provides greater bandwidth or channel capacity and enables signals to travel distances without amplification. Cable operators soon switched to Hybrid Fiber/Coax (HFC) cable technology (Parsons & Friedman, 1998, p. 103). HFC uses fiber for trunk and feeder lines. It sends several fiber lines directly from the headend to neighborhood hubs, from which mini-tree-and-branch coaxial networks deliver programming to hundreds of homes.

In 1975, cable systems began using satellites for the delivery of signals to headends. This enabled them to offer more stations and specialized programming than terrestrial stations could. The satellite distribution system makes individual stations available to cable subscribers across the country. This new mode of delivery revolutionized cable television and made it even more appealing to subscribers.

DEVELOPMENT OF CABLE

The origins of cable can be traced back to 1948. E. L. Parsons, an engineer from Astoria, Oregon, and John Walson, a lineman for Pennsylvania Power and Light Company, led the way with their own versions of community antenna television (CATV) systems. Bob Tarlton, another appliance leader from Pennsylvania, and Milton Jerrold Shapp, who later became the governor of the state, developed master antenna systems (MATV) using coaxial cable and boosters to wire whole townships.

In the 1950s, cable operators began to use microwave technology to bring signals from distant cities. Consequently, cable companies were able to offer more channels than standard terrestrial broadcasting companies. Between 1950 and 1960, the number of cable systems grew from approximately 30 to 400. In 1962, more than 700 cable systems were serving 850,000 subscribers. However, the increase in the number of broadcast stations resulted in a freeze in the growth of cable in major markets.

The history of cable television in the United States is closely associated with government regulations. As long as community antenna television systems were boosting the reception of local television stations, broadcast television saw cable as a means to reach more viewers. However, once cable systems began carrying programming from distant markets and started producing their own programs, broadcast television began lobbying for the regulation of cable.

The first regulation of cable by the Federal Communications Commission (FCC) was issued in 1965. It required that cable systems carry the signals of all local TV stations and that programs imported from distant stations not duplicate programs offered by local stations. These were known as "must carry" and "program exclusivity" rules. In 1968, the Supreme Court upheld the FCC's jurisdiction over cable television, and, subsequently, the commission issued the 1972 Cable Television Report and Order. A major provision of the act was that cable companies provide "access" channels for members of the local community, municipal governments, and schools.

Although the goal of the 1972 regulations was to stimulate the growth of cable while protecting broadcast television, the act also eased federal, state and local restrictions on franchising. 1972 also witnessed the launch of the first pay-TV network, Home Box Office (HBO), by Sterling Manhattan Cable. HBO pioneered the use of satellite technology to beam its programs to cable operators in North America. This enabled cable to carry more original programming and independent stations from across the country. By the end of the 1970s, more than 15 million households in the United States had become cable subscribers.

The 1984 Cable Communications Policy Act of the U.S. Congress resulted in further deregulation of the industry. Cable rates were deregulated and cable companies were allowed to adjust rates without local government approval. It relaxed franchise requirements and prohibited common carriers such as AT&T from owning cable systems in markets in which they operated telephone services. This resulted in a boom in cable television. Between 1984 and 1992, the industry invested billions on wiring the nation and billions more in programming. This was the golden period of cable. As a result, 53 million homes were subscribing to cable by 1989. The number of cable program networks rose from twenty-eight in 1980 to seventy-four in 1989.

Steep and steady rate increases and consumer complaints led to the 1992 Cable Television Consumer Protection and Competition Act, which gave regulatory authority to the federal government (Grant & Meadows, 1998). The act required program providers to sell their services to cable competitors such as direct broadcast satellite systems (DBS), multipoint multichannel distribution services (MMDS), and satellite master antenna television (SMATV) systems. As a result of this act, the FCC ordered a 15-percent rate reduction for most cable systems. The act also gave local television broadcasters a choice between "must carry" and "retransmission consent," which prohibited cable operators from carrying a television station without permission.

The Telecommunications Act of 1996 deregulated cable rates once again. Most cable systems were granted immediate deregulation. Deregulation of larger markets was spread out over a three-year period ending on March 31, 1999. The act also opened up telephony and data services to cable companies, while opening up cable to telephone companies.

CABLE PROGRAMMING

Cable television provides a variety of services to its customers (Willis & Aldridge, 1992, pp. 117–120). The basic service consists of over-the-air broadcast signals from commercial and public television stations, superstations like WTBS, and satellite services such as CNN, C-SPAN, and ESPN, all covered by the basic monthly subscription.

Premium satellite services, also known as pay satellite services, include channels such as HBO, The Movie Channel, and Cinemax. Most of them are national and some are regional. Subscription television or pay television has been in existence since the 1940s. While premium channels like HBO offer programming for $10 or more per month, some others, like the Food Channel and the Sci-Fi Channel, charge a low monthly fee of $1 to $3 and are known as minipays.

Pay-per-view (PPV) television services offer single movies, sporting events, and rock concerts for a set price. They consist of individual programs purchased by the subscriber. Prices range from a few dollars for a movie to $50 or $60 for major boxing matches (Grant & Meadows, 1998).

Near video on demand (NVOD) or enhanced PPV is an outcome of expanded bandwidth. It uses dozens of channels to show movies at staggered times (Parsons & Friedman, 1998). The same movie is shown simultaneously on several channels with different starting times. Some multiplex movie theaters do the same. This way, the subscriber does not have to wait for hours for a particular movie. Video on demand (VOD) enables customers to order programs such as movies and television shows at any time, and gives them the ability to watch them at their own pace by fast forwarding, rewinding and pausing the program at will. It is very similar to home viewing of videotapes. VOD will need interactive technology, which is not yet available to most cable subscribers.

Most cable systems also provide ancillary services, such as news, weather, and community bulletins. Some of them also offer classified advertising of real estate and other commodities (Willis & Aldridge, 1992).

Public access channels, required by the 1972 Cable Television Report and Order, provide channels for members of the public as well as to municipal government and educational institutions. Many cable systems dedicate one of the unused channels for this purpose.

The 1972 regulations also required cable systems with more than 3,500 subscribers to set up two-way cable capability. Even cable systems that are wired for it do not necessarily carry two-way services. A few experiments, such as the QUBE system of Warner Amex in Columbus, Ohio, did not last long. However, the advent of digital television will enable cable systems to provide interactive services, such as advanced forms of pay per view, home shopping, and opinion polls.

ALTERNATIVES TO CABLE TELEVISION

Just as cable has become a major alternative to broadcast television, other delivery systems have become alternatives to cable (Willis & Aldridge, 1992, pp. 121–124). Some of them, like the direct broadcast satellites, are beginning to challenge the dominance of cable. No discussion of cable television can be meaningful without an overview of these systems.

Subscription Television (STV)

Broadcast television can send scrambled signals to the subscriber's home directly. Signals are unscrambled with the help of decoders attached to the TV set. Viewers can be charged for individual programs or the whole service. Subscription TV, also known as pay TV, goes back to the 1930s. The 1950s and 1960s witnessed the rise and fall of pay-TV enterprises by Zenith, WOR-TV in New York, and KTLA in Los Angeles. These and other subsequent attempts had very little success, especially in areas where cable was available. However, with the advent of digital television, broadcast television is threatening to go back into the pay television business.

Wireless Cable or Multipoint Distribution Service (MDS)

Multipoint Distribution Service, also known as wireless TV, is used to distribute television signals to subscribers via microwave channels. Wireless cable is a misnomer because there is no physical connection between the headends and the subscribers in this system. They offer programming over the air through microwave channels.

In 1963, the FCC allocated a small portion of the microwave spectrum (2.150 GHz to 2.162 GHz) for commercial distribution of television signals. MDS was meant to be a cheaper alternative to broadcast and cable television. Initially, one or two channels were made available in each market and most of them were used for niche programming, such as adult entertainment programming and hotel information. In 1983, the FCC allocated eleven additional channels, making the expanded Multichannel Multipoint Distribution Service. It also allowed MDS operators to lease unused educational channels (Willis & Aldridge, 1992). This brought the range to thirty-three channels. The development of compressed digital technology makes it possible to convert the thirty-three analog MMDS channels to one hundred thirty-two channels. As of October 1998, there were 250 MMDS systems in the United States with 1.64 million subscribers. However, that number had fallen to 700,000 by the end of 2000 (NCTA, 2001).

Local Multipoint Distribution Service (LMDS)

LMDS is a new wireless technology that will be able to deliver several channels of wireless cable along with wireless telephony, data, and interactive services. It uses low-power transmitters that cover a radius of two to six miles. A digital LMDS could carry several hundred channels of programming. Within a few years, LMDS is likely to become more popular and replace MMDS, which is an older technology with no interactive features (Pappalardo, 1998).

Direct Broadcast Satellites

In the early 1980s, individuals began tapping into satellite television signals directly by using satellite dishes. It was a one-time investment, which involved a service fee. However, satellite programmers started scrambling their signals, forcing dish owners to pay a fee to receive clear signals.

Direct broadcast satellites can deliver better quality picture and sound. They can also offer a wider range of channels. Most of the subscribers live in rural areas where cable is not available. Lack of access to local broadcast stations and high installation costs used to be the major limitations of DBS. Today, the dishes have become smaller and less expensive.

However, DBS and direct-to-home satellite TV (DTH) have made a comeback since the mid-1990s. Companies such as DirectTV, PrimeStar, and Echostar have led the way. Use of digital technology enables these services to provide sharper pictures and more stations than most cable operators do. In October 1998, Direct Broadcast Satellite reached 7.83 million customers. By the end of 2000, it had cornered 16.23 percent of the multichannel video providers with 14.1 million subscribers.

Television Receive Only and Satellite Master Antenna Television Systems

In the 1970s and 1980s, C-band satellite receivers or television receive only (TVRO) were popular, especially in rural areas where cable was not available (Parsons & Friedman, 1998, p. 151). Dish owners were able to get most program signals unscrambled for free. Once cable operators began scrambling the signals, dish owners were forced to pay a monthly fee. This, along with the rise of DBS, led to the decline of TVRO. The number of subscribers dwindled from more than 4.5 million customers in 1986 to 1.8 million in 1998. SMATV is another version of TVRO used to bring satellite programming to apartment complexes and hotels. As of October 1998, there were 1.98 million SMATV subscribers in the United States.

The total customer base of noncable, multichannel video distributors totaled 18.68 million in 2000. This includes the 430,000 customers of local telephone companies involved in the cable business (NCTA, 2001). It is a considerable increase from 3.09 million customers in December 1993. Of these, direct broadcast satellites seem to be the biggest threat to cable in years to come.

THE STATE OF THE INDUSTRY

Cable television is a thriving industry with tremendous growth potential, and is poised for substantial growth in new areas, such as telephony and high-speed data services. At the same time, it is an industry with a troubled relationship with its clientele. Cable companies have a negative image among the public due to constantly rising costs and poor customer relations.

In 2000, the industry invested $12.43 billion for infrastructure upgrades and facility improvements. Since the 1996 Telecommunications Act, a total investment of $41 billion has been made (NCTA, 2001). This has significantly increased the bandwidth of cable systems, and has also increased their channel capacity. About 80 percent of cable systems were able to provide more than 100 channels by 2001. In addition, 75 percent of cable providers are equipped to offer two-way interactive service.

March 31, 1999, marked the end of cable regulation. Cable operators will be able to increase their rates without any interference from local governments or the FCC. If the past is any indication, cable rates are bound to go up in the near future. Former FCC chairman William E. Kennard said that FCC policy to allow cable companies to pass on cost of programming to customers is bad for the public (Farhi, 1998).

CURRENT TRENDS

Cable systems are also positioning themselves to take advantage of the 1996 Telecommunications Act and enter the fields of telephony and data transmission. The possibilities are enormous in the Internet market. The industry is also bracing itself for the advent of High Definition Television (HDTV), which will be mandatory for broadcast television by 2006. The cable industry has been spending billions of dollars on upgrading its infrastructure for digitization.

The immediate challenge for cable systems is to decide whether they should expand their operations to areas such as telephony, digital set-top boxes, and high-speed data services, including the Internet and video on demand. Different cable companies are focusing on one or more of these.

Just as cable operators are allowed to enter telephone and data delivery businesses, phone companies are allowed to deliver cable programming. Telephone companies such as AT&T are entering the cable business through mergers and acquisitions, not to be major players in cable, but to use cable lines to expand their telephone business and provide broadband connections to personal computers. Such major mergers will have a tremendous impact on the future of the industry. By the end of 2000, nine of the nation's largest cable systems already offered residential and commercial phone services in forty-five markets. Cable operators had also reached into connection agreements in forty states and the District of Columbia (NCTA, 2001).

In 1999, Congress and the FCC had to make several major decisions which affected the cable television industry. First, the FCC specified that cable operators are not required to carry broadcast television's analog and digital signals while making the transition from analog to digital broadcasting. Second, in November 1999, Congress passed the Satellite Home Improvement Viewing Act (Albiniak, 1999, p. 4), allowing direct broadcast satellite services to carry local programming. The FCC was also expected to determine whether the Internet operations of cable systems should be subjected to telephone-style regulation.

Digitization could expand cable's channel capacity from dozens to hundreds. Digital compression makes it possible to fit up to a dozen channels in the space occupied by one analog channel. This will lead to a proliferation of cable channels. In 1992, John Malone, CEO of Tele-Communications Inc. (TCI), promised that cable TV will deliver 500 channels in the immediate future. Although this has not become a reality, the channel boom is well on its way. Already most major cable program providers, such as Discovery, A&E,

MTV Networks, and Nickelodeon, are adding new channels. This will result in the fragmentation of audiences, as well as advertising revenues for the mother networks (Gay, 1998).

Cable is experiencing more competition than ever. While the 1996 regulations have opened new avenues to cable, they have also opened cable to its competitors. Telcos and public utilities are rapidly entering the field. Of late, municipal utilities are going into the cable business. More than seventy municipalities are building telecommunications systems with fiber-optic and coaxial cable to compete against local cable television, data communication, and telephony providers (Powell, 1999). Starpower Communications Inc., a joint venture of Potomac Electric Power Co. and RCN Corp. of Princeton, New Jersey, a phone company, is the first full-service telecommunications company to challenge District Cablevision Inc., which has dominated the District of Columbia for fourteen years. Ameritech is overbuilding cable systems in several big markets and Bell Atlantic is moving to wireless cable in others.

Internet providers such as America Online are lobbying lawmakers to require that cable TV lines be opened to all competitors who want to provide high-speed Internet service via broadband technology (Gruley, 1999, A20).

Competition from direct broadcast satellites is going to be stiffer than ever. In November 1999, Congress passed the Satellite Home Improvement Viewing Act, empowering DBS to carry local stations. DBS will also be able to offer more channels than cable and develop interactive and high-speed data services. Until cable goes digital, it will not be able to offer the picture quality DBS can offer.

The threat of DBS and other delivery systems like MMDS is serious. In 1997, cable cornered 89 percent of the market of subscription-based TV, but this went down to 68.21 percent in 2000 (NCTA, 2001). At the same time, there has been a steady increase in cable rates. Cable will not be able to keep pace with its competitors without a competitive price structure (Jessel, 2000).

Broadcast television, which is undergoing the transition from analog to digital, is threatening to compete with cable in offering specialized network programming on a subscription basis, without the services of the cable systems.

CABLE IN 2025

Predicting the future of a mass medium like cable television in the middle of a communication revolution is a risky proposition. Convergence of information technologies and mass media amounts to a media meltdown. Changes are taking place at a pace no one ever dreamed of. The development of the Internet and digitization of television make it extremely difficult to make even short-term predictions. However, it is amusing to make some educated guesses about the future of cable over the next quarter of a century.

Convergence is the operative word in forecasting the future. According to media futurists, over the next decade or two, convergence will lead to the merger of telephone, cable television, broadcast television, and voice, data, fax, video, and image services. "Future cable operators will upgrade their infrastructure and become one-stop telecoms and distribution companies providing telephony, cable television, interactive video, video on demand, home shopping, on-line/Internet access, gaming, telemedicine, and tele-education. Acting as enablers to other content providers, they will offer these services on bundled or individual basis" (Janowiak, Sheth, & Saghafi, 1998).

In the meantime, cable television will experience some decline in subscription and revenues. Major telcos such as Ameritech, GTE, Southern New England Telephone, and Bell South are already involved in the cable business. Direct broadcast satellites, which will be able to add local broadcast television to their programming schedules in the near future, will cut into the customer base of cable.

Revision

Digitization will make cable more attractive to its customers. As of September 30, 2000, an estimated 7.8 million homes subscribed to cable digital service. That number is projected to grow to 50.1 million homes in 2006 (NCTA, 2001).

High-definition television will be a problem for many cable operators. One major problem is that HDTV reduces the channel capacity of cable systems. Cable companies are not too enthusiastic about this new version of broadcast television (Gay, 1998).

Proliferation of channels, on the other hand, could result in a shortage of content. The question is what programs these channels are going to carry (Jankowski & Fuchs, 1995). The additional cable channels will also fragment the audience and advertising revenues of cable and broadcast television.

Evidently, the future of cable lies not in an increase of channels, but in interactivity. Pay-per-view services, on-screen TV guides with marketing features, and video on demand will be available to most cable customers within a few years. Through interactive services, subscribers will be able to navigate the Net, order movies on demand, and e-mail friends through interactive television. Interactive TV needs a pipeline to carry digital signals and a set-top box to receive and translate digital signals for the subscriber's television set. At present, "advanced analog" boxes can handle digital and analog signals. The next generation set-top box will cost between $150 and $200. At present, interactive TV adds $40 to $60 to monthly cable bills. The challenge is increasing the number of interactive cable customers from 40,000 today to millions within the next decade.

Cable telephony will be the wave of the future for cable operators. Today, telephony is a $200-billion business, while cable is only $42.1 billion. Cable operators who can bundle and market the right mix of digital programming, high-speed data, and telephony at the right price will be the winners. People who depend on the cable company for telephone service are less likely to cancel, and that is expected to reduce the churn rate by half (Mermigas, 1998).

Cable companies are examining technology that will allow millions of phone calls to travel on the Internet instead of the regular phone network. Mergers between telephone companies and cable systems will be the major trend of the future. The $48-billion merger of AT&T and TCI, and the $11.3-billion merger of US West and Continental Cablevision are just the beginning of a slew of mergers and acquisitions. AT&T is not really trying to get into the cable business through takeovers and partnerships with cable companies. It wants to use cable's broadband pipeline to expand its telephone dominance. Other phone companies are sure to follow the lead and pursue cable-related mergers, acquisitions, or alliances in the near future (Mermigas, 1998).

Cable telephony, both circuit switched or digitally transmitted through the Internet protocol telephony, will be one of the most lucrative operations for cable operators. This is why AT&T is trying to secure long-term, full-service telephony agreements with Time Warner, Comcast, and other major cable operators, in addition to acquiring TCI cable system.

The future of cable also lies in on-line and other ancillary services using the increased bandwidth. The challenge of the cable industry is to put cable operators at the forefront of the Internet wave in five years. Cable modems instead of modems connected to phone lines, will be able to deliver services up to 1,000 times faster. Internet access through cable modems will also solve the current problems with dial-up telephone modems.

Cable television in its present form may not survive the information and communication meltdown. Leo Hindrey, president of TCI cable, does not think that there will be any such thing as cable in the next five years:

Current largely coaxial-plant cable companies will be broadband distributors of seamless entertainment, data and telephony services. With some also being entertainment and data content owners and some being just distributors. "Cable" will be replaced by "broadband" in describing the industry and entertainment-only offerings will be replaced by seamless telecommunications offerings, very broadly defined and mostly digital or IP in nature. (Greenberg, 1998, p. C13)

The day when a single corporation provides the customer telephone, cable television, and high-speed data services such as the Internet through an interactive and multimedia services on a television or computer monitor has arrived.

REFERENCES

Albiniak, P. (1999, November 28). At long last, local. *Broadcast & Cable, 129* (48), 4–6.
The cable connection: The role of cable television in the national information structure. [On-line]. Available: http://www.cablelabs.com/Wpapers/cableNII.html.
Cauley, L. (1999, March 22). The small screen—ready to roll. *The Wall Street Journal*, p. R10.

Elstrom, P. (1998, January 11). 1999 to be another year of heavy regulation. *Business Week*, p. 98.

Farhi, P. (1998, January 14). FCC report on cable. *The Washington Post*, p. D11.

Gay, V. (1998, November 30). Changing channels. *Media Week*, pp. 28–31.

Grant, A. E., & Meadows, J. H. (1998). *Communication technology update* (6th ed.). Boston: Focal Press.

Greenberg, D. (1998). The hurdles ahead. *Broadcasting & Cable, 128* (47), C13–C15.

Grover, R. (1999, January 11) Media & entertainment: Prognosis 1999. *Business Week*, pp. 100–101.

Gruley, B. (1999, January 26). AOL leads lobbying campaign to gain access to "broadband" cable-TV lines. *The Wall Street Journal*, p. A20.

Haley, K. (1998). On the threshold of a new world. *Broadcasting & Cable, 128* (47), C5–C9.

Jankowski, G. F., & Fuchs, D. (1995). *Television today and tomorrow*. New York: Oxford University Press.

Janowiak, R., Sheth, J., & Saghafi, M. (1998). Communications in the next millennium. *Telecommunications, 3*, 47–54.

Jessel, H. A. (2000, December 4). Cable's future is now. *Broadcasting & Cable, 130* (50), 22.

Lyle, J., & McLeod, D. (1993). *Communication, media and change*. Mountain Field, CA: Mayfield.

McConnel, B., & Albiniak, P. (1998). 1999: Big year for cable regulation. *Broadcasting & Cable, 128* (49), 98–104.

Mermigas, D. (1998, November 23). Telephony will transform cable. *Electronic Media*, p. 10.

National Cable Television Association (NCTA). (2001). Cable television industry overview 2000. [On-line]. Available: http://www.ncta.com/home.html.

Pappalardo, D. (1998, April 23). A wireless future. *Network World*, p. 30.

Parsons, P. R., & Friedman, R. M. (1998). *The cable and satellite television industries*. Boston: Allyn and Bacon.

Powell, J. (1999, January 30). The power of choice: Starpower bursts on the cable TV scene. *The Washington Post*, p. H1.

Willis, E. E., & Aldridge, H. B. (1992). *Television, cable, and radio: A communications approach*. Englewood Cliffs, NJ: Prentice Hall.

————————3

Computers

Curtis R. Holsopple

Communication has involved some form of technology ever since one cave-man threw a pebble to get another caveman's attention during a hunting party. Human communication across time and space was limited by our physical senses, but people have created devices and methods—technology—to help messages overcome these limitations (McLuhan, 1996, p. 3). Computers are only the most recent in a long list of technological developments used by those who wish to record history and pass along the news of the day (Crowley & Heyer, 1995, p. 322). Ever since cave-dwelling humans first painted herds of animals on a rocky wall, people have recorded and preserved stories. These people are called journalists.

Preservation of stories is not enough, however. As people have reached out beyond the cave and the village, the need for mass communication has grown. The computer age has been a watershed experience for the mass media that compares to the telegraph or photography in impact. Journalists have already seen much change driven by technological advances, but they are far from realizing all the benefits and liabilities of computers. The changes in the world of journalism are indicative of the revolution in mass media overall.

JOURNALISM'S TECHNOLOGICAL DEVELOPMENT

Within the past twenty-five years, computers have taken over many news-rooms and publishing houses, and in the last decade laptop and notebook computers have become commonplace enough to make computer-based writing truly mobile.[1] As journalists contemplate the next millennium, advances in computer technology promise to give the craft new and powerful tools. The craft of good writing is still an utterly human art, however. The new technology involved just makes it easier to apply words to a page.

Changes in technology have changed journalism already. What lies ahead for journalists living in a fully computerized age? The electronic descendants of the quill pen and ink bottle have already made a difference in writing styles, and editing has been streamlined with computer-assisted word processing. In the past twenty-five years, the computer has gone from being a massive and expensive bit of corporate and military hardware to a small, portable, and relatively inexpensive appliance commonly found in the business, home, and vehicles.

This revolution has precedent. When the telegraph matured in the 1840s, it revolutionized our society in many ways, yet fewer than 15,000 telegraph offices were established within the first thirty years of Western Union's operation (Czitrom, 1982, p. 23). The relatively small cadre of experienced telegraph operators knit together a nation. Through their electric dots and dashes, news and commercial information traveled between distant places. The telegraph made possible fast railroad operations, and regular train schedules facilitated the wide distribution of newspapers. A new national identity was born due in large part to the telegraph and its implementation into journalism.

A similar technological revolution is happening now as computers become commonplace. A generation ago, the personal computer was an arcane engineering tool. Now it is a household appliance. Thanks to parallel growth in the telecommunications industry, more than 65 million people now enjoy some form of computer-mediated communication via the Internet. Traffic on this new medium doubles every hundred days ("Internet Usage Doubles," 1997, p. A3).

The technology of writing down one's thoughts progressed slowly over many thousands of years. Within the last two centuries communication technology has accelerated with the advent of electricity, following quickly by the telegraph, telephone, camera, radio, teletype, and television. Each of these developments has had a significant impact on journalism, because they have all helped journalists improve productivity and extend their reach. As literacy became widespread in the nineteenth century, people shifted their trust away from words spoken by local human authority figures to the authority of the printed word (Illich & Sanders, 1989, p. 35). This permitted social organizations to move beyond a face-to-face village culture to achieve a national and global framework (Stevens & Dicken-Garcia, 1980, p. 74; Emery & Emery, 1992, p. 116; McLuhan, 1996, p. 255).

Mass communication on a global scale has depended on computerization. Thanks to computer technology, digitized telephone circuits permit fast and convenient dialing across the planet, and the telephone's formerly poor audio quality is now excellent. In 1962, television viewers saw shaky pictures of the Eiffel Tower in Paris and the Statue of Liberty in New York transmitted through Telstar-I and linked together on a split screen. The first commercial communications satellite suddenly made faraway places seem much closer, and this development inspired Marshall McLuhan (1996) to coin the term "Global Village" (p. 93). The military-based rocket technology that permitted the launching of Telstar was utterly dependent on computer technology for guidance and control. Hardware designed for mass destruction soon became a central ingredient in mass communication (Von Braun & Ordway, 1975, p. 164).

By the mid-1970s, computers were beginning to invade newsrooms and publishing houses, pushing typewriters and linotype machines out as word processors and electronic typesetting came in. Gone were the arduous retyping and physical cutting and pasting of manuscript sheets. Formerly, writers had to think through their stories in a very linear fashion before committing words to paper, or they suffered the consequences through much retyping of manuscripts.

Thanks to computerized word processing, however, an article, story, or book can be composed in a fragmented random order if that suits the writer best. By allowing random-access writing, computers have fostered a fundamental change in thought patterns for journalists, allowing them to write as inspiration and resources become available. Journalists are still free to think and write linearly, but changes in available technology have allowed comparable productivity from writers who use nonlinear thinking as they write. Computer power and software are now sufficient to permit direct voice access to the computer, eliminating the barrier of typing skills that has limited some writers. Calling this technological determinism would not be fair. The changes in technology have broadened the options, not delimited them.

This is quite a change from the days of Horace Greeley and the first truly national newspapers of a century ago. Yet journalists have some enduring qualities that they apply to their work, regardless of the tools available. Advances in technology do not necessarily change everything in mass communication.

JOURNALISM'S FIRST PRINCIPLES

Perhaps one of the oldest descriptions of good journalism comes from the Bible itself. In the opening lines of the Gospel according to St. Luke, the writer explained that he had "carefully investigated everything from the beginning, [and] it seemed good also to me to write an orderly account for you . . . to know the certainty of the things you have been taught." So a first principle for journalists is to tell the story truthfully in such a way that others may obtain certain knowledge of events to which they were not personally a witness. Readers expect journalists to provide the truth.

Communication scholar Walter Fisher (1989, p. 3) said that human beings are storytellers by nature. For one person to accept another's story as true, the recipient exercises an innate human trait of testing the story for narrative probability: If the story has internal coherence and also appears comparable to other stories known to the recipient, it will be accepted. In the modern scientific mind of Western culture, Fisher noted that rational knowledge "was a product of empirical investigation of physical nature" (p. 32). But Fisher also said that people accept as truth material that goes beyond rational scientific fact. The human condition is not always rational, measurable, and predictable, yet the stories we share can be truth telling in their description of irrationality. Not all truth contains verifiable data. Fisher asserted that truth must also appeal to emotions, imagination, and value systems (p. 75). Journalists need to know people, and good journalism is clearly a description of the human condition in all its dimensions. According to Fisher, a story will be accepted as truth when it "exhibits narrative probability and fidelity across time and culture" (p. 78). Journalists are expected to relate the human narrative faithfully, and the question of whether the trade uses a quill pen or laptop computer is irrelevant to this standard.

John Milton (1992, p. 41) raised the issue of freedom of expression in the 1640s when England attempted to license and restrict the press. Journalists of that day were not to write anything without the approval of the government, and Milton argued that society would be better served if the press were free to act as a conduit for free discussion among all members of society.

The ethics and values journalists bring to the job are most strongly influenced by parents and early home life (Endres, 1985, p. 47). Once on the job, journalists find their value systems are refined and cemented through newsroom experience and the influence of journalistic colleagues (Willis, 1990, p. 13). Objectivity is a laudable and guiding goal for journalists, even if it is not always attainable. But journalists strive toward the objective ideal by applying a sense of balance to a story, recognizing that there are usually two sides that deserve fair representation (pp. 22–23). A sense of fair play transcends the technology being used.

Like all mass communication, journalism comes at a cost. Someone must pay for the reporter, the publishing equipment, and the distribution costs. Whether a news service is a government-owned monopoly operated at taxpayers' expense or based entirely on free enterprise and commercialism, a major danger to journalism is the urge to provide a tangible return on the investments. Truth may suffer in the face of commercial gain or economic necessity. This flies in the face of many who demand that journalists have a social responsibility to fight injustice and to pay special attention to the needs of minorities.

For hundreds of years the enduring qualities of truth, balance, and social justice have evolved. If journalists lack integrity, they lose the trust of their audience. Computers have permeated the page-layout departments and writers' desks, and they are quickly finding their way into the streets and beats where the news is collected. But at the heart of it all is the journalist who still seeks out and writes a believable and trustworthy story.

AN ERA OF RAPID CHANGE

Perhaps the advent of computerization has been the answer many have been waiting for. Newspapers in the late twentieth century became relatively scarce and controlled by a few. When mass communication media are relatively scarce, the lowest common denominator often receives the lion's share of the media's attention. With computerization has come a renewed broadening array of parallel channels of communication. Cable television and satellite communications systems have provided multiple opportunities for broadcast journalism, and the Internet has multiplied further the lanes on the information superhighway. Traditional newspapers and magazines are quickly appropriating the global communication network for on-line publishing, bringing sound and motion to the printed page (Endres 1997, p. 1). This melding of mass media is called "media convergence" (Head & Sterling, 1998, p. 5), and it is a hallmark of mass media in the near future. All of this rides on the back of computer technology.

Advances in technology must have practical application to become popular among journalists themselves (Willis, 1990, p. 3). The old railroad telegraph of the 1800s involved an acquired skill in sending and receiving Morse code, a technique that few journalists bothered to embrace personally. But the utility of long-distance communication was an obvious advantage for journalists seeking to gather news from distant places quickly. The very journalistic convention of writing in the "inverted pyramid" form grew of necessity: Civil War–era reporters experienced frequent outages while telegraphing stories from the battle front, and the most essential information was packed into the leading sentences (Itule & Anderson, 1994, p. 58). As the telegraph linked America's urban East to the far-flung West, another change occurred. In 1884, Simon N. D. North reported on the state of the American press. He wrote, "The influence of the telegraph upon the journalism of the United States has been one of equalization. It has placed the provincial newspaper on a par with the metropolitan journal, so far as the prompt transmission of news—the first and always to be chiefest function of journalism—is concerned" (Czitrom, 1982, p. 18). Whereas the newspaper was once localized, provincial, and opinionated, the national web of telegraphic intercommunication changed journalists into more dispassionate disseminators of news. As rural papers emulated their urban counterparts more closely, mass communication begat mass culture.

The implications of computer technology continue to grow. A 1986 study by Henke and Donohue revealed a crucial consequence of computerization. They found that consumers are impatient with balky delivery systems, and early computerized information-delivery systems were annoyingly slow and inflexible. Any computer-based newspaper must meet expectations regarding quality of graphics, user-based control of "page turning," and overall convenience of use (p. 542). Simply put, a traditional newspaper is still convenient. It can be read in the bedroom, backyard, or subway. Computer-based news-delivery media must be similarly flexible, and the images and print quality must be equal to or exceed that of the traditional newspaper. Viewers of television news waited decades to graduate from the brief and rigidly scheduled evening news programs to twenty-four-hour news networks. Now television programming of all kinds can be delivered on demand at any time (Head & Sterling, 1998, p. 179).

Consumers expect instant access, and computer-based journalism can and must meet that expectation. As all-news radio and TV outlets have already discovered, providing a twenty-four-hour service requires constant updating of the program material. The daily deadline of the print-based newspaper has yielded to the minute-by-minute revisions possible with cyberpublishing.

Carrying a computer-based newspaper around was not possible until recently. Computers had a large cathode-ray video display, an item that is costly, heavy, and power hungry. This type of display delayed the trend in miniaturization found in all other aspects of computer technology. In the 1990s, however, new solid-state video screens changed the world of computers. The most obvious change has been the advent of the laptop computer, made possible by liquid crystal "flat panel" displays. According to Fidler (1994), this aspect of computerization is a major breakthrough for journalists.

The light-weight portable computers now so commonly used by business and professional travelers would not have been possible without flat panels. However, the most important uses for flat panels may not be as mere replacements for picture tubes. Just as the solid-state transistor transformed electronics in the 1950s and 1960s, the flat panel has the power to transform communications, and with it all forms of mass media, in the next two decades. . . .

While these devices may seem insignificant at the onset, they represent the first wave of products and services that are likely to emerge in the next two decades from the implosive convergence of computer, communication and information technologies. . . . Ultimately, these devices can be expected to combine the readability and ease of using paper with the interactivity of personal computers and the compelling qualities of video and sound. (pp. 27, 29)

Apparently, actual technology is catching up to an earlier vision. The mass media are now equipped to gather pictures, sound, and text on a global basis, update them many times a day, and distribute them electronically to consumers who can access this material in a mobile environment. But McLuhan's (1996) catch-phrase of the 1960s was "the medium is the message" (p. 7). Such truisms may not fairly describe all media or all messages, but there is a bit of truth here worth considering.

REPORTING THE NEWS, OR CREATING IT?

While the enduring qualities of good journalism may not change with the advent of new technology, the events considered newsworthy have changed. Erik Barnouw (1990) mentioned the impact of television on acceptable newsgathering values, noting that television's visual element incited a paradigm shift for journalists. Instead of reporting what happened, the availability of mass communication now makes some of the news happen, and this makes some people very uncomfortable. Barnouw blamed journalists for being too quick to eat from the trough of news releases filled by the government and corporate entities:

They took cues from news agencies and newspapers but also from announcements of planned events: proclamations, meetings, press conferences, celebrations, anniversaries, award ceremonies, cornerstone layings, battleship christenings, and revelations of new inventions and products. Since the advent of television most of its news images have been of events created for cameras. Daniel Boorstin had dubbed them "pseudoevents" but viewers had become fairly oblivious to this aspect of the invented event. . . . The most common disasters, such as murders and car crashes, were likely to be symbolized by *events created afterwards* as photo opportunities: officials inspecting the scene, television newsfolk visiting the victims. A "news" item of this sort was less an event than an artifact. (p. 523, emphasis added)

Barnouw's concern is a valid one. Too often, both electronic and print-based "news" reports are not of the news event itself but of official commentary after the fact. Television technology has even created news events where newsmakers deliberately stage their activities with the press in mind. One might say that television has helped bring a far-flung nation closer to the activities of its governing body. But one might also ask whether the government has been reshaped by the press through the use of new technology. As journalists contemplate the further computerization of their craft, vigilance is warranted in tracking how mass media technology affects the functioning of society.

In the First Amendment to the U.S. Constitution, mass communication was charged with a responsibility to keep the government and the governed informed of each other's activities. But the government does not want to know everything about each citizen's comings and goings. Likewise, the citizenry has little interest in or need to know all the minutia of governmental activity. Some kind of intelligent filter is needed in the news pipeline. Itule and Anderson (1994) explained this long-standing tradition among journalists: the function of "gatekeeping." They wrote, "There is no scientific formula for deciding what is news and where it should be placed in a newspaper. At several junctures in the process of gathering and writing news, decisions to include or exclude information are made. Reporters and editors, consciously or unconsciously, often rely on time-honored news elements to help them make these decisions" (p. 30).[2]

But new technology has cut a hole in the fence, and the gatekeepers can't always control the flow of news anymore. As computers have led to sophisticated communication satellites, cable networks, and the Internet, the raw and unfiltered events of the day have bypassed experienced writers and editors on their way to the ears and eyes of the public. Some of the gatekeepers claim this new-found freedom-of-information flow is resulting in a loss of civility and social order (Cohen, 1998, p. A21).

How can journalists continue to provide an orderly account of events if stream-of-consciousness data floods past the journalists and inundates the general public? Will journalism's enduring qualities of truth, balance, and social responsibility survive the computer revolution? How will journalists in the year 2025 conduct themselves, given the technological advantages they will have over their forebears?

A GLIMPSE INTO THE CRYSTAL BALL

Assuming the population of Earth avoids a major catastrophe that destroys civilization, further computerization and miniaturization of communication technology is likely. Already, voice-recognition technology is on the market. Journalists may soon be able to take recordings of newsmakers' words and have the computer give typed transcriptions.

The laptop computer is likely to continue to shrink, although some typists with fat fingers may not like the trend. Lighter, more power-efficient computers will bring the journalist's office back out into the streets, and this is likely to improve mass media's interactivity with the audience, a rather significant shift from the one-way street broadcasters and publishers currently use.

As the various electronic communication technologies converge, the journalist of 2025 is likely to have a pocket computer linked via satellite or cell-phone technology into vast reference works, facilitating the research phase of story writing. The functions of today's broadcast news camcorders will be absorbed into the telephone-linked computer, improving the speed and portability of spot news coverage. Similarly, personal computers will graduate from desktop to purse and pocket, making consumers more likely to receive the products of mass communication with the same flexibility and mobility now reserved for paperback books, newspapers, and portable radios.

The real-time broadcasts now enjoyed by all-news radio will benefit from expanded pager and cell-phone technology, giving electronic newspapers the ability to be upheld constantly in a mobile environment. And these pocket-sized cyberpapers will be interactive. Not only will users be free to do some of their own gatekeeping by setting filters to include or delete certain sections of the paper, they will also be able to send e-mail responses back to the publisher. Thus, the letters to the editor section of the traditional newspaper have already evolved into a large on-line discussion group in which the people chat among themselves about the news of the day. This development may prove to be a heyday for advice columnists and public-opinion pollsters. It could also signal a return to true direct democracy, the Areopagus of ancient Greece, and the free-flowing marketplace of ideas envisioned by John Milton.

Reporters will continue to benefit from lighter and more flexible video and audio recording equipment. When this merges with portable text-editing and cell-phone technology, all newsgathering in mass media will experience a richer information flow. Good journalists try to show rather than tell about the news. Whereas the traditional newspaper might give us a snapshot of a news event, cyberpapers of the future will permit full-motion video with sound. The user may see a snapshot initially, but the opportunity will be there to select additional still frames or extended audio or video clips. In other words, the newspaper and CNN will look more like each other all the time, with increased viewer control over which, when, and how much of each story is viewed.

The mere thought of a paperless newspaper has economic implications. On one hand, some experienced press operators and paper-mill workers will find themselves out of a job. On the other hand, perhaps the growing environmental impact of logging operations will be reduced.

Unfortunately, cyberpublishing and interactive consumption of the mass media has a frightening implication: loss of privacy. Already, cell-phone technology permits the tracking of people without their knowledge. While a book or paper may be read in complete privacy, a cyberpaper supported by wireless Internet technology could be tracked, and a reader profile of astounding detail would be available for surveillance purposes and commercial exploitation. Private citizens may not want their reading habits exposed to that extent, especially if it occurs through technology too complex for them to understand or control.

An increased quantity of news does not necessarily promise an increase in quality. Journalists are likely to find computerization, miniaturization, and portability the hallmarks of their trade. But computer-generated transcriptions may be little more than stream-of-consciousness descriptions of events: raw data. This is not journalism; we still need the senses and intellect of an experienced journalist to provide a carefully crafted narrative, complete with background information and explanation of how events are significant to the readers and viewers.

If journalists access computers verbally, they may partially forsake the centuries-old skills of the writer and return to expressing thoughts orally. Walter Ong (1982) wrote,

Electronic technology has brought us into the age of "secondary orality." This new orality has striking resemblances to the old in its participatory mystique, its fostering of a communal sense, its concentration on the present moment, and even its use of formulas. . . . But it is essentially a more deliberate and self-conscious orality, based permanently on the use of writing and print, which are essential for the manufacture and operation of the equipment and for its use as well. (p. 136)

Mass media are completely dependent on the availability of advanced technology, and at their heart is electricity itself. If the power system fails, electronic interaction stops, and society immediately returns to the cave and village mode of face-to-face communication. Humankind should not shrink back into the cave voluntarily because equipment occasionally fails, but people need to be aware of their dependency on mass media technology.

Newspaper columnist Tony Gabriele (1998) offered a humorous warning about becoming too dependent on communication gadgets:

I have just had both of my hands cut off. It's the fifth or sixth time it has happened this week.

Well, not *literally*, of course. Experienced readers will no doubt realize that I am employing a figure of speech. . . .

For that is really what it feels like, when your computers go down—like you've had your hands cut off.

At our office—and probably at yours, too—we read stuff on the computer, we write stuff on the computer, we file stuff on the computer, we talk to each other on the computer. Our whole workday is built around the computer. The only thing we don't do on the computer is take coffee breaks, although they're probably developing the necessary software as I write this. (p. D1)

CONCLUSION

Miniature cameras, recording equipment, cell phones, the Internet, and pocket-size computers are all wonderful. They have made mass communication less rigid, and the possibility for interactivity is exciting to those who will be able to access the new mass media of 2025. But nothing in all of this hardware can replace the subtlety of human eyes and ears, and a pencil and reporter's pad still work when all else fails.

NOTES

1. One writer who loves bicycling has combined his two loves into one. Steve Roberts constructed BEHEMOTH (which stands for Big Electronic Human Energized Machine . . . Only Too Heavy). It is a bicycle that includes two computers, a cell phone, a global positioning satellite receiver, solar cells, alarm systems, and amateur radio equipment, among many other technological wonders. Using a special keyboard built into the handlebar grips, Steve can enter text into his onboard computer while pedaling down the road. Apparently it works—he has logged more than 7,000 miles on BEHEMOTH (Kleinschmidt, 1992, p. 25).

2. Itule and Anderson (1994, pp. 30–31) listed the traditional news values that the gatekeepers apply to choosing and arranging the news: *timeliness, proximity, conflict, eminence and prominence, consequences and impact* and *human interest*.

REFERENCES

Barnouw, E. (1990). *Tube of plenty: The evolution of American television* (2d rev. ed.). New York: Oxford University Press.

Cohen, R. (1998, September 17). Gatekeepers no more. *The Washington Post*, p. A21.

Crowley, D., & Heyer, P. (Eds.). (1995). *Communication in history: Technology, culture, society* (2d ed.). White Plains, NY: Longman.

Czitrom, D. (1982). *Media and the American mind: From Morse to McLuhan.* Chapel Hill: University of North Carolina Press.

Emery, M., & Emery, E. (1992). *The press and America: An interpretive history of the mass media.* Englewood Cliffs, NJ: Simon & Schuster.

Endres, F. (1985). Influences on the ethical socialization of U.S. newspaper journalists. *Newspaper Research Journal, 6*, 47.

Endres, F. (1997). The magazine in cyberspace: A "site" to be a "zine." *Electronic Journal of Communication, 7.* [On-line]. Available: http://www.cios/getfile\ Endres_V7N297.

Fidler, R. (1994). Newspapers in the electronic age. In F. Williams and J. V. Pavlik, (Eds.), *The people's right to know: Media, democracy, and the information highway* (pp. 25–43). Hillsdale, NJ: Lawrence Erlbaum Associates.

Fisher, W. R. (1989). *Human communication as narration: Toward a philosophy of ransom, value and action.* Columbia: University of South Carolina Press.

Gabriele, T. (1998, 12 March). Hands "lost" in crash of computer. *The Daily Press (Newport News, Va.)*, p. D1.

Head, S., & Sterling, C. (1998). *Broadcasting in America: A survey of electronic media* (8th ed.). Boston: Houghton Mifflin.

Henke, L. L., & Donohue, T. R. (1986). Teletext viewing habits and preferences. *Journalism Quarterly, 63*, 542.

Illich, I., & Sanders, B. (1989). *The alphabetization of the popular mind.* New York: Vintage Books.

Internet usage doubles every 100 days, study says. (1997, April 16). *The Daily Press (Newport News, Va.)*, p. D1.

Itule, B. D., & Anderson, D. A. (1994). *News writing and reporting for today's media* (3d ed.). New York: McGraw-Hill.

Kleinschmidt, K. (1992). Life on a megacycle. *QST, 76* (4), 25–30.

McLuhan, M. (1996). *Understanding media.* Cambridge: MIT Press.

Milton, J. (1992). *Areopagetica.* Santa Barbara, CA: Bandanna Books.

Ong, W. (1982). *Orality and literacy: The technologizing of the word.* London: Routledge.

Stevens, J. D., & Dicken-Garcia, H. (1980). *Communication history.* Beverly Hills, CA: Sage.

Von Braun, W., & Ordway, F. L. (1975). *History of rocketry & space travel* (3d rev. ed.). New York: Thomas Y. Crowell.

Willis, J. (1990). *Journalism: State of the art.* New York: Praeger.

4

Magazines

Leara D. Rhodes

Magazines have been a most resilient medium, readily adapting to shifts in taste and fashion, stimulating new technology in printing and graphics, and weathering the gyrations of the nation's economy.

Regional K. Brack, Jr. and Donald D. Kummerfeld

As a mass medium, magazines will celebrate their 260th anniversary in the year 2001. Two magazines were started in 1741. In 1999 there were more than 22,000 magazines published in the United States. From magazines' early beginnings in 1741, the industry has developed patterns. One such pattern has been how to beat the competition. Andrew Bradford's *American Magazine, A Monthly View of the Political State of the British Colonies* started February 13, 1741, three days before Ben Franklin's *General Magazine and Historical Chronicle for All the British Plantations in America*. A Philadelphia editor, John Webbe, was to be Franklin's editorial assistant. Webbe, however, jumped ship and gave Franklin's idea to Bradford (Mott, 1938). Competition started.

Even though Bradford's magazine folded after three months and Franklin's lasted only six months, the history of magazines had begun, a history that includes launches and failures, new magazines, and revitalization of old ones.

These starts and stops enable new ideas, new forums for dialogue, new looks at American culture to emerge. Therefore, to look at the future of magazines we must first look at the historical patterns to find constants. These constants will demonstrate that magazines have managed to find a balance to remain strong in spite of wars, economical disasters, changes in societal mores, and introduction of media like radio, television, film, video, and now the Internet. These historical patterns will then be used to examine the present state of magazines. The transition between what exists now on the newsstand shelves and what may be there in the year 2025 will be speculated on in the last section, based on the projections of the historical patterns.

The magazine industry is a changing one. The changes come from two sources: tradition and ability to meet the problems of introducing new innovations. According to Wolseley (1969, p. 19), there has been a tradition within the industry since the early 1800s of having to adapt to change and new concepts of society. How the magazine industry adapts to changes is how it remains strong.

HISTORICAL PATTERNS PROMPTING MAGAZINE FLEXIBILITY

Historical patterns of magazine adaptation include the following: building a relationship between the magazine and its readers, providing information not found readily in other places, adapting to societal changes, having advertisers pay the cost of publishing, adjusting to war shortages and economic limitations, and contributing to shaping the public discourse by defining the major issues of our society. These patterns can be traced through the stages of magazine development.

Early magazine editors and printers had a commitment to publishing information germane to the colonists and not just reprints of articles from Europe and Great Britain. The important relationship between the editor and the reader had begun. These early magazines wanted to be American publications, but more important, editors and printers wrote about issues affecting the colonists with the intent to influence opinion. The early start of magazines in Philadelphia made that city the hub of the magazine publishing industry. By 1800, almost 100 publications had been founded (Wolseley, 1969, p. 26). At the time, magazines were distributed mostly within the city of publication and had short lives.

Along with the news, these early magazines published essays and literary works. There were few outlets except for magazines to publish the works of Edgar Allan Poe, Ralph Waldo Emerson, Henry Wadsworth Longfellow, Harriet Beecher Stowe, James Fenimore Cooper, Nathaniel Hawthorne, and Walt Whitman. Magazines that published short stories and poems of American writers were creating a forum for this new nation's voice. The tradition of providing information not found in other places developed during this early history of magazines.

Events promoted changes to magazines. Whereas the early magazines published news, opinion, and literary essays, the pre–Civil War magazines were in tune with what was happening in the country and published different information for its readers. These included articles about public affairs, religion, current events, and the antislavery movement.

Magazines have followed national trends and multiplied. The number of periodicals grew from 700 in 1865 to 3,300 in 1885 (Mott, 1938, p. 5). This was in large part due to improvements in transportation and mail service. As the westward movement accelerated, magazines followed. Farm magazines were started to provide information to the pioneers turning America's heartland into farmland. Magazines could be distributed nationally and became the ideal medium for national advertising. Improvements in printing technology helped magazines increase their national circulation. This increased circulation encouraged competition among the magazines for the advertiser. Advertising, not the reader, carried most of the cost of the magazine. Thus, the tradition was built among American magazine readers that someone else would bear the cost of producing their favorite periodicals (Click & Baird, 1990, p. 3).

All the technological advances in industry-produced magazines were designed for both business owners and factory workers. This history of the magazine industry demonstrates how magazines have provided information people want to know but also shaped the public discourse and helped to define the major issues of our society. Whereas the first magazines campaigned for colonists' rights, others later began campaigning for women, workers, and immigrants. They wrote about societal as well as industry problems.

Women's magazines attempted to raise the consciousness of their readers, educating them on their role in society. One example is Sarah Josepha Hale, editor of *Godey's Lady's Book*. The magazine was published to provide women with information they had not been receiving. Hale had written the poem "Mary Had a Little Lamb," and through her talents made the magazine one of the most successful of the time. She championed female education and advocated that women be allowed to practice medicine. She is given credit for creating the national celebration of Thanksgiving (Wolseley, 1969, p. 30).

During World War I, *Good Housekeeping* and *McCall's* both led food conservation efforts. When the liberated women in the 1970s wanted to express their views about women's rights, a group of them invaded *The Ladies' Home Journal* offices to express their aims. Token response came promptly and space for their opinions was given, with more lasting changes coming later. However, *New Woman* and *Ms* appeared to fulfill what the older magazines were charged with failing to do (Wolseley, 1973, p. 6).

Workers and their rights were examined in magazines that took stands on social issues. *McClure's Magazine* went after Standard Oil Company, and writers like Ida Tarbell transformed the reporter into a "muckraker." *The New Yorker* wrote a series on DDT and chemicals used in maintaining lawns and changed how Americans care for their yards. Other magazines, such as *Collier's, Hampton's, The Independent, Success,* and *Cosmopolitan,* wrote about controversial issues (Peterson, 1964; Tebbel, 1969). By writing about these topics, magazines influenced national policy. Workmen's compensation laws were passed, the Pure Food and Drug Act became law, the insurance industry and railroads were regulated, tenements were cleaned up, and occupational safety standards were devised.

Whatever the economy, whatever the situation, magazines adjusted. Women entered the workforce and new magazines appeared. Immigrants became a new workforce and more magazines appeared. All these social changes affected publishing. The cost of materials and labor, higher taxes, and increased postal rates took their tolls. Both newspapers and magazines lost advertising revenue to radio and then to television (Wolseley, 1969, p. 38).

Adjustment happened again when *Time* magazine appeared and helped shape the course of American domestic and foreign policy. After World War II, newfound leisure in American life created a need for magazines teaching hobbies and offering diversions. Magazines contained articles about inventions and pollution, and informed readers of the wonders and dangers of science.

After 1945 and the end of World War II, mass-circulated magazines were replaced by specialized magazines. Commercial television grew from an infant industry to a national institution in less than two decades, but it did so mostly with new advertising money rather than reallocations of money taken from magazines and newspapers. Magazine circulation increased 21 percent between 1950 and 1960, and advertising revenue increased 86 percent (Click & Baird, 1990, p. 3). From its inception, the magazine industry has been characterized by change, which continually produces a better and stronger industry. New magazines appear and existing magazines merge, are sold, or are discontinued, with the births overall outnumbering the deaths (p. 4).

Whereas previous wars had deprived some magazines of circulation, the war in Vietnam helped to reshape the way magazines were written. Reporters went into the battlefields and television recorded every move. The concept of "New Journalism" emerged, with writers like Tom Wolfe, Norman Mailer, Truman Capote, Gay Talese, Tom Morgan, and Gail Sheehy. This genre gave writers a narrative voice when writing about news events. No pretense was made of objectivity. The writer injected his or her own reactions and views into the material.

Freedom of expression emerged in magazines, mirroring the mood of the nation. In the 1970s, the rise of personality journalism emerged through publications like *People,* which interpreted the news of the day through profiles of celebrities and others making the news. Along with the personality journalism came the revolutionary or underground press. Traditional magazines were accused by the 1960s generation of stressing false standards and goals, and ignoring rather than facing problems. The underground press met the needs of the under-thirty readers. Some traditional magazines, like *Harper's* and *The Atlantic*, adjusted to the revolution in society and survived. In tune with the tone of American life, they published articles on minorities' civil rights, poverty, the rise of soul and rock music, the revolt against certain religious tenets and practices, the environment, dubious government policies, and cynicism about the war in Vietnam (Wolseley, 1973, p. 7).

The history of magazines is one of fluidity and movement. Their starts and stoppages reflect the interests of their readers. The real uniqueness of magazines, however, stems from the fact that they are more than the sum of their ink and paper. Personal relationships are built among the writers and editors and their readers (Click & Baird, 1990, p. 5). These relationships appear to forge a union unbroken by war, transitions, upheavals in the economy, or changes in society.

PRESENT STATE OF MAGAZINES

Magazines have a strong business presence worldwide. The relationship of magazines to their readers remains strong. The rising level of education of the American public increases readership of magazines, with studies indicating there is a direct correlation between education and magazine reading (Abrahamson, 1996, p. 49). Spending the day at the office staring at the computer screen may offer workers the printed form of a magazine as a refreshing change. The personal allure of magazines may give the medium an advantage over the high-tech sterility of a computer screen (Frydlewicz, 1998, p. 8).

Another major change, and one that will continue to grow, is the increase in the number of publications aimed at specific ethnic groups. By far, the Hispanic population is the fastest growing in the United States, and magazine publishers are trying to ride the wave. Magazines such as *Glamour*, *People*, and *Woman's Day* started Spanish editions in 1998. Now there seems to be at least one magazine for every race, ethnic group, minority, age, and level of education, from preschool to pregrave (Husni, 1999, p. 1).

Many magazine markets are showing great growth potential, especially in the developing economies of Asia and Latin America. Growing literacy and improving distribution networks are widening the pool of potential readers, and economic growth is building a demand for magazines within this pool (Zenith Media, 1998–1999, p. 1). Many publishers seek growth through brand extensions, both in print and in electronic media. To increase their business, both consumer and business titles are expanding publishing operations outside the United States.

Magazines accounted for 13 percent of worldwide ad expenditure ($37.4 billion) in 1997. Advertisers value magazines for several reasons. Magazines build relationships with readers, who become very loyal. Magazines provide relevant editorials and offer high-quality production. The more specialized magazines allow advertisers interested in certain types of readers to target them specifically (Abrahamson, 1996, p. 70; Zenith Media, 1998–1999, p. 1).

Based on the history of magazines and their capabilities to adapt to changes, how will magazines be affected by the advancing new media? "New media will open new possibilities, developments and opportunities," says Dennis Escrow, editorial director of Cahners in New York (personal interview, February 4, 1999). John Wickersham, president and CEO of Bill Communications in New York, sees most publishers as information providers. They are in the publishing business, not the printing business. "In the future," says Wickersham, "publishing will be more multifaceted. Each medium can be used to cross-promote others. The biggest issue will be the complementary use of the mediums" (personal interview, February 5, 1999).

TRANSITION TO THE NEXT CENTURY

The magazine industry is mature, strong, and stable. Internet publishing and new media are not viewed as threats to print but rather as complementary media that offer great potential for magazine brand extensions and transactions. Most magazines have active Web sites; there are 1,750, according to the Magazine Publishers of America (Jeffrey, 1998–1999, p. 65). Revenue is derived from advertising, sales of products and services, and in some cases subscription fees. While most magazine Web sites are not yet profitable, many are. The prospects for profit from business-to-business magazine Web sites are generally greater than for consumer-based sites (Zenith Media, 1998–1999, p. 2).

In addition, according to NetSmart Research (Jeffrey, 1998–1999, p. 65), magazine readers are not substituting on-line forms for printed copies. In fact, on-line versions probably serve as an adjunct, rather than a replacement, enabling potential readers to sample magazines free before deciding whether to make a monetary commitment. On-line magazines may extend the audiences of titles. And an on-line version may help a magazine further strengthen the relationship with readers by offering more in-depth information on topics of interest to their readers and even allowing readers to give immediate feedback (questions and comments) (Frydlewicz, 1998, p. 7).

A study in 1998 by Strategic Record Research showed that 25.1 percent of Americans had access to the Internet (Jeffrey, 1998–1999, p. 65). Jupiter Communications, an on-line research company, said that 28.4 percent of Americans were on the Net (Jeffrey, 1998–1999, p. 65). And research commissioned by MTV determined that new media had not pushed aside the old; the two were, in fact, coexisting. For instance, 36 percent of teens were not only heavy viewers of cable TV but also frequent radio listeners (p. 65). So the old arguments that TV did not kill radio and that video did not wipe out movie theaters may have some relevance in the age of new media (p. 89).

Through MediaFinder (http://www.mediafinder.com), many publications have been introduced to a growing computer-savvy audience, showing that computer literacy is not replacing literacy but extending it (Striplin, 1999, p. 3).

Internet users are some of the magazines' best customers. According to MRI (Frydlewicz, 1998, p. 5), Internet surfers are 21-percent more likely to read magazines than the general public. This statistic is largely a function of the group's better education and high income. More than eighty magazines are read by Internet users at rates 50 percent or more above that of the general public. Some of these magazines include the following, shown with the percentage of readers who are on-line users (cited in Frydlewicz, 1998, p. 5):

Scientific American	63.7
Outside	62.0
Skiing	57.5
Business Week	51.3
Fortune	50.3
Barron's	46.5
Conde Nast Traveler	45.7
Atlantic Monthly	44.8
Premiere	42.7
Money	41.7
The New Yorker	41.5
Smart Money	41.4
Architectural Digest	37.1
Bon Appetit	36.9
GQ	35.2

Newsweek's management launched a combination of videodisc and Macintosh hypertext software as CD-ROM special editions in 1992. The results of this launch indicated that the *Newsweek* audience was equally comfortable with print and with the Web. Hence, newsweek.com posts 100 percent of the content of *Newsweek*'s domestic and international print editions. In addition, it has Web-only features, including hyperannotation of names and concepts in each week's cover story linked to articles from the *Encyclopedia Britannica Online*, a gallery of photos with narration, and a personalized business-news portfolio to reflect a reader's investment interests. Its initial advertisers are telling as well, including such print sponsors as Compaq and Lockheed Martin. The appearance of such advertisers in both media reinforce the perception that the news magazine's print readership now routinely surf the Web (Ditlea, 1998, p. 62).

To maintain prominence though, according to Husni (1999, p. 1), the visual impact of print will have to dominate, forcing editors and publishers to focus more on writing for the eye and more titillation of the senses in order to captivate the reader. Major new titles such as *Maxim*, *ESPN Magazine*, and *Bizarre* are doing just that with their design.

Calming the soothsayers' prophecies of doom is the fact that print is thriving in many different ways, not in spite of new media but because of it (Anthony, 1998, p. 2). Television is fueling magazines. ESPN produces a show and if the viewer wants more information about the sport, they get a magazine. Net sites, "Web-zines," are gathering readers on-line, then launching physical editions of their magazines. Individual television programs, from *Seinfeld* to *Star Trek*, are spawning their own magazines (p. 2). *Mr. Food*, a cooking and recipe magazine based on a TV show, had a circulation of 400,000 in 1999. The bottom line is to provide readers with information they cannot get in other places. There is only so much time on TV to offer information; if people want to know more, they turn to magazines. New magazine titles generated by popular television programs and personalities are becoming more popular (Zenith Media, 1998–1999, p. 2).

This TV sparkle is, however, not reflected in the total audience coverage between TV and magazines. There are a number of magazines that have higher coverage and ratings than popular TV shows. These titles include *National Geographic*, *Reader's Digest*, *Better Homes & Gardens*, *People*, and *TV Guide*. The average issue of *People* reaches 27.4 percent of women eighteen to forty-nine, while their favorite TV show, *ER*, reaches only 19 percent. In fact, six other magazines have larger audiences than *ER*. *Reader's Digest* reaches nearly twice as many people as *ER*; they have the same audience demographics. This fact disputes the notion that magazines are significant only for pinpointing audiences (Frydlewicz, 1998, p. 3).

FUTURE OF MAGAZINES

Technology is too bold to distinguish the patterns of magazines created through the past two-and-a-half centuries without careful examination. There are evolutions taking place as new trends push aside CD-ROMs for DVDs, MP3s, and tailored-to-the-reader specialized magazines that include audio and video highlights. There will be a time when newsweeklies will no longer be newsweeklies. Frequencies are defined as different periods during which repeat visitors tend to space their return. These periods are getting closer and closer together. In 1999, an examination of the newsweek.com site revealed features for real-time fans (breaking news), daily visitors (Today's *Newsweek*), weekly aficionados (*Newsweek*'s print content), and even once-every-three-weeks special-interest types (fresh Web-only features on health, money, and technology) (Ditlea, 1998, p. 64).

The deluge of technology forces new issues into the public arena. America is changing. Issues affecting the majority of Americans include aging, family changes, ethnic growth, lifestyle changes, and social concerns. The median age in the United States was twenty-eight in 1970, thirty in 1980, and thirty-three in 1990. The median age is predicted to be thirty-six in 2000 and forty in 2020. Middle-age America will undergo both psychological and physiological developments (Zenith Media, 1998–1999, p. 3). A mature nation will emerge, with less emphasis on things and greater emphasis on relationships. They will have a greater sophistication about the way the world works, greater self-reliance, and a mistrust of easy answers. As people age, new terms will enter the vocabulary, like "granny flats" and "ECHO housing" (Elder Cottage Housing Opportunities) (p. 3). People will be more practical minded, will want more hands-on control of their lives, and will have a greater concern about health and posterity issues.

Families will be more important in the coming years. As the baby-boom generation matures, people will marry at older ages and have children later. The number of nontraditional families will increase. Nontraditional households will surpass traditional households by 2010. Growth of ethnic communities will continue. The Hispanic population in the United States will be 11 percent by 2000. By 2008, Hispanics will be the largest U.S. minority (Media Analysts, 1998).

As the country ages and diversifies, the pace of life will begin to slow. Clutter will grow as new technology beckons to be seen and heard. The affluent will be willing to trade money to save time. People will want to feel in control of their lives. A trend will emerge toward manufacturing products that satisfy and address real physical, emotional, and artistic (quality-of-life) needs. The enlightened consumer society driven by back-to-basics values will replace the society manipulated by Madison Avenue's "hidden persuaders."

Social concerns will include more awareness of the global community. The environment will become a priority as the green consumer movement grows. According to the Conference Board, Special Consumer Survey Report (1998), serious concerns of Americans were cost of medical care, 88 percent; drug abuse, 88 percent; crime, 81 percent; and pollution, 80 percent.

Advances in communication will create a new environment to attract consumers and empower them. Convenience will be a necessity. Lifestyle and lifestyle identification will be the best ways to target consumer groups. The mass market will fragment (Zenith Media, 1998–1999, p. 120).

The more self-contained nature of magazines presents an opportunity to position the medium as a refuge from a data overload. Editors are paid to edit, to decide on the most appropriate pieces of information, and to present it best to their readers.

CONCLUSION

Patterns developed throughout history indicate that the relationship between magazines and their readers is important. So important is this relationship that the traditional letter to the editor is gaining in popularity. Whereas hundreds of letters were received by magazines each day prior to gaining an electronic link with its readers, now thousands of e-mails are received by editors of national magazines as a result of the content of those magazines.

Readers will continue to want a dialogue with their magazines (Tebbel, 1969). *Time* already can give a personalized cover to its readers.

Information in magazines—analyses, trendy recipes, how-to's—is not found in other places. This information gains importance in the readers' eyes because they accept and encourage the editor to select relevant information on specific topics to save them, the readers, time.

The cost of producing magazines is being revolutionized. In traditional print media, the advertisers carried the brunt of the cost of producing the magazine. The Internet has not yet achieved financial viability as an advertising product, but with cross-promoting in different media, and by marketing on-line products as added value to the advertiser, magazines can adjust to the economic demands incurred with electronic publishing.

Finally, magazines continue to shape public discourse by defining major issues of society. The Starr Report was published on the Internet; there were simply too many pages to publish the material in a magazine. However, the analyses and the debates resulting from the report have been covered in great detail in magazines. The future of magazines will be one where they adjust to the new technology and provide information to readers in new and exciting ways, just like they have been doing for more than 250 years.

NOTE

The Magazine Publishers of America in New York provided valuable assistance through the use of its information resource center. I am grateful to Suzie Ross of the Magazine Publishers of America and Joanne Calabrese of the American Business Media for their help in arranging interviews with several top-ranking executives in the magazine industry.

REFERENCES

Abrahamson, D. (1996). *Magazine-made America: The cultural transformation of the postwar periodical*. Creskill, NJ: Hampton Press.

Anthony, T. (1998). Living periodically: For professor, a magazine a day isn't enough. In *The National Directory of Magazines 1999*. Lanham, MD: Oxbridge Communications.

Brack, R. K., & Kummerfeld, D. D. (1999). *Magazines*. New York: Magazine Publishers of America.

Click, J. W., & Baird, R. N. (1990). *The magazine industry: Magazine editing and production* (5th ed.). Dubuque, IA: Wm. C. Brown.

Conference Board. (1998). Special Consumer Survey Report. [On-line]. Available: www.conference-board.org.

Ditlea, S. (1998). News you can browse. *Brandweek, 39* (42), 62–64.

Frydlewicz, R. (1998). Magazines in the information age. In *Media Research Report*. New York: FCB.

Husni, S. (1999). Magazines enter the 21st century alive and kicking. In *The National Directory of Magazines 1999*. Lanham, MD: Oxbridge Communications.

Jeffrey, D. (1998–1999). New media dominated '98 and not without controversy. *Billboard, 110* (52), 65, 89.

Media Analysts. (1998). Research Director, Marjorie MacDonald in Stamford, CT. Available at Philmorr@aol.com.

Mott, F. L. (1938). *A history of American magazines* (Vols. 1–5). Cambridge: Harvard University Press.

Peterson, T. (1964). *Magazines in the twentieth century.* Urbana: University of Illinois Press.

Striplin, D. (1999). Introduction. In *The National Directory of Magazines 1999.* Lanham, MD: Oxbridge Communications.

Tebbel, J. (1969). *The American magazine: A compact history.* New York: Hawthorne.

Wolseley, R. E. (1969). *Understanding magazines.* Ames: Iowa State University Press.

Wolseley, R. E. (1973). *The changing magazine: Trends in readership and management.* New York: Hastings House.

Zenith Media. (1998–1999). Introduction. In *World Magazine Trends 1998/99.* London: Royal Mail.

5

Newspapers

Randy E. Miller

At the beginning of the twentieth century, newspapers were numerous and were the most timely mass medium available. At the end of the twentieth century, more than a few critics are sounding a death knell for the newspaper industry, which has conceded its timeliness edge over the century to radio, then television, and now the Internet. One can define the present state of the newspaper industry in the United States by discussing the changes that have metamorphosed and will continue to metamorphose in recent times. In considering this transmutation, we may use this milestone: Twenty-five years ago, most newspapers were either adopting or about to adopt "cold type," the process of using computers and paper to replace the linotype machine and lead in the printing process. There may still be functioning linotypes somewhere, but for the newspaper industry, they might as well be passenger pigeons or some other extinct species.

The number of morning and evening newspapers has steadily declined since 1950 (NAA, 1998), as shown in the following:

Year	Total U.S. Daily Newspapers
1950	1,772
1955	1,760

1960	1,763
1965	1,751
1970	1,748
1975	1,756
1980	1,745
1985	1,676
1990	1,611
1992	1,577
1995	1,533
1997	1,509

Televised news has long since surpassed newspapers as the primary news source for most Americans. The steady disappearance of afternoon newspapers (from 1,450 in 1950 to 816 in 1997) has generated a lack of competition for many American metropolitan dailies. Houston, the fourth-largest city in the United States, is served by only one newspaper, as are Miami, Atlanta, Dallas, San Antonio, and St. Louis. Only the advent of joint-operating agreements through the Newspaper Protection Act of 1970 has preserved other two-newspaper situations.

Many in the newspaper industry, however, continue to declare an optimistic future for themselves: "At some point in every journalism conference nowadays, indignant defenders of the faith inform sundry and all that newspapers are not dinosaurs" (Feola, 1998, p. 45). They may point to an established home-delivery system, to the portability of newspapers or the tactile familiarity of newsprint, or to the maximized profitability of an industry without significant local competition. Still, some in the newspaper industry have been exploring alternatives and other means of producing journalism. Some of these efforts fall under the 1990s buzzwords, "media convergence."

At least some of the concern over the future of the newspaper industry has been met by the push of many newspapers to create on-line sites of their own. Two of the earliest newspapers to venture into this forum, the *Raleigh News and Observer* and the *San Jose Mercury News*, quickly established reputations among the on-line community. Today, hundreds of daily newspapers maintain Web sites and lists can be obtained through several sources, including the American Journalism Review Web site and www.newspapers.com, as well as simply typing the newspaper's name into a search engine.

In addition, some newspapers are beginning to forge alliances with their former competitors in television. One alternative to traditional print reporting can be observed in the *Sarasota Herald Tribune*'s launching of local cable broadcast news programming within the newspaper newsroom. Reporters produce print and broadcast versions of local stories. The print reporter then serves as an on-air reporter. Still others, like the Media General–owned *Tampa Tribune*, are constructing newsroom facilities that share office space with a television station; in this case, the Media General–owned WFLA-TV. The *Tribune* and the broadcast station have occasionally worked together on large projects, such as a print series about depression augmented by broadcast stories that included a telephone number for viewers to call a panel of psychologists. Shared facilities ought to lead to increased convergence.

For others, the most important shift at the end of the twentieth century has been the triumph of a bottom-line-oriented management model in newsrooms. Doug Underwood (1993) notes, "It's probably no surprise that in an era of mass media conglomerates, big chain expansion, and multimillion dollar newspaper buyouts, the editors of daily newspapers have begun to behave more and more like the managers of any other corporate entity" (p. 15). While the critics understand the need for profits, they think a commitment to reporting has been lost.

Licensed by publishers, MBAs have been granted positions of power in many newsrooms. These men and women, who have never been reporters, depend upon polling and focus groups to shape the news package. They are responsible for the endless meetings, with their charts and abstractions, that consume so much of the time that was once used by editors to inspire and instruct the young and push the seasoned veterans to better stories. They slice and pare and trim in the name of the holy bottom line, extol the virtues of "reader-driven" journalism, and in the process witlessly reduce the possibilities for long-range growth (Hamill, 1998, p. 16).

Marketplace journalism has devoted less "shelf space" to stories that seek to reform or to crusade against powerful institutions. The emphasis on the bottom line also affects the way newspapers cover—or don't cover—certain stories: "Many journalists are finding it tougher to question authority out in the world when they are being pressured to become loyal corporate soldiers inside their organizations," Underwood (1993, p. 15) says. One result is that morale among reporters and editors has fallen over the last twenty-five years. Pease's (1992) survey of more than 1,300 newsroom workers found that 46 percent wouldn't want their children to pursue a career in newspaper journalism.

The modern newsroom certainly seems more sterile than its predecessor. *The New York Times* journalist R. W. Apple has noted, "I look out around the *New York Times* newsroom, it looks like a law firm" (Hertsgaard, 1988, p. 80). For those journalists who remember the sense of excitement conveyed by the noise of typewriters, teletypes, and telephones, the MBA newsroom, replete with carpeting and cubicles, sounds as quiet as a library. Underwood (1993) and others point out that the sanitized newsroom does not tend to foster the creative iconoclasts who used to populate journalism.

One factor contributing to the increased role of market-based journalism has been the decline of independently owned newspapers throughout the century. Of approximately 1,500 dailies in the United States, only about 300 remain independently owned today. In 1940 there were some 1,300. These days fewer companies own more and more papers. They trade them and cluster them to consolidate operations and to achieve maximum market clout (Overholser, 1999).

Bagdikian (1983) is the foremost critic of this trend to place more and more newspapers under the control of fewer and fewer companies. He explains why this trend almost certainly will not change: "Ideas that would reduce the imbalance in media power are not difficult to suggest. The difficulty is that the most effective solutions would require that the giants lose their giantism. That is not in the nature of giants" (p. 229).

Consider also the trend in journalism toward what has come to be known as public or "civic" journalism, even though, as some academics note, there seems to be little agreement as to the exact definition of that phrase. Killenberg and Dardenne (1997) explain that the lack of a universal definition is due to the fact that public journalism takes forms or morphs, as in the technique used by filmmakers. The definitions seem to generally describe the notion that reporters and editors should take a more active role in the community by working with community groups and organizations. Those who support public journalism talk about its ability to build communities and for newspapers to actively set agendas that will benefit the public. They see it as a means to combat irrelevant, complacent, and lazy traditional journalism. The critics, in turn, see public journalism as, at best, another marketing ploy, and, at worst, an ill-advised attempt to sleep with the enemy by becoming coopted to government and other institutions.

Another change attempting to make headway within American newsrooms is the dismantling of copy desks. While the traditional horseshoe-shaped desk has long since vanished from most newsrooms, a few papers, such as the *Wichita Eagle* and *St. Paul Pioneer Press*, have reassigned their copy editors to reporting teams (Russial, 1998). With the advent of the computer into the newsroom in the 1970s, the copy editor's role has changed to include many typesetting duties formerly handled by backshop personnel. This transformation of job roles has been helped by "pagination" systems that allow layout personnel to handle tasks on a computer screen rather than on a dummy sheet. With those responsibilities, the editor's time to spend on traditional copy editing tasks has decreased. Instead, the copy editor spends a large portion of the workday worrying about copy-fitting stories to fit a newshole designed through a computerized system.

The desk is also more concerned about graphic presentation and design than it was in previous years. Spurred by *USA Today*'s efforts in the 1980s, many newspapers now actively seek to use infographics on key stories. And some newspapers have hired page designers who only work with the visuals, not words. In some cases, the emphasis on visuals helps tell the stories. The *San Jose Mercury News* was awarded the Pulitzer Prize in 1990 for earthquake coverage that included well-done maps and diagrams, says Smith (1992), but "in (some) other cases, the drive for better design has been at the expense of comprehensive reporting" (p. 236). Certainly, many newspapers have shortened their news stories (though the first of the ten-inch-story kings, *USA Today*, has actually lengthened some of its stories).

Other newspaper traditions should be disappearing shortly. Technology now exists that enables publishers to deliver a specialized news product to different markets. Blankenburg (1992) calls this process the unbundling of the newspaper. He said in the early 1990s that "with advanced presses and computer-aided pagination, editorial and advertising modifications during press runs will become more feasible" (p. 117). Sophisticated collation devices can assemble sections for particular neighborhoods. Because marketers have been able to identify numerous neighborhood types, each with its own demographic breakdown, publishers are beginning to deliver specialized products within a city. Blankenburg predicts that editors "will maintain a package of news for general distribution: major news from a distance, consequential news from nearby, and human-interest features of wide appeal. These topics could constitute one section supported by the kind of advertisers who seek a broad reach" (pp. 117–119). However, beyond that, editors will have the option of delivering tailored news and advertising sections to individual households. If the family on the corner is particularly interested in science news, the editor can bundle in a section featuring the latest science news daily. If the residents across the street want news about golf and investments, a newspaper may be crafted for them as well, and through use of bar codes, delivered by the same carrier who just tossed the science news onto the driveway.

THE TRANSITIONAL PERIOD

The transitional period has begun for newspapers. It will almost certainly continue, and the following are some of the factors that will bring about the transmogrification. As technology allows changes, those changes will occur. When technological advances occur, society tends not to ignore them. In the 1990s, *The New York Times*, known as "the Gray Lady" for its adherence to old-fashioned layout and the lack of color on its pages, ran its first color news photographs. The change may be attributed to the *Times* joining the twentieth century just as it ends or to a new direction in editorial policy, but the reality begins with the *Times*'s purchase of new presses in the early part of the decade. When *Times* management began to shop for the presses, it learned that only color-capable presses were being manufactured. The managers could not have purchased a new black-and-white-only press because such a device was no longer on the market.

When technology allows change, then one does well to predict that the change will eventually occur. American journalism has reached another allowance point much as it faced in 1975 with the advent of cold type. The most important factor in the transitional period will be the audience's increased ability to serve as its own editors. It is not unrealistic to predict that television viewers will soon have available the equivalent of a switcher so that they may not only choose from hundreds of channels, but may select which camera shot to use. Already, numerous Web sites allow people to send search queries into cyberspace and retrieve information, including news stories, on almost any topic imaginable. Some sites update the reader with any new topical stories every fifteen minutes or so. These topics are chosen by the user to match whatever suits his or her fancy.

By doing so, the computer serves as another method to break down the concept of place, as discussed by Meyrowitz (1985) in *No Sense of Place*. Meyrowitz argues that television as a medium, as opposed to television content, helped break down the concept of place as location and the concept of place as social standing. Television does so because its nature takes us behind the scenes to places we have not been or experienced. This technological change, he argues, was an important factor in the civil rights movement, the women's movement, and in the termination of political heroes.

It seems obvious that as the Internet metamorphoses as rapidly as it has in the previous decade, it would appear to have the ability to drastically change the sense of place as much as, if not more than, television has. The Internet contains an array of visual images combined with ever-increasing speed of use and the ability to "take" the user anywhere in cyberspace. It is just as apparent that the Internet will converge with a number of other media and media technologies, such as high-definition television and fiber-optic cable. The newspaper industry will be faced with adapting to compete against or join forces with whatever form of evolution this media becomes.

As newspapers continue to adapt, they will face an audience that has become familiar with the editing function once reserved for journalists. Some audience members will quickly become proficient at editing their own media product and others will require guidance from someone or something on the Internet to make sense of this new world. This ability to construct one's own newspaper and news programming will serve to further fragment an audience, which has become exceedingly fragmented in the last twenty years. Only 5 percent of Americans watch a network news broadcast four nights a week (Braestrup, 1992), and the percentage of the total adult population that reads newspapers fell from 77.6 percent in 1970 to 58.7 percent in 1997 (NAA, 1998).

Newspapers, long the most comprehensive source among daily media, may well no longer be the primary agenda-setter for the public, on the grounds that a fragmented public will fragment the agenda. The lack of a centralized news product may well lead to a change in government practice. It may be difficult to conduct a democracy when there is no common ground for discussion and little desire to encounter viewpoints different from one's own. The new newspaper may well lead to decline in tolerance of any idea that doesn't mesh with those nebulous community standards or of anyone who is different in any way.

One must also question whether the bright, new newspaper will be available to everybody. Certainly one can argue that newspapers have not often been attuned to meeting the needs of the economically disadvantaged, and that trend has been increased throughout the news-as-marketing era. One would expect an even greater disinterest among newspaper publishers to meet the needs of groups who are left behind on the information superhighway. These disenfranchised will be served instead by those media who currently serve their needs: specialized weekly newspapers, magazines, and radio.

Finally, the newspaper industry will have to decide whether it will continue to use newsprint. Some in the industry are quick to praise paper for its flexibility, its portability, and the tactile sense of the newspaper, though in fairness nobody seems to go for the tactile explanation as much as industry traditionalists. Newsprint has yet to disappear, but the amount bought will depend on the growth—or perhaps the reduction—of portable computers and the cost of computer chips. Knight-Ridder has actively researched and expects a time when media products are available on a pocket-size, mobile, flat display panel (Underwood, 1993, p. 158).

During the transition period, we should see some innovations make an appearance in the marketplace. It may well be that newspapers become a multimedia operation in more ways than one: Not only will publishers produce print and Internet products simultaneously, but the products will also use different approaches to news. One medium may become the company's "magazine journalism" product and the other may well become the traditional short newsform product.

The reporters themselves will see drastic changes during the transition. As some reporters already do in certain large markets, they will no longer routinely travel to the newspaper's central office. Instead, with portable newsgathering units, they will work out of homes or small bureau offices. This change almost certainly will not come easily, because the prevailing notion that working downtown ranks above bureau work will be difficult to allay. But as large newsrooms become more antiseptic, the culture will begin to change. The reporters will submit stories and receive feedback and assignments. They will communicate with others at the newspaper by cell phone or Internet chatrooms.

The copy editors themselves will continue to become even more production oriented than before. One would expect a reduction in traditional copy editing as spellcheck programs get more and more accurate and intelligent. We should understand that copy editors will have little problem becoming adept at editing Web stories just as former copy editors managed to adjust to video-display terminals after years of handling copy paper. Most copy editors will begin to work a schedule already in operation in some newspapers, four days a week with ten-hour shifts.

The toughest adjustment will come after the stories leave the newsroom. Because there will be an increase in demand for the on-line product and a decrease in demand for the newsprint product, labor negotiations with the press operators could become particularly troublesome. Backshop, pressroom, and mailroom jobs would become scarcer and, in one scenario, it's not hard to visualize a major strike at a large newsroom. After an impasse, a fire breaks out one morning in the pressroom—neither side claims responsibility—and management then announces that it doesn't plan to replace the presses at all, but will go all electronic. An uneasy peace is formed, but it's clear the unions have lost again.

THE NEWSPAPER IN 2025

A rumination about time.[1] Most of the changes discussed earlier in this chapter are based on the concept of time. Shorter stories? Readers have less time. Converging media? The audience has a decreasing amount of time. The death of afternoon newspapers? Unable to keep up in a more hectic time for traffic and readers.

One of the more interesting facets of Internet journalism, as practiced before 2025, is the disappearance of deadlines. The time crunch necessary for a newspaper to be produced and distributed almost completely vanishes with the Internet. When a story has gone through the editing process, it can simply be placed on a Web site at that moment. No backshop. No stereotyping. No press run. No delivery truck. One might say the new media of 2025, which includes newspapers, has diminished the sense of time as much as Meyrowitz's (1985) television diminished the sense of place. When news is instantaneous, when the competitive pressure to be first is lessened because of the nature of news, then deadlines are dead. Readers who have access to whatever Internet information sources are available can get updates throughout the day.

The newspaper has always been defined by time, as can be seen through some of the jargon associated with the field: first-day and second-day stories, advances, weekender, A.M. and P.M. papers, weeklies, embargo, and so on. The daily meeting of editors that determines front-page stories is often referred to in newsrooms by whatever time that meeting should begin (e.g., a "4-o'clocker"). Even the repository for old stories—the morgue—had its own certain connotation of time.

Most important, stories had to make it through the production process in time to be read at the doorstep. And in the old days, when newspaper competition was commonplace, it was important to be the first paper on the doorstep, not the second. With the newspaper of 2025, that concept is as dated as a linotype machine or copy boys.

Our 2025 reader likes a morning paper with breakfast. As she wakes, her printer (leased from the communication company, it will also print magazines) begins issuing her customized newspaper of the day, with just the sections and features within those sections that she requests. Her front page includes an index to the editor's selected news of the day and she may opt to tap one of those stories, which then billows from the printer. If not, she reads her local news stories, followed by extensive news of Ireland, her personalized stock quotes, the comics, and women's basketball stories. She takes a look at a long feature story on Orlando's star player and wants to know more. She taps a button and prints the transcript of the interview. She also has the option to view the interview through her Web cable unit. The next story looks too long for her to read now, but one tap reduces it to a headline and blurb.

She also takes note of the electronic coupons offered by businesses in conjunction with credit- and debit-card companies. As a newspaper subscriber, any purchase with a Visa card at Joe's Pizza automatically registers a 10-percent discount. The use of the card automatically triggers any subscriber discount. She takes note to stop at Joe's on her way home from work.

Her husband, who has slept in, doesn't have time for his morning paper and heads to work. He has the option of ordering a specialized section at a news kiosk or buying the old-fashioned copy. Their teenage daughter, however, chooses to scan headlines quickly on her portable display unit while the music from the hot band of the month plays through the unit; she tends to read stories after school ends. Her Uncle Larry, on the other hand, is a traditionalist who likes a printed newspaper delivered to his home, and indeed, walks outside each morning to fetch the paper from the lawn. However, as opposed to modern practice, Uncle Larry pays a rather hefty premium for this additional service. Over the years, with a decline in the number of readers requiring a newsprint version, the cost of newsprint has dropped, but the price of production and delivery has risen markedly, especially after the labor strife with the pressmen's union about ten years ago. Most of the pressmen have managed to find work as unskilled laborers at the news kiosks.

Meanwhile, a reporter prepares for the day. He covers suburban education and thus lives some fifty miles from the central news office, which, as a telecommuter, he visits maybe four times a year. He brushes doughnut crumbs from his lapel as he checks the battery on his handheld audio–video recorder, which produces broadcast-quality material that can be downloaded back to the design desk. He double-checks his assignment on his handheld computer unit and quickly scans previous stories about his subject as well as optimum directions to minimize time in traffic.

It seems like a simple enough assignment, but the demands on the reporter have changed. He will not only produce a basic localized story, but will also write a brief version that will fit on one screen and will download a video version that includes a package of shots from the high school in order to attract a local audience. Even more, because he works for a newspaper that is part of a large chain (one of only as few, as Bagdikian [1983] has predicted) and because his chain beat is suburban education, he will then communicate by what we today call visual telephones with other sources from around the country in order to produce a national story. Any subscriber to a chain paper can access that story or, indeed, any story from any reporter who works for the chain.

The chain's reporters thus contribute to a system that provides intensive local coverage, but also expands greatly the number of potential beats and thus potential audiences. A Knight-Ridder sports reporter in 1999, for example, might cover a collegiate soccer match. In 2025, that reporter might cover the local college soccer team as well as collegiate soccer nationally.

Meanwhile, back to our story package. As the reporter hits the send button, the package travels to the central office, where a package editor receives it and the editing functions begin. A copy editor, to use the old terminology, does actually read the stories after subjecting them to an artificial-intelligence spellchecker, which flags any potential problems (the thing ought to be perfected soon, the editor grumbles). Meanwhile, a video editor has scanned the video portions of the package and done a light editing job. At that point, one version goes to the newsprint desk and another version goes to the electronic desk, which composes a relatively short headline and a one-sentence summary before quickly placing it through a program that indexes it throughout the chain's Web sites. It is then placed on the suburban "page," which manages to look an awful lot like a traditional newspaper layout. But when readers click the story, they get a package that gives them several options, including the link into the electronic library for additional stories on the subject.

While the newsprint version goes through the traditional route—additional reading by copy editors, crafting of headlines and cutlines (off a photo lifted from the video package)—the story is already on-line. The reporter has returned home and, wisely, chooses to read the finished version. He spots an error and contacts the desk immediately and watches as the correction is made before his eyes. (He swears the mistake was introduced by the desk, which naturally blames him—some things never change.) He also double-checks that the newsprint desk is informed about the error—mistakes in that version can't be corrected as easily.

The reporter continues to contact sources, but takes a break to read an article in the latest journalism magazine. It claims that, in 2050, some expert says that journalists won't need all of that equipment, but will instead have a special chip implanted into their heads that will enable their bodies themselves to serve as camera and audio recorder, and may even introduce the senses of smell, taste, and touch into news stories.

Yeah, like that could happen, he thinks. Everybody knows change comes slowly to newspapers.

NOTE

1. This admittedly speculative section is based on past trends as well as discussions with several colleagues, particularly Rick Wilber and Jay Friedlander, and a rampant imagination.

REFERENCES

Bagdikian, B. H. (1983). *The media monopoly*. Boston: Beacon Press.

Blankenberg, B. (1992). Unbundling the daily newspaper. In P. S. Cook, D. Gomery, & L. W. Lichty (Eds.), *The future of news* (pp. 111–120). Baltimore: Johns Hopkins University Press.

Braestrup, P. (1992). Epilogue. In P. S. Cook, D. Gomery, & L. W. Lichty (Eds.), *The future of news* (p. 241). Baltimore: Johns Hopkins University Press.

Crichton, M. (1993). Mediasaurus. *Wired, 1*, 4.

Feola, C. (1998, June). Don't forget lessons of T. rex. *Quill*, p. 45.

Hamill, P. (1998). *News is a verb.* New York: Deirdre Enterprises.

Hertsgaard, M. (1988). *On bended knee: The press and the Reagan presidency.* New York: Farrar, Strauss, Giroux.

Killenberg, G. M., & Dardenne, B. (1997, October). Why professionals hate public journalism (and why academics love it.) Address to the Society of Professional Journalists national convention, Denver, CO.

Meyrowitz, J. (1985). *No sense of place.* New York: Oxford University Press.

Newspaper Association of America (NAA). (1998). *Facts about newspapers 1998.* NAA.

Overholser, G. (1999). Editor inc. *American Journalism Review, 20* (10), 48–65.

Pease, T. (1992). Newsroom 2000: Not my kid! Journalists leery of industry's future. *Newspaper Research Journal, 13* (2), 34–53.

Russial, J. (1998). Goodbye copy desks? Hello trouble. *Newspaper Research Journal, 18* (2), 2–17.

Smith, C. (1992). How news media cover disasters: The case of Yellowstone. In P. S. Cook, D. Gomery, & L. W. Lichty (Eds.), *The future of news* (pp. 223–240). Baltimore: Johns Hopkins University Press.

Underwood, D. (1993). *When MBAs rule the newsroom.* New York: Columbia University Press.

6

Public Relations

Julie K. Henderson

Public relations is often said to be an American invention. Although its roots date back to ancient times, the professional practice of public relations flourished during the twentieth century in the United States during a juncture of the emergence of the mass media with a thriving democracy dependent upon input from all segments.

A historical overview of the development of American public relations usually begins with a discussion of the American Revolution and the public-relations tactics used at that time, such as staged events (the Boston Tea Party), and the proliferate use of pamphlets, sermons, and slogans. Public relations evolved through various stages since that time.

The earliest and least sophisticated stage of public relations is the publicity model, in which the goal is simply to get the client's name exposed. Later stages included a one-way model, based on simply getting a message out with no concern for feedback, followed by the two-way model, in favor today. Under this model, relationships are built; that is, an organization does not seek to simply influence its surroundings, but seeks to be a community partner.

Part of the public confusion over the definition of public relations arises from the fact that as a new stage evolved, the former one did not universally die out; thus, all stages are still practiced today, not just the latest. For example, an agent for an athlete or an entertainer may simply be seeking to get his client's name in the media, at any cost, and may call himself a public-relations person, when actually he is a publicity agent.

The relationship between public relations and the mass media is curious. Public relations has prospered partly because of the mass media; today public relations still involves much work with the mass media, and yet it has failed to promote its own story. The term public relations is mostly used derogatorily in the mass media, frequently implying that its practitioners are trying to corrupt democracy or the channels of communication, or cover up an error or accident (Henderson, 1998). This remains one of the great challenges facing public relations in the next century: clarifying its role and purpose.

WHAT IS PUBLIC RELATIONS?

Put twenty-five public-relations practitioners in a room, and thirty definitions of public relations are likely to emerge. By 1985, one public-relations educator had compiled more than 500 definitions of public relations (Wilcox, Ault, & Agee, 1995). As defined by a popular textbook, it is "the management function that establishes and maintains mutually beneficial relationships between an organization and the publics on whom its success or failure depends" (Cutlip, Center, & Broom, 1994, p. 6). A task force of the Public Relations Society of America (PRSA) offered two other definitions: "Public relations helps an organization and its publics adapt mutually to each other," and "Public relations is an organization's efforts to win the cooperation of groups of people" (Seitel, 1998, p. 6).

In terms of what a public-relations person does, there are many misconceptions. For example, one is that public relations deals chiefly with placing items in the news. This is publicity. Public relations is much more complicated. The chief executive officer of a major public-relations firm outlines some of the numerous aspects of public relations by noting its practice can "help to build a brand by enhancing the reputation of the parent company. It can strengthen the value of the brand through coordinated investor relations. It can avoid embarrassment to the brand through vulnerability assessments and crisis management. And through internal workplace programs, public relations can stimulate greater loyalty and productivity among the workers who create products and services" (Drobis, 1998, p. 3).

As advisors or counselors to chief executives, public-relations people serve many roles, including advocate, translator of a company's message, conscience of the organization, and manager of issues and crises.

PUBLIC RELATIONS AT THE TURN
OF THE CENTURY AND MILLENNIUM

The practice of public relations has seen steady growth throughout the 1900s. By 1996, public-relations specialists held about 110,000 jobs in the United

States, according to the Public Relations Society of America, the largest professional group in the world. In 1997, the top twenty-five public-relations firms generated $1.7 billion in revenue, an 11-percent increase over the previous year (Drobis, 1998). More than 200 colleges and about 100 graduate schools offer degrees or emphases in public relations. The *1998–1999 Occupational Outlook Handbook*, published by the U.S. Bureau of Labor Statistics, notes that employment of public-relations specialists will increase faster than average for all occupations through 2006, but that keen competition is expected for entry-level jobs.

A variety of societal developments toward the end of the twentieth century bode well for public relations, and indicate it will continue to grow during the next century. These include the following:

1. Information overload.
2. The increased importance of communication.
3. Constant changes in society and business that require adaptation and the need for collaboration.
4. Globalization.
5. The speedy flux of public opinion.

INFORMATION OVERLOAD AND COMMUNICATION INEFFECTIVENESS

Individuals, businesses, governments—all are overwhelmed by the information available today, especially in trying to sift out the data that are relevant to crucial, immediate decisions. The public-relations department may become communication central for its organization, the place where all people go to get information. One strength of the public-relations professional will be the ability to take in the overwhelming amount of information available, sort it, condense it, and put it into a format that others can use. And to do this quickly.

On the flip side, public relations will be looked to as the home of communication experts, the place to turn to when a message needs to be created quickly and accurately and appropriately to the audience, based on an understanding of that audience. Technology is a tool, but the message is still crucial. One of the conundrums of modern life is that a fax can be received from China in thirty seconds but neighbors still can have trouble talking to each other.

Changes

Nothing is constant but change, and change is a constant in all organizations, only to become faster and more urgent in the future. Change often means some people benefit, others lose. The result is conflict, and dealing with conflict is another attribute of the professional public-relations person.

For example, think of the workforce and the workplace in 2025. The oldest baby boomer will be seventy-nine, the youngest sixty-one. Will this segment have moved into retirement, or will the age for retirement have been extended for them? Yes or no, the so-called Gen Xers and Yers will be in the prime of their work lives, but may have different approaches, as they have different ideas about values and expectations concerning their jobs (Grates, 1998).

In addition, the boomers will be voting for high taxes to keep Social Security and Medicare going, while Gen Xers will not, again aggravating social tension. Thus, the increased need for collaboration to achieve any forward movement, and the increased importance of public-relations people in their roles as negotiators.

Globalization

The concept of globalization has been discussed in depth in many forums. The public-relations department again will be called upon to deal with culture clashes (see the section on women and minorities).

Public Opinion

A chief area of concern for public relations is public opinion, which has never been so volatile, so quick to turn. Likewise, never have so many people demanded a voice in decisions affecting all aspects of their lives. Keeping the pulse of public opinion will be another important role public relations can fill for management.

This is especially important for businesses that sell products. Consumers in the future are expected to be more cognizant of the civic reputation of the companies from which they purchase goods. "Organizations will be judged less by their products and services and more by their policies and behavior related to those values that are 'hot' or 'politically correct.'" Already today, "The modern corporation is no longer perceived solely in economic terms, but as an institution which contributes to society as a whole. These changes in public expectations and in the perception of business are transforming public relations practitioners from ancillary roles in the corporation to an essential one" (Thomsen, 1997, pp. 14–15).

Scott Cutlip, an author of the first widely used textbook on public relations and of two books on public-relations history, summed up the possibilities:

Given the speed and obsolescence of innovations in the Information Age, it is risky to predict anything. My hunch is that the public relations function will remain essentially the same whatever the developments in the Internet, inter-global economy and global politics and crises. But the pressures on the function for more precision and more swiftness of responsiveness will expand exponentially.

Institutions and industries will still require the two-way interpretive function in order to adjust more quickly to the public's changing views and changing needs for goods and services. A society more interdependent beyond the dreams of the 20th century will more urgently require the functions of communication, two-way, and conciliation that arrives at a consensus of the public good. The increasing speed of communication and the resulting volatility of public opinion will require talents almost beyond the capacity of ordinary mortals. (Scott Cutlip, personal communication, December 15, 1998)

Not all the signs are auspicious for the practice of public relations, however, either today or in the future. A significant problem is the confusion over the definition of public relations and the poor job public-relations practitioners have done in educating the public as to their function and worth. "Lawyers are people who call themselves lawyers or attorneys. Doctors are people who call themselves doctors or medical doctors. Architects, who are certified, call themselves architects. People know what they do. They have not the vaguest ideas what we do . . . and that process will not be improved until we stop coining new terms and titles each week of the year," noted Frank Winston Wylie, professor emeritus of journalism at California State University at Long Beach (personal communication, December 21, 1998).

One in a long list of terms confused with the practice of ethical public relations is the currently overused term "spin." Spin was coined in a 1988 *Time* magazine article, and has haunted the public-relations profession ever since. Spin is used in the media as a synonym for public relations, but also is often implied to be "the twisting of messages to create the appearance of performance, which may or may not be true" (Seitel, 1998, p. 2). That is certainly not how professional public-relations people view their practice.

As public relations fights the misuse of the term, one of the main hurdles in the misunderstanding of the practice itself is the fact that public relations cannot be called a profession, and its practice cannot be limited, because there is no regulation. For example, Tom, who enters the market from an accredited university with a degree in public relations, three internships, and numerous awards, and Dick, who enters the market after dropping out of high school, can both call themselves public-relations practitioners. A quick glance at any newspaper's help wanted column reveals how frequently public relations is part of a job description, from receptionist to sales clerk. One response to limiting the people who can call themselves public-relations practitioners has been the movement toward accreditation and licensing.

WILL THE PRACTICE BE LIMITED BY 2025?

The Public Relations Society of America and the International Association of Business Communicators (IABC) both offer accreditation examinations for their members. PRSA began its program in 1964; in 1998, it joined with the Agricultural Public Relations Council, the Florida Public Relations Association, and the Southern Public Relations Federation to form the Universal Accreditation program. Later, the Maine Public Relations Council, the Society of Healthcare Strategy and Market Development, and the Texas Public Relations Association also joined. The transition process is expected to be completed by December 31, 2002.

The IABC will revoke accreditation of a member who does not abide by generally recognized standards of professional conduct and performance. The PRSA also maintains the right to punish its members and to revoke accreditation for unethical behavior. Both associations have their own codes of ethics, and accreditation is closely tied to ethical behavior. However, taking away someone's accredited status does not mean that person cannot still call himself or herself a public-relations person.

The debate over accreditation continues. Some people feel the accreditation provided by the PRSA is of little value because few in the business world acknowledge its value in terms of hiring and promotion. Others see it as a crucial step in the evolution of public relations into a profession, especially because of the emphasis in the examination on the code of ethics (Hearle, 1996; Graham, 1996).

No career is considered a profession unless members have their right to practice taken away, such as when an attorney is disbarred. Public relations does not have this procedure, and is not likely to in the future. Until a stronger method of labeling legitimate members, such as licensing, is made uniform, it is unlikely disreputable practitioners will be eliminated.

Frank Wylie notes that the purpose of licensing is to protect the public and that licensing of professionals is under the aegis and authority of the state, but is usually managed by members of the profession. "While many claim that they oppose licensing, they should also admit that without it, public relations will never be regarded as a profession. If PRSA and IABC were to cooperate, they could start the process of licensing by the states," Wylie said. Should public relations be licensed? "Yes, if it does half the things we claim for it in our commentaries, it does indeed have the potential to wreak serious havoc with the client or firm/corporation/non-profit agency. Because it has that serious potential, it needs to be licensed to protect the public. If we care about the public, we should care enough to offer them logical protection against the ravages bad public relations can cost" (personal communication, December 23, 1998).

The practice of public relations may be limited in another sense in the future, according to Thomas A. Schick, APR, a fellow of the PRSA, and coordinator of the public-relations major at Xavier University. "Public relations may be severely limited in its potential to serve its employers and clients by those employers and clients themselves, who restrict resources for public relations or who constrain public relations to narrow inanities like integrated marketing communications; public relations may also be limited by practitioners who subvert the scope and potential of our profession by focusing on carrying out employer/client mandates, instead of constantly keeping in mind the public interest" (personal communication, December 18, 1998).

WHO WILL BE THE PUBLIC RELATIONS PRACTITIONER OF 2025?

Today's ideal public-relations person is often described as a Renaissance person, someone who knows a little about everything, knows how to do everything, and has the eternal curiosity to keep learning. All the evidence indicates those requirements will only multiply:

Public relations practitioners have always needed to be highly educated persons, with a strong sense of history and knowledge of current events, who are taught to think in a certain way and to solve problems in a certain way. However, tomorrow's public relations practitioners will also need to be far more culturally astute and cosmopolitan—that is, particularly sensitive to the multicultural and international nuances of their organizations' diverse publics. Public relations practitioners—if they prove worthy of the task—will be called upon to be corporate—that is, organizational—interpreters and ethicists and social policymakers, charged with guiding organizational behavior as well as influencing and reconciling public perceptions within a global context. (Kruckeberg, 1995–1996, p. 37)

Specialist or Generalist?

Who will be more successful, the generalist or the specialist? The evidence seems to be leaning toward the specialist. While it is important to master the general skills of communication, future practitioners understand they must become generalized specialists who "are particularly conversant in and knowledgeable either of a specific aspect of public relations work—investor relations or government relations or speech-writing—or of a particular industry—computers or health care or sports or the arts. . . . Increasingly in the future, specific public relations jobs will be awarded to the practitioner who demonstrates specialized expertise in the particular area at issue" (Thomsen, 1997, p. 15).

In 1999, the three fastest-growing areas of public relations were high tech, financial, and health care. The National Investor Relations Institute is the fastest growing national public-relations association (Seitel, 1998).

One trend pointing toward specialization in the 1990s was outsourcing, the hiring of public-relations agencies or individuals to do public-relations activities. In a 1998 survey of public-relations corporate departments, 73 percent said they did outsourcing, often for special knowledge (Bisbee, 1998). Another trend was mergers that produced agencies too big to provide specialized help. "Mega-agencies cannot give personal services to hundreds of different clients at one time. This is a violation of the very tenets of the profession. Future trends will be toward small, specialized agencies looking after the needs of a handful of select clients," according to John Budd (Thomsen, 1997, p. 15).

One scenario is that corporate departments may become the homes of generalists, while individuals and small agencies will become the homes of specialists:

A generalist must have the detailed knowledge and expertise of the specialist when dealing with problems . . . which have far-reaching legal, social, political and economic implications. Only the specialist can know in full detail what interest groups will be aroused by a particular stand on an issue or by a particular decision. Only a specialist can know how a specific social issue is affecting a country in Europe and might, therefore, affect the U.S. or a country in the Pacific area. . . . It is this combination of generalist managers and specialist counselors that will characterize a successful public relations profession over the next decades. (Thomsen, 1997, p. 16)

The role for generalists cannot be overlooked, as "the need for specialists will grow: high-tech, financial, fund-raisers, speech writers and such; but the need to be an all-around communicator, thinker and counselor will be greater than ever. Especially the counselor part, if we want to get to—and stay at— the table (B. Adams, personal communication, December 15, 1998).

Technician or Counselor?

Most newly graduated public-relations majors enter the field in technician roles; that is, creating public-relations tactics: newsletters, news releases, organizing special events. However, as a profession, public relations seeks to aspire beyond that role, to a counselor function. This often takes additional education and experience. As Dr. Doug Newsom, professor at Texas Christian University, observes, "No one is really practicing public relations today unless he/she is affecting policy. If practitioners are not involved in counseling clients or their company, they are performing creative and clerical tasks that are part of public relations tactics" (personal communication, December 20, 1998). Another educator suggests an interesting scenario for the future:

The public relations function will probably be much as it is now within the organizational structure, but that structure itself will undergo some changes due to the dynamics of business. For example, my guess is that more and more executives will be hired guns, going from one company to another for quick fixes, and taking their top public relations people with them. We know the era of the 40-year executive is long gone; job-hopping no longer has the same meaning; loyalties have gone the way of the dodo and the mega-merger, so public relations people of the future will have to be even more flexible and mobile than ever before. By 2025, it's hoped the public relations person will be thought of as just another top executive, at the CEO's right hand, just as is the lawyer, the human resources person, top economics exec, and the accountants. (B. Adams, personal communication, December 15, 1998)

Another educator sees unlimited personal opportunities within economic boundaries:

The public relations scope will increase. Currently it is only limited by the ability of practitioners to convince others to let them prove their worth in exciting new ways. The opportunities really are boundless. But, we must note that cost control will continue to accelerate in the U.S. that will place more burdens on all leaders including or especially those in public relations. The code will be this; do more, for less, faster and more effectively. That's how the future will be played. (F. Wylie, personal communication, December 4, 1998)

Educational Preparation

In defining curriculum, public-relations educators face a continuing balancing act between skills and theory courses. How much of precious class time should be devoted to technical training that will be out of date in five years? Yet employers want employees who can hit the ground running, and so a certain amount is needed to avoid a disadvantage in the competitive job market.

While the ability to write well remains, as Cutlip (personal communication, December 15, 1998) terms it, the "admission ticket" to public relations, the future public-relations major will also need to address other areas of education, especially the social sciences, communication theory, history, law, and business. Former PRSA president David Ferguson noted,

Public relations will never reach the status of a profession as long as people can get into the field and prosper without having completed a fairly rigorous course of study in the field. And, until education in public relations becomes sufficiently broad to include study in such subjects as economics, philosophy and the law . . . any attempt to expand the vision and reach of public relations education must include significant involvement in international affairs and the international business climate. (Thomsen, 1997, p. 16)

In 1998, the Educators Academy of the Public Relations Society of America held its first International Interdisciplinary Conference, focusing on the need for public-relations education to relate to other disciplines—business, communications, and the social sciences—in sum, endorsing Ferguson's position.

Bill Baxter, APR, a fellow of the PRSA and associate professor emeritus at Marquette University, says the public-relations person in 2025 will, like today, be the communication conduit between companies–organizations–individuals and their constituencies–publics. And, like today, there will be a need for expert communicators: writers, photographers (print and electronic), graphics people, editors, makeup–layout specialists, speakers, media-relations types, special-event managers, and so on. But for those public-relations communicators who truly want to progress to management levels, to be counselors to decision makers and an integral part of the leadership heart of a company or organization, there are certain traits that must be espoused and mastered. Baxter cites such traits as a can-do attitude, being well prepared, an understanding of news media and public opinion, an understanding of organizational politics, and good judgment and taste (personal communication, December 5, 1998).

This type of broad-based education may lessen two of the problems facing public relations today. One is the influx of non-public-relations people placed in charge of the public-relations function, such as lawyers. The other is low wages. "The university student of 2025 will probably face the same low-income future for starting jobs as the student of 1999 does; why not? The wages are about the same now for openers as they were 10 years ago; lousy. Something needs to be done to ensure a living wage, or we're going to start losing graduates to other disciplines" (B. Adams, personal communication, December 4, 1998).

THE ROLE OF WOMEN AND MINORITIES

As this is written, in 1999, the majority of people entering the public-relations field, the majority of those practicing public relations, and the majority of students majoring in public relations are all women. Some view this as a negative trend, believing too many women will lower the salary scale for public relations and too many women will handicap the future growth of public relations.

Will so many women harm the profession? No, says Wylie:

The future of public relations will depend on the competence of the job holder far more than it will on any sexual preference by bosses. When the choice must be made between sexism and greed, the outcome will favor greed about 95 percent of the time. If persons have the talent, they will get the jobs and the promotions.

There is no such thing as too many good or superior quality public relations persons at any level. Our sexist society forces women to become better listeners and communicators. They develop these skills at an earlier age. And, they're better at them. Their language, presentation and writing skills tend to be very good indeed—public relations does not suffer from too many women, it benefits. Quality performance is the most urgent need in public relations. Those who can deliver and grow will win. Those who play a pat hand will lose. (F. Wylie, personal communication, December 4, 1998)

But with visibility comes responsibility. "If public relations is to achieve the higher destinies its leadership regularly projects for it, women are going to be the catalyst because they will increasingly represent numerically the majority of practitioners. The professional gauntlet is theirs to pick up" (Thomsen, 1997, p. 15).

The increasing number of women and minorities will change the face of public relations, even at the upper-management level now dominated by white males:

It's becoming more obvious that women will soon be the majority in public relations (if it hasn't happened already) and that minorities of all stripes and colors and creeds and nationalities will soon have a bigger slice of the public relations pie. It's only natural, as our nation becomes more of a melting pot. If women continue to eschew the traditional role of mother and workplace dropout, they'll naturally ascend to positions of greater management responsibility. Positions, by the way, they would have already ascended to in greater quantity if they hadn't assumed those traditional familial roles over the years. By 2025, the majority of top jobs (of any kind) will most certainly not be filled by white males. (B. Adams, personal communication, December 15, 1998)

In a poll reported in the spring 1995 issue of *Public Relations Quarterly* (Kotcher, 1995, p. 7), which questioned 257 public-relations practitioners, most said that the public-relations industry will have to become more sophisticated in regard to communicating with multicultural audiences, and the way to do so is to have staffs that are more gender diverse and ethnically diverse. Utilizing spokespersons whose backgrounds are the same as targeted audiences was cited as an effective means for reaching diverse external audiences. And nearly all respondents said the public-relations field needed to recruit more minorities, something that perhaps is occurring because the profession is becoming more of a "mainstream career" than it was twenty years ago (L. Duffey, personal communication, January 22, 1999).

CONCLUSION

There is no doubt the practice of public relations will exist, and probably flourish, in the next decades. As Lee Duffey of Duffey Communications in Atlanta notes, "As long as there are people and as long as there is a conflict of opinion and different viewpoints, public relations will definitely exist in 2025" (personal communication, January 22, 1999). What is less certain is that the practice will be known by that name.

The founder of one of the largest and best-known agencies in the United States sees good things ahead for his chosen profession: "The public relations field has come a very long way in my half-century in the field. It's essential, not an option. We're offering a much wider range of services. Budgets are breaking new records. We're attracting higher-quality young men and women than ever before. The future is bright," says Daniel J. Edelman (1998, p. 1), chairman and founder of Edelman Public Relations.

REFERENCES

Bisbee, J. (1998). The survey says . . . Outsourcing of PR activities on the rise. *Public Relations Tactics, 5* (2), 13.

Cutlip, S., Center, A., & Broom, G. (1994). *Effective public relations.* Upper Saddle River, NJ: Prentice Hall.

Drobis, D. (1998). *Still young at 25* (copy of speech given at the University of South Carolina on October 7, 1998). New York: Ketchum Public Relations.

Edelman, D. J. (1998). The future is bright. *Celebrating 50 years of PRSA* (supplement to *Public Relations Tactics*), 5 (2).

Goldman, E. (1998). 21st-century sea change in public relations careers. *The Strategist, 4* (1), 43–45.

Graham, J. (1996). Why accreditation makes sense. *Public Relations Strategist, 30*, 32–33.

Grates, G. (1998). Seeing through new eyes: A view on optimizing the future. *Public Relations Quarterly, 43* (2), 7–11.

Greenberg, K. (1998). Job outlook 2000: A forecast for the next century. *Public Relations Tactics, 5* (2), 20.

Hearle, D. (1996). Why accreditation doesn't make sense. *Public Relations Strategist, 31*, 34.

Henderson, J. (1998). Negative connotations in the use of the term "public relations" in the print media. *Public Relations Review, 24* (1), 45–54.

Kotcher, R. (1995). Diversity in today's workplace and marketplace. *Public Relations Quarterly, 40* (1), 6–8.

Kruckeberg, D. (1995–1996). The challenge for public relations in the era of globalization. *Public Relations Quarterly, 40* (4), 36–39.

Marcus, Jon. (1996). Spinning to win: Some frank advice from behind the headlines. *Academe, 82*, 29.

Seitel, F. (1998). *The practice of public relations*. (7th ed.). Upper Saddle River, NJ: Prentice Hall.

Thomsen, S. (1997). Public relations in the new millennium: Understanding the forces that are reshaping the profession. *Public Relations Quarterly, 42* (1), 11–17.

U.S. Bureau of Labor Statistics. (1998). *Occupational outlook handbook 1998–1999*. Washington, DC: U.S. Government Printing Office.

Wilcox, D., Ault, P., & Agee, W. (1995). *Public relations strategies and tactics*. New York: HarperCollins.

7

Radio

Edward Turner and Paula Briggs

THE DIGITAL IMPACT ON RADIO

In the year 2025, the listener is accustomed to getting what he or she desires in an instant. The world of digital technology allows the consumer to custom design with ease his or her daily listening habits. Digital broadcast stations and digital receivers allow for manipulation of program reception. Webcasting on the Internet also provides a means of customized listening. The radio station owner divests and develops alternative sources of revenue in order to ensure the financial success of his or her operation, utilizing a variety of technologies.

The digital broadcast signal contains not only audio information, but a variety of data useful for the consumer. The type of informational data are decided upon by the station. Stock quote updates, weather, traffic patterns, airport schedules, bus schedules, train departures, school information hotlines, movie viewing information, overnight ratings of television shows, and so on are choices made by the station. The idea of information on command from a radio service inspired the creation of a privately-held company based in Redwood City, California.

BUYOUTS AND CONSOLIDATIONS

U.S. radio was not doing well at the start of the 1990s. According to *Reason* magazine, "More than half of the radio stations in America were losing money. Many were going dark—the industry's poetic term for leaving the air" (Walker, 1999). Some feel this is a result of a Reagan-era rule called Docket 80-90, which relaxed the rules regarding how many stations a company could operate in a market. This resulted in 689 new outlets opening up on the FM dial.

Here is the dilemma. There is a set number of advertisers. Now there are more stations competing for the advertising dollar. The outcome: Broadcasters' profits fell because the price of airtime declined. Stations were going dark because of the competition. The solution was to license fewer stations and let existing owners consolidate their holdings. This consolidation took the form of "duopolies" that allowed owners to have two stations in the same market. Duopolies were legalized in 1992 (Walker, 1999).

One reason advertising revenues increased after 1992 is because chains owned more formats in a particular market. The Telecommunications Act of 1996 made it legal for corporations to own an unlimited number of stations nationwide. They can own as many as eight stations in most markets (Walker, 1999). Since passage of the Telecommunications Act, 4,000 of the 11,000 radio stations in the United States have changed hands, many of them gobbled up by small chains or media conglomerates. The result has been a rapid dwindling of local programming in favor of standardized music, talk, and news, often packaged in distant corporate headquarters (Hornblower, 1998, p. 25). Also, station owners have shrunk by more than 700 since 1996 because of a series of industry buyouts. This has left four corporations in control of more than 1,000 stations nationwide (Walker, 1999).

Thus, stations were able to force advertisers into buying time that they otherwise might not buy. With these "must-buy deals," advertisers bought time on a chain's popular station but had to buy time on the unpopular station as well. Increased automation and the nation's booming economy also spurred radio's rising revenues (Walker, 1999).

Advertisers have an advantage in exposing their products to potential clients by a variety of ways offered by the nontraditional radio station. Not only can their wares be marketed over the airwaves, but also on the Internet, on electronically triggered highway billboards, and on super large display monitors throughout the market landscape. Alternative streams of revenue are generated by taking advantage of additional exposure by one company in the business of getting the word out about the products the client has to sell, using an abundance of methods.

Success depends on the creation of sales, acquisition of program sponsorship, or increasing membership support for noncommercial radio stations. The demographic profile of listeners and the all-important ratings continue to be pivotal decision-making tools used by most agencies, consumers, and businesses. The number of qualified potential clients exposed to the message of the buyer translates into good business investment. The comparison with other media outlets, however, and unique contributing factors also play an important role in investment choices.

PROGRAMMING

The delivery of the message, whether selling a product or providing a public service, maintains its form of voice and/or pictures. The routing of this message, however, continues to change. The world has grown significantly smaller with the continued advancement in technology. Studio-quality production spots are transmitted routinely via integrated services digital network (ISDN) phone lines, satellite feeds, and Internet connections. The standardization of file configuration allows any studio to communicate its product all over the world in a matter of seconds. Live satellite, microwave, phone-line, and Internet broadcasts provide the listener with up-to-the-minute knowledge of events.

Program-delivery systems reside in a well-guarded, air-conditioned facility with qualified computer operators, programmers, and satellite technicians. Fiber optics, laser technology, and massive files of music and data on large hard drives are in place. Advanced software, hardware, and fiber-optics technology allow for ultra-fast streaming of data.

Programming now transmits both ways, by the user as well as by the program provider. The user selects music, news, sports, weather forecasts, stock quotes, business news updates, gambling results, and traffic updates in the manner he or she prefers. The provider makes this happen by employing the people who research, write, record, and produce this information. Module packages with this information can be stored on hard drives to be retrieved by consumers. Live connections, temporary buffered downloads, or hard-drive downloads will provide the prescribed data for the subscriber. The commercials, underwriting spot announcements (for noncommercial radio), company promotional spots, and jingles will all air within a prescribed format within the download.

Corporations are buying and selling stations on a grand scale. Independent programmers have been swallowed up by these huge radio corporations. For example, CBS Radio purchased sports and talk provider Westwood One and Jacor Communications acquired the Premiere Radio Network. Premiere distributes personality-driven shows like Dr. Laura Schlessinger and Rush Limbaugh (Schwirtz, 1998).

Programming is suffering in American radio because of consolidation. The fact that one company can own several formats in one market is putting a tight squeeze on independent programming. Ron Hartenbaum, CEO of Jones International Networks' radio division, calls this "the quieter consolidation" (Schwirtz, 1998). Hartenbaum has firsthand experience with buyouts. Jones bought his company, Media America. "In turn, Jones has partnered with Capstar Broadcasting, now a part of the Chancellor Media Corp., to produce a country music show called Nashville Nights. The new world order says that the old concept is out the window and competitors are working together on projects," said Phil Barry, vice president of Jones Programming (p. 12).

Corporations are working together, as Barry states. They are also developing their own content providers. Chancellor Media Corp., a 400-plus station operation, formed the AMFM Network this year. AMFM owns the ubiquitous *Casey Kasem Top 40* show, and two other personality-driven shows. The classic-rock show is hosted by actor Kevin Bacon and RuPaul hosts the other program (Schwirtz, 1998).

AMFM has affiliates in all the top-ten markets. These stations run programming produced by AMFM. This cuts back on the content provided by independent syndicators to affiliates (Schwirtz, 1998). It's not easy for independents to find outlets to run their programming. Kraig Kitchins, resident of Premiere Radio Network, says, "Syndicators today gather 25–30 stations on average where once it was easy to get 200 affiliates" (p. 12). As a result, advertising costs may rise. Companies can tie up the market "and then build a stable of popular syndicated programming. Westwood One for example, is the only place to buy NFL since the merger between CBS and Westwood One gave the syndicator rights to both football conferences, said Sam Benrubi, the network's executive VP. He notes that rates increased 'by a couple digits' as a result" (p. 12).

MICRORADIO

The consolidation of radio has resulted in a few corporations running the airways. They decide formats, programming, advertising rates, and so forth. Some people are becoming quite prosperous, and as long as the government continues its current practices of easing restrictions on combinations, they will continue to flourish. Jesse Walker (1999), associate editor for *Reason* magazine, states that mainstream radio "has long relied on the government to protect its biggest players, shore up their profits, and ensure that the competition doesn't get too unruly while making it steadily harder for startup stations to challenge the chains" (p. 1).

Former FCC Chairman William Kennard has addressed this problem. "As we move into the Information Age, we at the FCC will have to change," said Kennard. "The top-down, command and control, regulatory model of the Industrial Age is as out of place in the new economy as the rotary telephone. As competition and convergence develop, the FCC will continue to streamline its operations, eliminate unnecessary regulatory burdens, and make it easier for the public to interact with the agency" (Silva, 1999, p. 4).

If access were made easier and unnecessary regulatory burdens were lifted, then more people would be able to start up stations legally. Right now, that is a very expensive and complicated procedure. So, radio pirates have emerged. In April 1998 it was estimated that 500 to 1,000 microbroadcasters operated nationwide (Hornblower, 1998). These microradio operators are not licensed by the FCC to use the public airwaves. Current FCC policy prohibits licensing a new station if it is less than 100 watts, and these renegade radio buffs "operate low-budget, low-power stations [less than 100 watts] without permission from the government" (Walker, 1999, p. 1).

Microstations connect with that part of the community often overlooked by the large conglomerates. They give more than a ten- to fifteen-second reader on community activities. Walker (1999) states that "they have covered high school sports, broadcast city council meetings and church services, and given airtime to local musicians; they have trained teenagers and retirees to be broadcast engineers, sponsored concerts and parties, coordinated flood relief, and exposed local corruption and crime" (p. 1).

In late 1997 the FCC intensified its crackdown on unlicensed stations. This did not deter this grassroots movement. "They defiantly declared that they'd put 10 more stations on the air for every one the government shut down" (Walker, 1999, p. 1). Consequently, the FCC is considering creating a legal microradio service. On January 28, 1999, the FCC issued a Notice of Proposed Rulemaking on microradio and invited public comment. Kennard thinks that microbroadcasting will counteract the recent trend toward consolidation. "It might also reverse the decline in the number of black-owned stations, a concern important to Kennard, the FCC's first African-American chairman. . . . Kennard's plan would create three new classes of stations, one operating at a maximum power of 1,000 watts, one at no more than 100 watts, and one—perhaps—at one to 10 watts. (The last category is more a tentative suggestion than a concrete proposal.)" (Walker, 1999, p. 6).

House Telecommunications Subcommittee Chairman Billy Tauzin is not happy with Kennard's proposal. Tauzin argues that the FCC has no power to create a microradio service without Congressional authorization. This isn't true and, amusingly, a conservative Republican fails to note that the new stations might eat into the audience for public radio (Walker, 1999, p. 1).

There is concern about whether the FCC has the right to make good on Kennard's pledge to see that minority and other groups desiring station ownership acquire them through the creation of new low-power FM stations. New technologies provide business opportunities. According to McConnell, "Many broadcasters also complain that it is unfair for government to create a class of potential competitors that can get into business cheaply after so many station owners have invested so much to get full-powered stations on the air" (quoted in Tedesco, 1999, p. 26).

Stephen Dunifer, pioneer radio pirate, is founder of Free Radio Berkeley, one of the country's most prominent unlicensed operations. Dunifer doesn't think much of Kennard's plan. He calls it a "bogus" scheme, "designed to invoke the splitting of the movement to reclaim the archives" (Walker, 1999, p. 3). With some assistance, Dunifer enabled microbroadcasters to set up their low-power stations by selling kits around the country. All anyone needed was a few hundred dollars to launch a station with a transmitter powered by fewer watts that a light bulb, often covering a radius of only a few miles. It is notable that the FCC could not get an injunction against Dunifer's station (its motto is "Turn On, Tune In, Take Over"). A federal judge in Oakland, California, turned the agency down on First Amendment grounds (Hornblower, 1998).

The FCC is operating under technical standards set in the 1950s. Thus, it will not allow a station to sell off part of its frequency. This would open up legal and financially viable avenues for the pirate radio operator. However, "the law says he has to sell all his ethereal territory at once, meaning that only another giant can agree to buy it. So the law encourages consolidation, which in turn encourages centralized, automated, prefabricated programming" (Walker, 1999, p. 11).

More of the "ether" would be available if broadcast stations were allowed to compress or split up their frequencies. Instead, they are limited to two artificial reservations, the AM and FM bands. Jesse Walker (1999) suggests, "Manufactures could sell down-converters—small devices that would attach to or sit near a radio and convert signals sent over other sections of the spectrum" (p. 12).

Microbroadcasters give their listeners coverage that most radio no longer delivers. They offer "genuine localism, eclectic music, politically charged debates" (Walker, 1999, p. 10). So, in addition to grassroots competition, mainstream radio will face competition from the skies. "A new satellite service is poised to take the standardized, placeless programming that dominates the AM and FM bands and do it better, with more options, more listening convenience, and no ads. In a few more years, Internet radio may start to do the same" (Walker, 1999, p. 3).

DIGITAL PLATFORMS

Webcasting and Internet simulcasting provide additional platforms for program exposure. They also provide additional sales and marketing opportunities for aggressive entrepreneurs. Internet users and clients take advantage of the advance technologies available to them within the cyberspace universe. Users of the Internet have the option of programming their listening by quickly downloading song selection files onto their hard drives or temporary buffer memories. The price of this download, however, includes commercial spots, station promos, and song-licensing fees.

The investment into Webcasting is perceived as an additional outlet to existing services, not competition for listeners. Several companies moved rather swiftly to set the pace for providing legal digital music access on the Web. Secure Digital Music Initiative (SDMI) and Microsoft established their business interests early, according to Tedesco (1999):

Secure Digital Music Initiate's portable device working group, which appears to be moving at hyper-speed toward introducing music downloading devices with its imprimatur in time for the 1999 Christmas season. It aims to complete specifications for portable music downloading devices by June 30. Reciprocal's digital right management system enables distribution of all forms of digital content, and payment for it, while offering the copyright protection at the heart of the SDMI initiative. Making legal music downloads possible is the most pressing e-commerce market need in an arena where Microsoft is particularly eager to play. Jupiter Communications estimates music downloading as a $30 million business by 2002. Microsoft and Reciprocal join a crowd of companies looking to define that market.

The popular Internet provider America Online realized the possibility of e-commerce and made significant investments in the possibilities: America Online made its first move into the online music space [by] acquiring online music programmer Spinner Networks and technology firm Nullsoft in stock swaps worth $400 million. The two deals immediately make AOL a major Web music player: The Spinner.com music service transmits 2 million tunes daily to PC users and Nullsoft owns Winamp, the most poplar MP3 player for PCs, and Shoutcast, an MP3 streaming audio system. So in a single harmonious stroke, AOL lands a top music Web site and a technology arm to fuel future music initiatives. (pp. 44, 70)

It took seven years for the first satellite radio service to get a license, in part because the satellite portion of the spectrum had not been established, and mainstream media put up a hard fight against it. Because of the small size of the spectrum, only two companies, CD Radio and XM Satellite Radio, have licenses (Walker, 1999). The FCC auctioned these licenses in 1997 at a cost of $83.3 million and $89.8 million, respectively (Bachman, 1999).

There are two schools of thought on point-to-point communication. Traditional terrestrial stations view it as serious competition. Direct Audio Radio Service states it would supplement, not replace, terrestrial stations (Walker, 1999). Satellite radio will cater to a national audience. Its programming will be as diverse as one could expect, according to Bachman (1999):

In terms of programming, their services should offer much in common—which is to say, plenty of variety. Both companies expect to offer 100 channels of crisp, CD-quality sound. The music channels will be commercial-free, and the talk channels will include commercials but will be peppered with lower spot loads than conventional radio (perhaps five minutes per hour).

Both services will offer the radio staples, but instead of just one oldies station, listeners will be able to chose from among a '70s station, a '60s station, a '50s station, and so on. Consumers will be able to flip to a channel featuring female country artists, blues, modern jazz, All Frank Sinatra All the Time. Plus there will be channels providing category-specific information on topics as diverse as gardening, home improvement and cooking. (p. 28)

Satellite radio has a pronounced advantage over terrestrial stations in that the listener can carry a signal across the country with digital clarity—no interference. David Margolese, founder of CD Radio, was fascinated with this idea. Margolese, a pioneer in cellular phones, sold his cell-phone company for $2 billion to start CD Radio. CD Radio was to have launched three Loral satellites in 2000. Its three-band audio system could offer 100 channels of digital satellite-to-car (STC) sound. CD Radio will be marketed directly to the automobile market and will position itself to adapt existing car radios for STC (Hogue, 1999, p. 20).

There are at least two other companies posed for this new service of providing radio adapters for cars. "Hughes Network Systems has a mobile satellite radio interface standard for mobile satellite services using geosynchronous earth-orbit satellites" ("Hughes Prepares," 1999, p. 18). "Delphi Delco Electronic Systems is now designing and marketing a factory-installed three-band car radio" (Bachman, 1999, p. 26).

CD Radio's negotiations with GM fell through. Instead, XM will provide STC service for GM cars. According to Bachman (1999), "XM is a subsidiary of American Home Satellite Corp., and one of the owners of AMSC is Hughes Electronics, a subsidiary of General Motors Corp." (p. 28).

XM is targeting a broader audience than CD Radio. XM wants to position itself as a third alternative to AM and FM. It plans on being available in various places. XM has also negotiated several exclusive programming deals with twenty-four-hour sports and talk networks One-On-One Sports, Bloomberg News Radio, C-SPAN Radio, and USA Today ("XM Satellite Radio," 1999). BET, Radio One, and Syndicated Communications will create four African American talk and music channels for XM (Hall, Harris, & Munson, 1999).

Domestic and International broadcast from satellite is scheduled to start in 2000. Domestically, the customer's investment in satellite radio is similar to cable. The one-time startup fee for both companies is roughly $200. Customers will then receive a small satellite dish and a card that will allow their radios to receive the signals. They will then have to pay a subscription fee of $9.95 a month (Walker, 1999). The switch here is that satellite radio, for the most part, will be predominantly subscriber supported. XM plans to attract some advertisers, but the bulk of its revenue will come from subscriptions (Walker, 1999). "CD Radio estimates that it needs about 2 million subscribers to earn a profit" (Bachman, 1999, p. 26).

Digital satellite radio receivers will make it possible for WorldSpace Inc. to provide satellite radio service internationally. WorldSpace was to have started broadcasting to Africa and the Middle East in 2000. AfriStar, the company's first satellite, will transmit three beams of digital-quality sound to listeners. Each satellite beam is capable of providing more than fifty channels of programming, WorldSpace claims. CNN International is contracted to provide programming on all three beams of AfriStar for three years. With other satellites planned, according to Noah Samara, WorldSpace chairman and CEO, WorldSpace should have programming for a majority of the world next year, Samara noted. Satellite radios will pick up receiver L-band programs as well as AM and FM local and regional broadcasts. In addition, domestic and international short-wave communications can also be picked up with digital satellite radio receivers. The receivers contain data ports that are used to receive multimedia programming ("Satellite Radio Rollout," 1998).

CONCLUSION

The production and daily operation of a radio station requires well-rounded individuals with computer expertise, audio-production skills, superb writing abilities, aggressive creative know-how, and the persistence to accomplish set goals within established deadlines. The tools needed to accomplish these tasks, however, no longer reside in a typewriter, tape recorder, or stand-alone personal computer. These are now fully integrated workstations that access research databases, the Internet, audio-stream files, video files, photo files, graphic files, mail-merge files, and live network feeds. The operator or programmer has the capability to establish a platform of operation by selecting and implementing performance tasks. This performance task can then be relocated to a remote site and enabled for operation. The workstation is then available for other tasks.

The need for listenership continues to fuel the competition among program providers. The aggressive innovator willing to utilize advanced technology often takes and sustains the lead in capturing new revenue. The logical merger of services and technologies present a "spoiled" society with innovative tools necessary to stay on board the highway of life without being bumped off for lack of up-to-the-minute knowledge and entertainment.

REFERENCES

AOL stakes out Net music turf. (1999, June 7). *Broadcasting & Cable*, p. 44.

Bachman, Katy. (1999). The next wave. *MediaWeek, 9* (15), 26.

Hall, T. C., Harris, P. L., & Munson, C. P. (1999). Innerloop. *Business Journal, 17* (34), 2.

Hogue, Leslie. (1999). Satellite-radio biz tunes in to autos. *Crain's Detroit Buiness, 15* (17), 20.

Hornblower, Margot. (1998, April 20). Radio free America. *Time South Pacific*, 25.

Hughes prepares GEO interface standard. (1999). *RCR: Radio Communications Report, 18* (18), 31.

Rhoads, B. (1999, April 12). The *Radio Ink* Internet Conference publisher's notes (1), 8.

Satellite radio rollout planned next year. (1998, December 14). *Electronic News, 44* (2249), 18.

Schwirtz, Mira. (1998). Fewer choices on the dial. *MediaWeek, 8* (35), 12.

Silva, Jeffrey. (1999). Kennard hints at more deregulation. *RCR: Radio Communications Report, 18* (2), 4.

Tedesco, R. (1999, June). *Broadcasting & Cable*, p. 32.

Troy, B. (1999, April 12). We must destroy internet-only radio, this may be your answer how. *Radio Ink*.

Walker, Jesse. (1999, June). Radio waves. *Reason Online* [On-line]. Available: http://www.reasonmag.com/9906/fe.jw.radio.html.

XM satellite radio adds sports talk. (1999). *MediaWeek, 9* (2), 3.

8

Recording

Steven J. Dick and Michael Lescelius

Prior to 1877, if you wanted to actually hear music or a speech, you simply had to be at the event on time. Of course, you could read the transcript or the sheet music (if available), but it couldn't really be the same as being there. In April 1877, Charles Cros, a minor poet and amateur scientist, described in a paper to the Academie des Sciences in Paris a process that "consists in obtaining traces of the movements to and fro of a vibrating membrane and in using this tracing to reproduce the same vibrations, with their intrinsic relations of duration and intensity" (Gelatt, 1971).

Later that year, on a tangent from another work, Thomas Edison and his minions in West Orange, New Jersey, built and demonstrated the first "talking machine." This first phonograph, which used tin foil wrapped around a cylinder, was an instrument of crude design and dubious utility. It could record only 150 to 200 words and even Edison later admitted "that no one but an expert could get anything intelligible back from it" (Gelatt, 1971).

Edison returned to talking-machine development in the summer of 1888, but he was not alone. Others had made several patented improvements on Edison's original design, including better sound and longer playing time. Though Edison's phonograph was not the best, his reputation and his company's quest for a better cylinder helped it carry the day in the infancy of the recording and record industry. It was during this time that both the gramophone (patented by Emile Berliner) and the phonograph became essentially playback units. Commercial recording of prerecorded music was under way by 1890 (Gelatt, 1971, pp. 64–68). From the late 1880s until the widespread use of radio in the early 1920s, the recording industry flourished because of the phonograph and the gramophone.

During the mid-1940s the tape recording as we know it today became a viable high-fidelity medium (Gelatt, 1971, pp. 284–285). German engineers invested over twenty years in the development of microphone, amplifier, and magnetic tape technology. Minnesota Mining and Manufacturing (3M) made subsequent improvements of magnetic tape. 3M also pioneered stereo recording techniques, such as "bouncing" or recording back and forth between two or more recorders to layer sound on sound. True multitrack recording followed and continues.

With the invention and refinement of computers in the 1950s, information could be stored and manipulated using millions of switches turning on and off very quickly, represented by binary numbers (Gates, 1996). Sound, being a form of information, was no exception. Instead of mechanical or electrical analogs of the frequency and amplitude of sound, audio signals are sampled at a very high rate (44.1 kHz to 96 kHz). The amplitude of each sample is then divided into discrete voltage steps, with each step assigned a binary number. These numbers are then arranged to form a binary word. This is known as "quantizing." Common word lengths for digital audio are currently 16, 20, or 24 bits. Sampling and quantization are to digital what frequency and amplitude are to analog (Huber & Runstem, 1990, pp. 129–134).

The quantization process was new because of a new step: translating waves into numbers. In reality, it was not all that different from the technology of AM radio. With AM, a high-frequency carrier wave is modulated so that its amplitude draws the shape of the lower-frequency signal. Since the frequency of the carrier wave remains constant, the signal is sampled at regular intervals. With quantization, the amplitude of the signal is sampled at regular intervals and described in numbers rather than by the wave.

PRODUCTION

A distinction must be made between professional and consumer sound technology. The difference can be defined simply. Equipment for the professional market is designed for the producers (composers, arrangers, musicians, engineers, manufacturers, etc.) of audio products, while the equipment for the consumer market is targeted toward the end user of audio products: the audience. Though they are connected and interdependent, there are many aspects of professional audio that are of little interest to the average listener.

A professional recording studio can be divided into the studio and the equipment. The studio is the actual physical space where the sound is produced. Studios vary in size, shape, and acoustic design in accordance with the personal tastes of the owners (Huber & Runstem, 1990). The goal is to design an environment that creates the desired feel for the musical style. Essentially, the studio is another instrument, a vibrating chamber of air that encourages some notes and discourages others. Since music is usually produced and always enjoyed in analog, the studio environment is likely to change very little. The equipment translates ideas, expressed by moving air, into a form that can be stored and re-created at a later time, independent of the actual performance. Components in all recording studios include transducers, amplifiers–attenuators, and storage systems.

A transducer is any device that changes one form of energy into a corresponding form of energy. The ear is a transducer that converts rapid changes in air pressure into corresponding nerve impulses. A guitar is a transducer that changes the muscle energy of plucking, hitting, or scraping strings into sound pressure waves. A microphone is a transducer that converts sound pressure waves into analogous electrical voltages. An analog-to-digital converter changes continuous electrical waveforms into corresponding discrete binary numeric values that represent analogous voltage levels (Huber & Runstem, 1990, pp. 8–9).

Unlike transducers, the input energy of amplifiers and attenuators is the same as at the output. An amplifier boosts the power of an energy source without undesirably altering it. In the world of audio, amplifiers have many applications. Employing either tube or transistor technology, they can be used to amplify, equalize, isolate, combine, or distribute audio signals. Attenuators do the opposite of amplifiers. Utilizing resistors of various types, attenuators attempt to decrease the power of an energy source without degradation. Amplifiers and attenuators in a recording studio provide means to control an audio signal.

Whether it's analog electromechanical grooves cut into plastic discs, electromagnetic flux on metal oxide tape, or binary code stored in a computer, all recording studios must be able to store audio information for later manipulation or reproduction. All practical methods of professional storage entail either magnetic (tape or hard disk) or optical media (CDs).

STUDIO RECORDING TODAY

Though analog vinyl records and compact cassettes have almost entirely given way to sonically superior digital compact discs in the consumer marketplace, many of those CDs are still initially recorded using analog magnetic tape machines. Five- to fifteen-year-old consoles and "vintage" microphones and outboard gear (compressors, equalizers, reverberation units, etc.) are still popular. Often these systems are older than the chief engineer. One reason for this apparent conservatism in such a fast-changing, technology-based work environment is the high cost of replacing major pieces of gear all at once. Another is that sometimes a manufacturer hits on a classic design that cannot be bettered (Michie, 1997). For example, microphones like the AKG C-12 and the Telefunken Elam 251, both designed and built in the early 1960s, are among the most sought after and highest-priced microphones on the market today (Webb, 1997).

Virtually all recording done in professional studios is "multitrack." The system or engineer makes multiple, simultaneous discrete recordings and combines them later in a mixing process to create a finished product. This is done so an artist, producer, or engineer can have complete control over the individual parts. Each part of the recording can then be modified or corrected without affecting the other parts. Overdubbing makes it possible to create the illusion of a larger ensemble with a limited number of performers (Alten, 1996, p. 126).

There are three main kinds of multitrack machines used in studio recording today: analog magnetic tape recorders, digital magnetic tape recorders, and digital computer-based recorders or digital audio workstations (DAWs).

Analog Recorders

Though slowly disappearing from the scene, analog magnetic tape recorders are still widely used and highly regarded for producing high-quality results. Twenty-four-track machines using two-inch wide tape running across a stationary recording head at fifteen or thirty inches per second (ips) was the industry standard for nearly twenty years until digital recorders hit the market. Offering a warm, full range sound, this format is preferred by many audio professionals over the competing digital options. Machines cost between $20,000 and $30,000, with tape costing nearly $200 for about twenty to forty minutes of recording time (depending on tape speed). This points out one of the drawbacks of two-inch analog recording: tape cost. Other disadvantages are the inherent tape hiss of any analog recording. With the use of advanced noise-reduction technology like Dolby Laboratory SR Noise Reduction, however, this problem has been minimized.

Other analog formats still in use include one-inch and half-inch sixteen-track and eight-track machines. In most cases, multiple machines may be synchronized to increase the number of tracks available for recording in a given session or project. Also, computer editing features exist that locate specific points on a tape and select the record mode as desired. This feature is referred to as "punching in/out." Other features include "looping," which is the repeated playing of a specific portion of tape for purposes of rehearsal prior to punching in.

Digital Recorders

Professional-quality digital recording machines can be categorized as digital audio stationary head (DASH), rotary head digital audiocassette recorders

(R-DAT), hard-disc recorders, and recordable compact disc (CD-R). DASH and R-DAT recorders rely on magnetic tape, similar to the type used in analog recording, to store the coded binary data. Hard-disc recorders use computer hard-drive technology to record audio in a nonlinear fashion, which allows for fast, random access and nondestructive editing and manipulation. Optical CD-R recorders are the first of a possible growing class of nonmagnetic media.

DASH recorders were the first digital recorders to be widely used in the industry starting in the late 1970s. Similar to analog reel-to-reels in design and using specially formulated quarter-inch or half-inch tape, they are usually configured to record twenty-four, thirty-two, or forty-eight separate tracks of audio. The cost of these machines was and is very high (anywhere from $50,000 to $400,000), so use has been generally limited to high-end studios.

First introduced in 1986, two-track stereo R-DATs brought digital recording to a large number of audio professionals for whom DASH recording was out of the question financially. Early systems were simply called DAT, but the recording industry objected to digital recorders in the consumer market. R-DAT distinguished the higher-price professional machines from play-only units that quickly failed in the retail market. R-DATs are rotary-head machines and similar in design to videocassette recorders. The data are stored diagonally across a tape in frames and housed in a plastic cassette. Unlike DASH machines, which record linearly at fifteen to thirty inches per second, R-DATs run at about one-third ips (Alten, 1996, p. 141).

The early 1990s saw the introduction of the first multitrack R-DAT recorders, known as ADATs, made by the Alesis Corporation. Available only in eight-track configurations, multiple ADAT machines could be linked to provide up to forty-eight tracks of recording. With each machine costing only around $2,500, high-quality professional multitrack recording had now become truly affordable. As a result, the age of the "project" studio was unleashed with a vengeance. Today, R-DATs come in several formats, including two-track stereo on four millimeter tape, eight-track multitrack on eight millimeter tape (Tascam DA-98, 88, and 38), and eight-track multitrack on half-inch tape (ADAT). R-DATs use 16-bit words at either 44.1 kHz or 48 kHz sampling rates and are generally used for mixdown master recording in place of quarter-inch analog machines.

Hard-disc recording has been gaining in popularity over the last few years. The first systems came in the form of stand-alone digital workstations in the early 1990s. They were expensive and limited due to cost of computer processing power. As computing power increased, storage devices cheapened, and hard-disc recording would overtake all other formats before too long. There are still problems to overcome, however, before the floodgates fully open (Katz, 1996).

The key to good digital recording lies in conversion from analog to digital and back again. The de facto standard in the industry has been 44.1 kHz 16-

bit conversion since the introduction of CDs in the early 1980s. Dissatisfaction with the edgy, sterile sound of digital has led to higher quantization (20 and 24 bit) and higher sampling rates (88.2 and 96 kHz). The higher sampling rates of CDs are still very expensive dollar- and memorywise, but well worth the cost (Ludwig, 1998). The problem is that the distribution (CDs) is still at the lower rate. Converting down still means loss of quality.

The new standard digital versatile disk or digital video disk (DVD) offers the opportunity to store a much greater amount of data. With standards still being set, it is difficult to determine the storage capability of the eventual DVD or recordable DVD. Even higher-storage-capacity systems will be developed. Higher-capacity storage could be used for mastering works or archiving.

Mixing Boards

Professional studio mixing boards or consoles are the nerve center of every studio (Alten, 1996). Mixing boards usually range from sixteen to seventy-two input–output channels. Prices range from a few thousand to a half-million dollars (and beyond), depending on the needs of a given studio and the ability of the board. Each input–output channel can have a number of features, including microphone preamplifiers, auxiliary routing of a signal for external processing, equalizers for boosting or cutting specific audio frequencies of a signal, dynamics processing (e.g., compressors, limiters), muting circuits, pan control, phase reversal switches, and output bus assignment switchers.

Some analog consoles use motorized faders (or flying faders) in conjunction with computers to automate signal mixing. Once given commands, a board will appear to set itself dynamically during a mixing session. Others made by Solid State Logic (SSL) employ computers and voltage-controlled amplifiers (VCAs) to automate functions such as panning, muting, and output level. Some consoles use computers to "take a picture" of the settings of a given session to be recalled later for use or modification.

Consoles are a dizzying array of lights, buttons, potentiometers, faders, and meters. They are essentially a routing matrix for all of the audio produced during a recording session. Most boards still deal with analog audio signals, but within the last five years a new class of mixing boards work with digital audio. Rather than employing a computer for automation and control, this mixing board essentially is a computer designed to handle audio as data. Priced anywhere from $1,000 to $800,000, there are now more than thirty digital consoles on the market with more to come (Petersen, 1997). Sharing (or emulating) most of the features from analog consoles, digital mixers are usually smaller in size than their analog predecessors. Interfaces are available for every type of digital recorder on the market, so once a signal has undergone analog-to-digital conversion, it can stay digital until it leaves the system through a pair of speakers.

RECENT DEVELOPMENTS AND FUTURE TRENDS

The prices for high-quality audio gear have been falling, making the number of small-project audio facilities grow like dandelions. Many top-selling albums have come out of situations not even dreamed of ten or twelve years ago. The trend has caused some venerable recording studios to close their doors, or at least slash their overhead to compensate for the loss of business. Competition for the recording dollar is fierce (St. Croix, 1998). As computers continue to grow in power and diminish in cost, this trend will continue or even increase. Major labels may be forced out of production and retreat into distribution, where their market power may keep them viable for many years.

Digital has invaded everything, but the wave of digital innovation has swept over the industry with an interesting twist: Vacuum tubes are the hot item in many new professional audio products. From microphones and preamplifiers to dynamics processors and compressor limiters, tubes have been called back into action to save audio from the sterility of the digital sound. The question becomes, "When to digitalize?" The product produced in the recording studio is affected by various factors, some effective and some perceived. The completely digital studio may be driven by cost at the low end, but older studios may be less willing to give up the proven sound of analog equipment. Due to the personal nature of some production methods, this segment of the industry should stay most resistant to a digital conversion.

Today's innovative telephone technology has enabled artists to "phone in" performances from remote locations to participate in studio sessions. Larger computer-industry designs for groupware (software that allows distant people to work together) are likely to allow a virtual studio, where performers may be in nearly any location and still participate in a live working session.

While quadraphonic (four-channel) audio had a brief and largely unsuccessful fling in the 1970s, the two-channel stereo format has had very little challenge in consumer audio. However, as video improves with the adoption of high-definition television, it is difficult to believe that audio will remain the same. If television adopts a higher-quality audio format, it will provide a market and a motivation to enhance consumer audio delivery. The combination of new formats and better compression systems should allow the industry to deliver content digitalized at a high quality. New storage devices should allow dynamic quality changes as desired by a producer. This will allow the producer to vary the quality to meet a special need or save space.

Purely digital production technology has not gone beyond the instrumental stage—yet. Musical Instrument Digital Interface (MIDI) grew out of the systems that combined synthesizers and keyboards to allow musicians to digitally imitate more traditional instruments. Apple fully installed MIDI support in the 1998 version 3.0 of Quick Time, a multimedia support software. The MIDI composer can choose between a couple dozen instruments. The resulting music may not be cutting edge or symphonic, but it can be marketable.

Plus, the files are small. The voices (or description) of musical instruments are stored on the receiver's computer so the creator must send only note and instrument choice. Normal development in this type of software could provide real power to low-end musicians and soundtrack creators.

CONTENT DELIVERY

Recording is not one but two industries, with individual forecasts and concerns. It is difficult to consider the production of music without considering its distribution. After all, it is the audience who pays the bills.

The technology of content delivery is the technology of consumer electronics. All content delivery is dependent on acceptance by the mass audience. Consumers must be willing to abandon old reception equipment (and some old music) in favor of the new. Therefore, consumers must be convinced of the advantages or convinced they have no choice. There are several possibilities in future content delivery, including variations on traditional discs and tapes, broadcasting, zero-motion players, and network delivery.

Compact discs have dominated music delivery since their introduction in 1983. Since that time, traditional vinyl albums have all but disappeared as a distribution format. While cassette tapes continue to be sold, they were endangered to the point of an industry-based rescue attempt in 1997 (*Billboard*, 1997). The fear was that the music industry would be left without a viable consumer record format. Emerging delivery choices can be divided between variations on the tape and disc technology.

Digital audio tape was introduced in 1985 by Sony and Phillips (Love, 1997). Due to fears of perfect digital copies, the recording industry attempted to force manufacturers to include strong anticopying measures. Failing to come to an agreement, the recording industry blocked a practical consumer market introduction through legal action. It is not entirely clear that DAT would have been successful in any case. Tape formats were more reliable (at least in the beginning) because they did not skip when the unit was in motion, such as in a car or personal mobile units. However, tapes were more prone to wear and breakage. Consumers could not as quickly or easily skip portions of the tape and go directly to desired cuts. DAT and other digital tape formats were never successful on the consumer audio market. However, variations were used for mass-storage backup in computer systems.

CDs were the first consumer digital format. CD manufacturers promoted them as a permanent nonlinear audio source with higher-quality sound and a fairly convenient package. Despite the fact that they could not record and early playback units were fairly temperamental, the advantages carried them into a successful market. When the computer industry needed more storage capacity, the audio CD was converted into the CD-ROM. Eventually, as computers installed better CD drives, the two formats became essentially one.

The most promising future formats are based on the success of CDs. The flat disc can be held and stored easily. CD-ROMs have proven the value of a cross-platform product. Future developments in disc distribution include recordability, size reduction, compression increase, and capacity increase.

The minidisc has made some inroads into the consumer market. It is recordable, higher capacity, and smaller than a regular CD. A built-in buffer allows the unit to correct for skipping automatically. A compression algorithm eliminates some frequencies from the minidisc. The value of the lost frequencies is a matter of debate. Sony (1999) maintains the lost frequencies are inaudible to the human ear because they are out of range or masked by other sounds. However, any loss in frequency response is not a selling point for audiophiles.

Recordable compact disc formats found their way to the consumer market after introduction in 1989 (Sony, 1999). They are usually associated with computer equipment but can produce audio CDs. Their strongest consumer-audio-market potential grows from audio downloaded from computer networks. CD-R offers no other advantages (other than recording), so it is likely to be a bridge to the next standard.

DVDs are the same physical size as CDs, but offer a tremendous increase in capacity and data flow rate. DVD is touted as the first format designed for audio, video, and data. CDs can provide 600 to 650 megabits of capacity, with a maximum data flow rate of 1.5 megabits per second. DVD increases capacity to 4.7 gigabits, with data rates reaching 11 megabits per second (Frost, 1997). Somewhat thicker DVDs will provide up to 17 gigabits of capacity. Recordable DVD formats are emerging with slight reduction in capacity.

The tremendous increase in capacity is great, but is not yet needed for most audio products. Current CDs already have the capacity needed to deliver standard-length audio albums without compression. While it is not necessary to fill a DVD, even to start requires a tremendous increase in content. The increased capacity may allow record producers to increase data rate, length, and channels. Producers may also add video, text, or computer programs, but all these extra data may come at a cost to consumers. It is unclear, given their options, that they will choose to pay for it.

Broadcast Distribution

Traditional broadcast stations have been a major partner in the distribution chain. Broadcast stations have traditionally determined market segmentation and helped separate the most popular music from the rest. One cannot fully understand the challenges faced by the recording industry without considering the changes within the broadcast community. There are two clear and somewhat counterintuitive trends growing in the broadcast community: consolidation and diversification.

The Telecommunications Act of 1996, the first complete revision of communication law in sixty-two years, allowed consolidation of radio stations under single corporate ownership. Within a few years, broadcast chains that were once limited to fourteen radio stations quickly grew into the hundreds. In addition, multiple stations within a market shared common ownership, which was previously taboo. Inevitably, major music formats will be programmed and counterprogrammed on the national level. Major decisions will be made further from the local market. It should become easier to promote choice artists to mainstream radio chains rather than so many individual stations.

Balancing the consolidation trend, there is the likelihood of new entrants in audio delivery. New consolidated entrants will come from cable television and direct broadcast satellite companies. Digital Music Express has provided multiple channels of audio on DBS for a few years. DBS has not impacted the broadcast community because of poor penetration, but cable companies are now switching to digital networks. Multiple audio channels will be a reasonable programming choice for the new capacity. In 1999, a new satellite service (digital audio broadcasting or DAB) is expected to deliver up to 200 channels of programming nationally. The service will require a subscription and a new radio, but, if successful, could be a powerful new competitor.

Less likely but possible competitors could come from broadcasting itself. As television stations switch to digital signals, increased capacity will require increased program content. It is within the spirit of the current Communication Act to allow television stations to deliver audio-only programming if they choose. If current AM and FM stations went digital, multiple channels of programming could come from them as well. Finally, the Federal Communications Commission has approved a new class of low-power FM stations (FCC MM Docket 99-25). If this proposal is ever granted, new entrants could grow out of the current illegal radio community.

Consolidation in the broadcast market will likely reduce the number of stations competing under any single format. New digital entrants also tend to encourage diversity of formats. It is unlikely that all new audio services will succeed, but the trend is for more channels and a greater diversity of programming. This trend is even more likely given developments in other parts of the distribution process.

Zero Motion

Physical storage devices such as CDs and tapes share a common problem. It takes motion to activate the recording or playback. The motion often causes wear on the storage medium and increased power requirements to operate motors. The motors have to be calibrated to move at the right speed over the long term and an exact relationship must be maintained between the medium and read–record heads. Finally, all moving parts take up space and add weight.

The natural progression of computer power and compression can solve all these problems by removing motion from the storage and playback process.

Zero motion players (ZMPs) have already been introduced, such as the Rio by Diamond Multimedia, with many more coming. Audio is stored in random access memory (RAM) or flash memory. Flash memory cards, about the size of a credit card, could be used for extra capacity or as prerecorded albums. The Rio is promoted as being smaller than an audio cassette and providing twelve hours of continuous skip-free sound on a single AA battery (MP3.com, 1999).

Physical storage devices are growing beyond the size needed for audio. A single DVD could hold over seven uncompressed CDs. Digital compression is already reaching ten-to-one with minimal loss. It is likely we will see much better compression rates in the near future. Zero motion devices could become popular for audio playback. DVDs could then be used to store a personal music library. ZMP personal stereos could be loaded with a day's music much as we load a personal digital assistant with data.

Networked

The popularization of the World Wide Web drew many people on-line with greater audio–video demands. It was not long before sites developed to serve the growing desire. At first, they were completely unacceptable. High-quality audio files were large and slow to download. Streaming, the process of transferring a media file and playing it after enough of a file buffer is on the user's system, increased accessibility but hardly quality. Eventually, a reasonable service will be established as compression schemes improve and network speeds increase.

On-line radio stations (many associated with over-the-air stations) stream programming out to a largely unknown and uncounted public. Other streaming sources, from sporting events to professional conferences, have also grown dramatically. The major streaming software, RealPlayer, claims an installed base of 50 million users in the first three years of its development. Now that most Internet service companies and computer manufacturers install either RealPlayer or its Microsoft competitor (Media Player) as part of a standard package, streaming audio is likely to become even more prevalent. Apple's Quick Time software has also introduced streaming software as part of the competition. As an added incentive, streamed audio may become more popular with the recording industry. Protocols can be created so that the receiver's computer never has the whole file at one time. The buffer could be discarded or encrypted as it is used. This way, program owners could have better control over their product.

Content is already being provided. The compression standard MPEG-3 (MP3) has been largely adopted as a means to transmit whole files to a quickly developing audience. A problematic side issue is that a growing population is copying files from their CDs and sharing them with others. By using MP3, an uncompressed three-minute song can be reduced to three or four megabytes. Some form of compression scheme is likely to continue for the near future. If network speeds increase as expected, compression may not be necessary for audio alone, except as an attempt to save money. However, file compression may be mixed with copy protection to relieve fears of copyright holders.

Copyright

The recording industry is constantly concerned with profiting from its product. Pirating (illegal duplication of the product) has been a long-standing problem. In the days of analog recordings, the duplicate was not quite as good as the original. It was not much of a defense, but it was something. The industry has the high ground on creating originals. In the age of digital distribution, the duplicate is virtually as good as the original.

The last real revision of the Copyright Act (1976) took nearly fifteen years to negotiate and pass. The big issues between 1961 (when work started) and 1976 were photocopiers and cable television redistribution. Photocopiers were expensive, cumbersome, and relatively poor quality. Cable television—another entertainment industry—was open to accommodation or regulation. In the end, the entertainment industry could do quite well without either of these technologies. Unlike photocopiers, it is usually easier to digitally copy the entire work rather than a part of it. Unlike cable television, the problematic copying is not being done by anything that could be considered a segment of the industry.

Digital technology, on the other hand, is quite valuable. Computer transmissions can carry everything from text to video with greater efficiency. The adoption of digital technology can be as good for the industry as it is for the consumer. It is not as easy to simply overlook the technology. Digital distribution could eliminate several expensive steps from the process. If music could be directly recorded in users' homes or retail outlets, there would be less need to preproduce. Wasted product and shipping could drop to near zero levels. When music is exported onto a storage medium (e.g., a CD), computer technology could create a customized product. It is not difficult to image a customized collection of songs. Custom publishers may go beyond this to offer varying tempo options, embedded names, or nonmusic content. Certainly there will always be the artist-controlled album, but other options offer new choices to marketers and consumers.

The problem is that adoption of the technology may cost the industry more than it can afford. Computers are already able to read music CDs and store their contents elsewhere. The digital copies are, in every important way, the same as the originals. If consumers can avoid paying by simply duplicating media products, the recording industry will face a piracy problem similar to that of the computer industry. In addition, even if antipiracy laws successfully reduce the threat within the United States, the interconnected nature of the network allows illegal copies to come from almost anywhere.

The recording industry has natural allies, with so much media content making the transition to digital. All entertainment industries face the same problems to some degree. The movie industry delivers its content digitally by DVD and has long faced pirating. Digital pirating of a DVD will be possible in the home as technology naturally advances. Many antipiracy schemes may only postpone the eventual copying. Paper publishing faces many of the same problems as recording, only with heavier products. Both industries must produce and distribute products on the expectation that a sale is possible. They must also accept returns of unsold products. Under this "sale on commission" model, unsold products create a huge waste for the industry. Digital systems could reduce waste and speed the time to market.

Next, consider the demographics of the people who have already adopted on-line systems. They are nearly ideal for both the publishing and home-entertainment industries. On-line consumers can (and most likely do) read. They have already agreed to spend money on a reception product. It is likely they would pay for content. In many ways, it is worth the industries' time to solve this problem.

The recording industry attempted to block the introduction of the Rio because of its ability to hold illegal copies of music. The industry was unsuccessful. Even if it had blocked Rio, it would not have stopped the problem of illegal digital copies. It is easy to either find or make illegal copies of current CDs. The industry is scrambling for schemes to limit illegal copies. Full-time monitoring of the Internet, new encryption standards, chip-based filters, and digital watermarks are all promoted as possible solutions. The eventual solution will have four requirements. First, it will be nearly invisible to the user. The recording industry cannot expect user participation. Second, it will not decrease audio quality—that is never an option. Third, it cannot inhibit legal copying. The ability to record is essential in new digital systems. Fourth, it must be effective over the long term. Whatever system is used, people will attempt to defeat it. The industry cannot afford to continually change formats.

A rather frightening development in the process of protecting copyrights and exacting payment is the potential to develop pay-per-view content. What is known as the "first-sale doctrine" allows the producer to profit from only the first sale of a copyrighted work. For example, if you buy a book, you may sell that book without further payment to the copyright holder. Instead of selling the work, PPV models license it, often for as little as a single use. PPV is quite popular in cable television and we already see the introduction of on-line jukeboxes. Communication networks will soon accept small payments (micropayments) profitably and the jukebox could become very real. Other systems, such as streaming and ZMP, could be created to allow access to material without selling it. Proponents argue that PPV allows distribution of content more cheaply, but it virtually eliminates first sale and fair use of copyrighted material. It could become the normal cost difference between buying and renting any product.

Free Music

There is a growing undercurrent in the music industry. Developing artists often pay their dues in garage bands and small clubs. Internet radio, music Web sites, and niche-service broadcast stations all crave music that is free of copyright entanglements. New or unknown artists are more than willing to provide content. The Internet has become a useful link between artists and people in search of content. MP3.com, a digital music community, claims that "tens of thousands of high quality songs from thousands of artists" are all legal copies (see www.mp3.com). Sites such as MP3.com create a community that encourages the unfiltered flow of music from creator to consumer; some even argue from creator to creator. Of course, "unfiltered" basically equates to "unpaid." Many people involved in on-line distribution promote a "free music" philosophy that rejects copyright protection (Samudrala, 1999). It is unclear whether free music will become a threat to the larger recording industry or a new minor league.

CONCLUSION

The recording industry is facing growing pains, but the essential nature of recording is unchanged and will stay unchanged. The goal is to deliver a product that stimulates the heart and mind. Whether it is a musician on a violin or a MIDI composer checking the playback, the process begins and ends in analog. The intervening steps are exciting, but it still comes down to a creator and an audience.

What will change by 2025 is content production and distribution systems. Digital technology will open new doors for distribution. As new doors open, copyright owners will want to protect their rights. Years of acrimony will likely lead us into a new market structure. The result will likely be an intricate demassified weave of overlapping genres.

In a way, the effect is healthy, with new formats, styles, and ideas. However, the total size of the audience will stay virtually the same, so the audience for each format should shrink. As audiences shrink, so will available money. Artists will have to be very popular in one format or reasonably popular in several to be successful.

REFERENCES

Alten, S. R. (1996). *Audio in media/the recording studio*. Belmont, CA: Wadsworth.
Billboard. (1997, October 25). Vol. 109, p. 66.
Frost, T. (1997). *DVD summit executive summary*. Stevenage, UK: Phillips Omnicom Conferences.

Gates, W. H., III. (1996). *The road ahead.* New York: Penguin Books.

Gelatt, R. (1971). *The fabulous phonograph: From Edison to stereo.* New York: Appleton-Century.

Huber, D., & Runstem, R. (1990). *Modern recording techniques.* Carmel, IN: Howard W. Sams.

Katz, B. (1996). *The secrets of dither* [On-line]. Available: http://www.digdomain.com.

Katz, B. (1998). High resolution audio [On-line]. Available: http://www.digdomain.com.

Love, M. (1997). DAT [On-line]. Available: http://bsuvc.bsu.edu/dat.html.

Ludwig, B. (1998). Everything I know about surround. *Surround Professional, 1,* 56–59.

Michie, C. (1997). Upgrading and restoring tape recorders and consoles. *Mix Magazine, 21* (10).

Miller, R., & Roger, B. (1982). *The incredible music machine.* London: Quartet/Visual Arts.

MP3.com. (1999). Rio PMP 300 [On-line]. Available: http://www.mp3.com/diamond/.

Petersen, G. (1997). Digital consoles: Audio's new frontier. *Mix Magazine, 22* (11).

Samudrala, R. (1999). *The future of music* [On-line]. Available: http://www.mp3.com/news/142.html.

Sony. (1999). Sony online [On-line]. Available: http://www.sel.sony.com/SEL/consumer/md/index.html.

St. Croix, S. (1998). More for less. Less for more. *Mix Magazine, 22* (3).

Watkinson, J. (1994). *An introduction to digital audio.* London: Focal Press.

Webb, J. (1997). Twelve mics that made history. *Mix Magazine, 21* (10).

9

Satellites

Steven J. Dick

Floating in space like so many stars, communications satellites represent some of the most difficult platforms in our communication infrastructure. They can also represent some of the most useful. Even though there has never been a practical application, a properly positioned satellite can theoretically serve one-third of Earth. The power and flexibility provided by a single satellite platform more than makes up for the difficulty.

Satellites should become even more important as technical issues are solved. In recent years, communications companies have been investing millions in new satellites and their related support systems. The number of communication satellites is growing dramatically. The growth is due in part to lower orbits that require more satellites and employ lower-cost launch vehicles.

THE BASIC SYSTEM

Satellite communication is a relatively old concept. Arthur C. Clarke (1945), a popular science fiction author, is normally credited with envisioning satellite communication. Clarke suggested that a radio receiver and transmitter could be positioned in a specific orbit over the equator. From this geostationary orbit (GEO), satellites travel at a speed making them appear to hang above a specific point on Earth below.

Despite the early start, practical satellite tests did not begin until the late 1950s. Spurred in part by the former Soviet Union's 1957 Sputnik test, satellites rode the early crest of the space race. The first American success at satellite communication was the 1960 launch of the 100-foot-diameter balloon called Echo I (Whitehouse, 1986, p. 149). Its metallic surface simply reflected signals whenever it was overhead.

Eighteen years after Clarke published his proposal in 1963, a satellite called Syncom achieved the required orbit. The following year a consortium of nations established Intelsat, an organization created to provide international satellite communication. The geostationary orbit was immediately adopted as the primary location for these satellites. The problem became one of parking places in this narrow band. Interference and lack of frequencies severely limited the number of satellites. Thirty-five years later, Iridium Inc. launched a constellation of sixty-six low Earth orbit (LEO) satellites and created a second satellite location with the market potential of the geostationary orbit.

While it is difficult to establish the platform, once done the system is rather simple (see Figure 9.1). An uplink antenna transmits the signal to the satellite. The satellite receives, amplifies, and moves (transposes) the signal to a different frequency. The area on Earth that can receive signals from the satellite is the satellite's footprint. The signal is then transmitted down to Earth and received by downlink antennas. The satellite creates a "bent pipe" transmission path that is fairly distance insensitive. Once the signal travels the long distance to the satellite and back, it matters little whether the receiver is hundreds or thousands of miles from the transmitter.

A successful satellite is really the combination of technologies. The most obvious division is ground-versus-space vehicle systems. However when analyzing the satellite industry, it is more useful to divide the systems on functional basis. For example, there is telemetry on both the satellite and the ground. It is not useful to look at these systems separately, since they must interact. A more useful division would include launch vehicle, spacecraft, station keeping, transmission, and reception systems.

Launch Vehicle

The launch vehicle is used to take the satellite out of Earth's atmosphere. In the early days, only governments supplied launch capacity. If you were not able to persuade the government to do the launch, the launch did not take place. In addition, few governments had the ability to launch the spacecraft.

While it may continue to be necessary to obtain government permission (often several governments) to place a satellite in orbit, more launch choices have become available. Governments have generally supported privatization of all aspects of the telecommunications industry, including launch services. The trend toward private and semigovernment launch services is likely to continue. There are also more governments attempting to create their own launch industries.

Figure 9.1
The Relationship between the Uplink, Satellite, Downlink, and Footprint

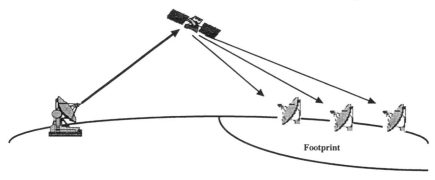

Footprint

Spacecraft

The spacecraft can be divided into main parts (Miller, Vucetic, & Berry, 1993). The spacecraft bus or service module consists of the structural, telemetry, power, thermal control, and location control subsystems. The bus moves the satellite into its final position and protects its valuable cargo.

The cargo or communications payload is what we normally think of with communication satellites (see Figure 9.2). The uplink antenna receives the signal. A low-noise amplifier adds power to the signal. The transponder translates the carrier frequency of the signal so the uplink and downlink signal will not interfere. A high-power amplifier prepares the signal for the downlink antenna.

Satellites are expected to grow dramatically in size. Lebow (1986) noted that weight of a twenty-four-transponder satellite was a little more than half a ton. *The Economist* ("Look Out," 1995) predicted four-ton satellites by 2010. Increased power and more transponders are likely to account for the change in weight. Batteries should be lighter in the future. Fuel may become more efficient and there will be new systems to refuel satellites rather than replace them.

Figure 9.2
A Typical Satellite Schematic

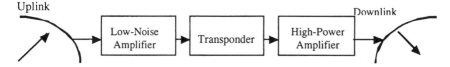

Station Keeping

For the satellite to remain useful, it must achieve and remain in its designated orbit. Telemetry systems help locate the satellite while the spacecraft's propulsion is used to push the satellite into position and maintain the orbit. A satellite's lifetime is often determined by the life of its propulsion system. Other parts of the satellite may break down, but a satellite can only carry so much fuel. When that fuel is gone, the satellite will eventually drift out of orbit.

Before widespread use of the geostationary orbit, telemetry systems helped guide ground-based antennas as they tracked satellites across the sky. Future low Earth orbit satellite systems may put "intelligence" in ground receivers to monitor signals and determine which satellite provides the best reception at any point in time.

Transmission

Transmission includes ground-based transmitters, antennas, and spacecraft antennas through the transponder. To the marketplace, maximizing satellite capacity is most important. Increasing capacity has been accomplished in three ways: increasing the number of transponders, multiplexing existing frequencies, and signal compression.

The transponder is the center of the satellite capacity. The number of available frequencies and the capacity of the spacecraft bus determine the number of transponders. More transponders require more frequencies, amplifiers, power, and backup systems. Each transponder is approximately equal to one uncompressed video signal. Early satellites had only twelve transponders. Later, twenty-four or more were likely.

Most attempts at frequency reuse amount to good signal planning. High transponder costs force strategic investment. Satellite signals can be polarized for double or triple channel capacity (Lebow, 1986). For example, waves can be produced so that they carry different signals on the horizontal and vertical planes. Polarizing elements in the antenna and their waveguide feeds can produce this effect. The signal must be carefully constructed to minimize mutual interference.

Satellites must compete for frequencies with many other services. In addition, given the distance signals must travel, high-frequency waves are best. They are less likely to be affected by atmospheric refraction. The same frequencies, however, are just as useful on the ground for point-to-point transmissions. The first satellite band, C-band, was commonly used for ground-based communication, so downlink antennas had to be placed outside major cities and power was limited to avoid interference. Other bands, Ku and Ka, can be seriously affected by bad weather. Finally, L and S bands have been used only in some emerging mobile satellite services. The following is a list of the satellite frequency bands and challenges associated with each:

Band	Service	Challenge
L Band, S-Band 0.5 to 1.7 GHz	DAB, PCS, GPS	Low Earth orbit and developing services
C Band 4 to 6 GHz	Telephone, broadcast, cable television, and business services	Interference with ground-based systems
Ku Band 11 to 14 GHz	DBS, telephone, and business communication	Attenuated by bad weather
Ka Band 17 to 31 GHz	DBS and business communication	Attenuated by bad weather

Satellite frequencies are under competing pressures. First, there is the desire to efficiently reuse or reallocate frequencies as much as possible. Second, for the sake of standardization, it is also desirable to dedicate a set of frequencies to a single service, despite its popularity. When you consider the vast difference in needed capacity, the problem becomes even more apparent. A single uncompressed television signal (6 MHz) requires the capacity of 1,500 telephone calls (4 kHz each).

Most satellites use digital signals and digital is excellent at compression. The simplest form of digital compression applies algorithms to remove redundant information from the signal. It may be easier to imagine a compressed video image. Compression may simply take something away from the image such as the number of frames of video, lines of resolution, or amount of color information. Other systems reduce redundant information within each frame (usually the background) or redundant information between frames (everything that does not change from one frame to another).

Reception

Satellite program distribution began in 1962. The people who operated downlinks were a select group of professionals. Satellite programming was not intended for the home audience and it was logical to think so. Reception equipment was expensive and bulky. Broadcast engineers thought only about reception at broadcast-quality standards rather than those desired by home consumers.

In 1978, Taylor Howard, an engineering professor at Stanford, published a how-to manual outlining his method for receiving satellite signals with relatively low-cost equipment (Parone, 1994). As word spread, the age of television receive-only antennas began. Even as they became popular, the antennas were too large and expensive for most consumers. TVRO was practical in rural areas, where cable did not reach and zoning laws did not prohibit the large dish antennas. In addition, many consumers understood that there would eventually be some kind of charge or encryption on the signal, even though many were told otherwise. Finally, the cable industry worked hard to keep the TVRO market from being successful. Considering all that was against it, TVRO did very well.

In June 1994, true direct broadcast satellite service began after eleven years of delays. DBS was a dramatic improvement over TVRO. Higher-powered satellites, access to programming, compression, and better home technology made the system small enough and cheap enough to compete directly with cable television. In 1998, Iridium launched a worldwide satellite telephone service based on a constellation of sixty-six low Earth orbit satellites. Later, a satellite-based digital audio broadcasting system was launched. In the same period, consumer use of the global positioning satellite (GPS) systems became commonplace.

In the five-year period from 1994 to 1999, consumer use of satellite-reception equipment became practical and marketable. It is likely this trend will only increase. As satellites systems continue to mature, other delivery systems will have to compete directly. Cable television, broadcast television, and radio industries are already preparing digital systems of their own.

SATELLITES IN MEDIA

Satellite systems can be used for several purposes that do not directly qualify as media. Military, space exploration, global positioning, weather, and remote-sensing satellites may affect communications. They may provide content and compete for space and frequencies. Any of these industries may have an unexpected effect on the satellite industry as society develops. For example, military applications may have a catastrophic effect on communication should conflict extend into space. Space exploration and space-based manufacturing may dramatically increase traffic in useable orbits, plus the desire for better disposal of waste products. These problems are beyond the scope of this chapter, so we will only consider communication services.

Service Class

Broadly defined, there are two divisions in future satellite applications. Broadband programming is the delivery of high-capacity content to consumers and distributors. Broadband content includes television, multimedia, and virtual environments. Telephony is all on-demand access to content or services, including telephones.

Broadband

Satellites are the perfect platform for the mass distribution of content. Direct broadcast satellites can now deliver more than 200 channels of programming. It is likely that further compression and satellite power would allow this number to increase. More than two hundred channels should allow enough capacity to provide mass program content for large areas. For the near term, it should even provide a simple pay-per-view system, with content determined by the provider.

A true direct broadcast satellite service was slow to start. Cable television interests and the technology itself conspired to keep companies from launching the service authorized by the Federal Communications Commission in 1983 (see 27 C.F.R. Sect. 100.19b). However, in 1989, the FCC declared that the companies authorized to build DBS had not done their job. The FCC reassessed and awarded DBS construction permits to a new group of companies (Carlin, 1998).

Two issues had a major impact on the failure of DBS. First, it was difficult to get programming at a reasonable cost. Shared corporate ownership between cable companies and cable networks combined with industry pressure to keep program costs high, if available at all. The Cable Television Consumer Protection and Competition Act of 1992 forced program content sales to DBS.

Second, a digital compression standard was necessary so that DBS companies could deliver enough channels to compete with cable television. In 1993, MPEG-1 (Motion Pictures Experts Group standard) was chosen as an international standard for video compression. This compression algorithm allowed eight digital video channels in the space on one analog. In 1995, DBS companies adopted MPEG-2, which allowed for broadcast-quality pictures and varying levels of compression. Once equitable programming and channel capacity was assured, investors could be found. The first DBS satellite was launched in 1994. By March 1998, DBS enjoyed 6.6 million subscribers for three companies.

The final step was to deliver local programming. Geostationary satellites, with a coverage area of most of the country, are not well equipped to deliver local television. The first plan was to deliver selected network affiliates. Networks and their affiliates objected and successfully limited the distribution of network television. Even if DBS companies could provide network programming, they could not provide local programming. The second plan was a technical fix to allow reception of local stations. The most promising was to place local stations on satellite capacity and deliver it to the communities where it would normally be received.

DBS has been left with few choices. One, disregard local stations (and network programming) and try to sell consumers on cable networks only. Second, fill satellite capacity with programming already in the customers' home areas. Third, use a ground-based system such as cable, wireless cable, or antennas to deliver local content. The first choice is unacceptable. The second choice is being followed today but expensive. The third choice may be workable if the satellite provider can partner with another company or buy ground-based capacity.

Satellites continue to be effective at providing networked content. Most broadcast and cable networks use a satellite distribution system. The problem develops as satellites attempt to deliver interactive broadband content. Satellite access to the Internet is growing, especially in rural areas underserved by cable. But cable access to the Internet is much faster. Plus, for most systems the return path must be through ground-based telephony.

Telephony

The FCC and other governing bodies have effectively created a tiered system of mobile satellites (Schwartz, 1996). Mobile satellite service (MSS) has been defined as that between (1) a mobile Earth station and a space station, and (2) two mobile Earth stations through a space station. In effect, all services that can be provided on the wired network will be provided on a satellite network.

More than simply being equal, futurists have started talking about the so-called Negroponte Switch (Negroponte, 1995). While it is suggested passively in his book, it is actively discussed in *Wired Magazine* and the *Wired* Web site (www.wired.com). The suggestion is that all communication that was wired (e.g., telephones) will be delivered over the air. Traditional over-the-air content (e.g., television) will be delivered wired.

In the past there has been a division between voice telephony and data services. As networks switch to digital distribution, this division is disappearing. Telephony will be defined (if not already) as any occasional or on-demand use of the network. This would include private networks that can be created and altered on demand. Telephony will be a major consumer of satellite services due to the relative ease of installation, alteration, and mobility.

Orbits

For all the interest in the geostationary orbit, it is easy to overlook the options of the past and soon the future. The original concept for a communication satellite envisions one that resides in a fairly narrow orbit above the equator. In recent years, new choices have been explored. These choices may make a dramatic difference in the services that can be offered and the convenience of satellite communication (see Figure 9.3).

Geostationary

The geostationary or geosynchronous orbit is sometimes called the Clarke orbit after Arthur C. Clarke, the person who proposed it. The satellite is placed in a circular orbit 22,300 miles (35,800 kilometers) above the equator. The satellite will take about one day to orbit Earth. In effect, it will seem to hang above a single point on the equator. The advantage over previous locations is that Earth-bound antennas can remain fixed on one point and do not have to move as the satellite tracks across the sky.

Figure 9.3
Satellite Orbits

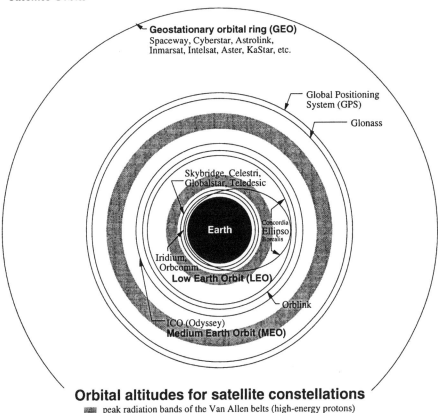

Orbital altitudes for satellite constellations

peak radiation bands of the Van Allen belts (high-energy protons)

Source: Lloyd's satellite constellations <http://www.ee.surrey.ac.uk/Personal/L.Wood/constellations/>.
Note: Orbits are not shown at actual inclination; this is a guide to altitude only.

GEO became a lightning rod for international competition and fairness. There were a limited number of useful spaces to park a satellite. Satellite spacing was dependent upon the power and frequencies used (Whitehouse, 1986). Satellites were originally spaced at four degrees apart and later upgraded to two degrees. GEO being a circular orbit, 360 degrees divided by two meant 180 parking places worldwide. Subtract parking places that are not over a major land mass, and the problem gets worse. More spaces were added as more frequencies were used, but the competition for these places remained stiff.

For GEO, a second problem is one of distance. The extreme distance requires highly focused intense signals to travel to our most distant communication orbit. Large antennas are often difficult to place because there must be a direct line of sight to the satellite. In northern latitudes the problem gets even worse, as the satellite is lower on the horizon. Higher-power DBS satellites help, but only bring the antenna size down to something that can be put on a rooftop. Indoor or nonvisible (inside the receiver) antennas are yet not possible.

For telephone systems, a related problem exists. The distance is so great that there is a delay for the signal to travel. The delay is only noticeable to human perception if a double hop or two satellite trips are needed to complete the call. Still, it is a limiting factor in highly interactive data exchange. As transmission rate and interactivity increase, the distance to any satellite will become a problem.

Eliptical

As mentioned, northern latitudes have a greater problem with receiving signals from the geostationary orbit. It is difficult to cut through all the atmosphere or find locations where antennas can be placed. The former Soviet Union, with its large northern landmass, dealt with the problem by adopting an elliptical orbit. For almost half the time it takes to complete the orbit, the satellite occupies the apogee, a high point over the satellite's footprint. Three satellites can serve the footprint effectively. On the ground, the antennas can still remain fixed, since a new satellite will take over as one moves out of range. In addition, the orbit even at its apogee is lower than the GEO satellites. New elliptical orbits can be designed to give special coverage to southern or northern countries.

Low and Medium Earth Orbit

Orbital paths other than GEO were not used because of the necessity to track satellites with ground-based antenna. Telecommunications engineers have learned a lesson from cellular telephones. A fixed network must track mobile cellular users. The logic can now be extended to satellites, where relatively fixed users must track a highly mobile network. It requires determining the strongest signal and moving from one point in the network to another to maintain signal strength.

The solution to the low Earth orbit and medium Earth orbit (MEO) problem suggests a second problem with lower orbits. The satellites keep moving, so more satellites are required—dramatically more. The Iridium LEO network was started with a constellation of sixty-six satellites and six spares. Teledesic, another LEO system, is planning a constellation of 288 active satellites (Wood, 1998). A compromise between LEO and GEO is the ICO MEO system, planned with only ten satellites. While the Iridium system failure may slow the deployment, LEO and MEO satellite orbits remain a viable alternative.

The difference between LEO and MEO is a matter of height. An LEO satellite will be placed at an altitude between 100 and 1,000 miles above the

Earth's surface. The MEO satellite is placed between 5,000 and 10,000 miles. Between the two orbits is the disruptive Van Allen radiation belt.

For both LEO and MEO satellites orbit height requires a trade-off (Schwartz, 1996). For a higher orbit, fewer satellites are required due to the larger footprint of each satellite. Less fuel is required to counter Earth's gravity. The satellite's lifespan is often determined by fuel consumption, so lower fuel requirements mean a longer projected life.

Satellites traveling in lower orbits can eliminate transmission delays. The satellites can be lighter and cheaper. Since more signal power reaches the ground, receiving antennas can be lighter, cheaper, and smaller. The FCC has mandated a class of little-LEO satellites that operate at the lowest orbits, frequencies, and power. These will be data-service satellites for business similar to the GEO very small aperture terminal (VSAT) services.

In the next couple of decades, we should see a race for these new LEO and MEO orbits. It may be similar to the development of the GEO orbit. With the proven success of GEO satellites and the ability to build satellites faster, the adoption of LEO and MEO should be even faster.

High-Altitude Long Endurance

In 1961, a group of university educators from the Big Ten Conference did something crazy. They loaded a DC-6 aircraft with two UHF transmitters, brand new AMPEX videotape machines, and a couple days worth of tapes. They flew the plane to an altitude of 23,000 feet above north central Indiana and started broadcasting educational television. For six years the Midwest Program for Airborne Television Instruction (MPATI) broadcast programming to parts of Indiana, Illinois, Ohio, Kentucky, Michigan, Wisconsin, and Canada. As crazy as that idea sounds, it is being revisited. The project lasted for four years before losing its experimental license from the FCC.

Advances in pilotless aircraft and dirigibles make it realistic to consider the placement of a communication platform above twelve miles (twenty kilometers) above Earth. These craft would stay in place for a week or two and be replaced for refueling. High Altitude Long Endurance (HALE) platforms would create a communication relay point similar to a satellite but at a lower cost and with increased flexibility. Initially, HALE would be designed for high-traffic areas like major cities. HALE could relay traffic back to the ground or to and from a variety of communication satellites.

CHALLENGES

Satellite communication has a promising yet complicated future. The incredible investment, scale, and inhospitable environment is unmatched in other areas of communication. To complicate matters, satellite communication is by definition international. Finally, the development of satellites in the next twenty-five years will take place within the framework of equal development on the ground.

Shortages

The biggest limiting factor for satellite communication is pure competition. Satellites must compete for frequencies, orbital positions, and customers. In addition to satellite communication, it is reasonable to believe that space will be exploited by other industries. The military, science, manufacturing, and travel industries may move into space. All will need satellite communication and will demand some of the resources.

However, satellites do have distinct advantages. Satellites can provide service where ground-based communication systems are either not established or difficult to install. Satellites can often offer quick solutions where installed. With cheaper, easier to build satellites, it is likely that new networks can be created faster, as long as there is space. Scarcity may work to the satellite industry's favor. Scarce resources may put a natural cap on the industry's investment, while driving up costs for those that need the service.

Service Classes

Current satellites amount to a patchwork of technologies and orbits. Satellite power, customers, and service classes are more an accident of history than a conscious plan. In the next twenty-five years, usable lifespans will expire and systems will be upgraded and replaced. Anticipating the future of satellite communication means understanding the real estate it uses. For the foreseeable future there are two major orbit classes: geostationary and nongeostationary. Given the advantages of each class, there should be three major service classes.

Mass Delivery GEOs

Geostationary satellites will hold the communication high ground. Their footprint is largest, while interactivity will be more difficult. Because they can operate in only one narrow orbit, the real estate they require should remain very valuable. Given their relative distance, GEO satellites are best suited for mass delivery of point-to-multipoint content. Each GEO satellite can serve one-third of the Earth. Efficiency dictates that these satellites should increase broadband capacity to serve the widest possible audience with the fewest signals. The caveat is that compression and power will dramatically increase the number of channels anyway. The next generation of satellites should be able to provide multiple footprints in its range. For example, a single satellite should provide content to both North and South America, rather than only one or the other.

Flexible-Use Non-GEOs

Non-GEO satellites should become more important for mobile and occa-sional-use systems. Increased power, decreased delays, smaller footprints, and cheaper systems should encourage the adoption of lower satellites that are adaptable and specifically designed. Smaller footprints should discourage mass distribution of noninteractive content. Too many satellites will be required to distribute a product over a large area.

Virtual Satellites

With increased compression and efficiency, excess capacity will become commonplace, both on satellites and on the ground. A market should develop that will sell excess capacity to users that can stand occasional delays or rollover onto higher-cost networks. These virtual satellites, or larger virtual networks, will use something akin to Internet protocols to select the lowest-cost net-work for transportation of communication resources.

CONCLUSION

The satellite segment of the communication industry has adopted techno-logical leaps first. Satellites are well on their way toward a market structure that will take them into 2025. Being there first has a certain advantage. Satel-lites can help secure their place as the "traditional" method of communica-tion delivery.

However, satellites must keep their advantage in mind. They best provide distance-insensitive communication to mobile communications. When pos-sible, there will always be more space on the ground to string cable than room in the air to park satellites. A single optic fiber can dwarf the capacity of the most powerful satellite. Cable and local broadcast can provide local content and local representatives better than any international satellite company. Keep-ing these limitations in mind, satellites should excel if they concentrate on the type of delivery they do best.

REFERENCES

Carlin, T. (1998). Direct broadcast satellites. In A. E. Grant & J. H. Meadows (Eds.), *Communication technology update* (6th ed., pp. 38–56). Boston: Focal Press.

Clarke, A. C. (1945). Extra-terrestrial relays: Can rocket stations give world-wide radio coverage? *Wireless World, 51*, 305–308.

Lebow, I. L. (1986). Satellite communications. In T. C. Bartee (Ed.), *Digital commu-nication* (pp. 49–85). Indianapolis, IN: Howard W. Sams.

Lewis, P. (1961). *Educational television guidebook.* New York: McGraw-Hill.

Lin, C. A. (1998). Satellite communications. In A. E. Grant & J. H. Meadows (Eds.), *Communication technology update* (6th ed., pp. 38–56). Boston: Focal Press.

Look out behind you. (1995, March). *The Economist*, p. 79.

Miller, M. J., Vucetic, B., & Berry, L. (1993). *Satellite communication: Mobile and fixed services*. Norwell, MA: Kluwer Academic Publishers.

Negroponte, N. (1995). *Being digital*. New York: Vintage Books.

Parone, M. (1994). Direct-to-home: Politics in a competitive marketplace. *Satellite Communications, 28*, 28–30.

Schwartz, R. E. (1996). *Wireless communications in developing countries*. Boston: Artech House.

Whitehouse, G. E. (1986). *Understanding the new technologies of the mass media*. Englewood Cliffs, NJ: Prentice Hall.

Wood, L. (1998). *Big LEO overview*. [On-line]. Available: http://www.ee.surrey.ac.uk/ Personal/L.Wood/constellations/tables/overview.html.

10

Television

O. Patricia Cambridge

It is the year 2025. You are sitting on the sofa in the family room, looking at a picture that hangs on your wall. But it is not a painting or a photograph. It is the heart of your communication center. Yes, you are watching a music video with CD-quality sound that you ordered through the Internet, but you have paused it to see the latest news at the top of the hour. Your doorbell has just rung and you see the visitor's face in the corner of the screen. You might just return to the room later to use your communication center to do some research for that paper you are writing.

What is this communication center? Is it your security system? Is it your stereo system? Is it your computer? Is it your telephone? Is it your radio? Is it your television? It is all of these. So, what happened to the television set? It will not disappear, but the way we use it will change. We are at the beginning of the era of media convergence, which is driven by digitization. By 2025, the distinctions that we now make among the television, the telephone, the computer, and other communication media will have disappeared. Will you be able to buy just a television set, or a telephone, or a computer? Yes. But you will also own systems that integrate all of these functions into one unit.

But how did we get there? Before we discuss television in the twenty-first century, specifically 2025, let us look at television in the twentieth century.

A BRIEF HISTORY OF TELEVISION

The twentieth century has been remarkable both for the number of technological innovations that have occurred and for the swift pace with which they have been adopted. Since the availability to many households in the second half of the twentieth century, television has changed the American home. What did individuals and families do before the arrival of television? From the early to mid-twentieth century, families gathered around the radio. They also began listening to the phonograph. Before this, they played pianos, in addition to reading books, newspapers, and magazines.

After television became the focal point of American homes in the 1950s, the media and their related industries underwent profound changes. Television not only offered fantasy, it offered new opportunities for advertisers to increase, as they could now demonstrate products for individuals to buy to enhance their lifestyles. The other mass media—books, newspapers, magazines, sound recording, film, and radio—were affected both in the way they were consumed by the public and in how they were organized.

These media often use television to promote their products. The film industry first saw television as a threat. Eventually, it coopted the new medium and began producing programming for it. Not only are movies promoted on television, but movie rights are sold to cable operators and networks after their first run in movie theaters. The industry has also accepted that many people will experience movies through their television sets, so video releases have become a considerable source of profits. As television captured mass audiences in the 1950s, radio became a formatted medium. Soap operas, dramas like *The Lone Ranger*, and variety shows hosted by entertainers such as Jack Benny and George Burns migrated to television, where audiences could see as well as hear their favorite stars. Radio then began to target local audiences with specific musical tastes, such as classical, hard rock, rhythm and blues, and country. Even the recording industry has not been untouched by television. The wide adoption of cable in the 1980s led to specialized music channels, such as MTV and VH1, through which the record companies promote their artists and their music.

Print media have changed too. Authors promote their books on television. Profits from books increase when television rights are sold, and made-for-television movies based on best-sellers, in turn, often spur consumers to buy books. Magazines have become more targeted because television was better at attracting general audiences.

Newspapers have suffered more than other media. More Americans now receive their news from television than newspapers (Hiebert & Gibbons, 2000; Wilson & Wilson, 2001). The availability of twenty-four-hour television news channels like CNN and Fox News has contributed to the decline in newspaper circulation. Although newspapers can provide in-depth information, they are unable to keep up with breaking news stories. Just think of the many twists and turns in the impeachment trial of President Bill Clinton. Events changed so quickly on some days that only radio and television could keep the public updated.

In attempting to stem declining circulation, newspapers have become more visually oriented. *USA Today* set a trend of being very colorful, with charts and graphs and short, easy-to-read stories that appeal to a television generation that has become accustomed to viewing news and entertainment in short chunks punctuated by advertising. According to Bagdikian (1997),

Broadcast news is widely watched because it is attached to family evening entertainment, and has thus evolved to meet entertainment standards. Newspapers, which for fifteen years have accelerated their entry into the entertainment field, have, to a lesser but still significant degree, adopted the same entertainment ethic in all their news. (p. 206)

Even the venerable *New York Times* and *Washington Post* eventually bowed to the new era and now have color. Even as television has changed the other mass media, the medium itself is about to go through a transformation, driven by advances in digital technologies.

Electronic television had its first major demonstration at the New York World's Fair in 1939. However, this was not the beginning of television. Paul Nipkow, a Russian scientist, had developed mechanical television in 1884, producing a picture with a resolution of 18 parallel lines per frame. Other scientists and inventors subsequently improved on this technology, eventually pushing the resolution to 240 lines by the 1930s, when the BBC offered its first regular television service. What was the problem with 240 lines of definition? If you compare it to the 525 that is the current analog standard, you will appreciate that mechanical television offered a fuzzy picture.

While experimentation with mechanical television continued, Philo T. Farnsworth and Vladimir Zworykin, a Russian immigrant, were working separately on electronic systems. Zworykin's inventions would form the basis for almost all of the television sets currently in use in the world. While working at Westinghouse in 1923, Zworykin invented the iconoscope. He later went to work for the RCA labs, where he would improve upon his invention with the kinescope. By 1939, when RCA showed off its electronic television set at the New York World's Fair, the resolution was 441 lines.

Television did not take off, however, until the 1950s. Two major circumstances intervened: World War II and the Federal Communications Commission's desire to set engineering standards. In 1941 the FCC accepted the standards set forth by the National Television System Committee (NTSC). The NTSC recommendation of 525 lines per frame and thirty frames per second have been the standard for U.S. television ever since. Of course, digital television will change this. The new standard will be 1,080 lines of resolution, offering a picture three times as sharp as what we are used to and with CD-quality surround sound. In July 1941 a few stations began broadcasting, but television growth stalled when the United States joined World War II later that year and industries were pressed into service to produce goods for the war.

By the end of the war in 1945, the FCC had to make decisions about allocating spectrum space responsibly to the many applicants for television licenses. It wanted to ensure that viewers would experience limited interference from the many competing stations. To resolve this problem, the FCC put a freeze on granting licenses from 1948 to 1952.

The freeze was lifted in 1952, and television finally took off. In 1953, the FCC decided on a color system developed by RCA, which had backward compatibility with existing sets. This meant that programs produced in color could be viewed on black and white sets, and programs produced in black and white could be viewed on color sets. ABC, CBS, and NBC became the dominant players in television. Having been successful in radio programming, they already had talent, experience in production, and established relationships with affiliate stations.

The networks do not actually broadcast programs. They provide programming to their affiliates around the country. The affiliates clear space in their schedules to carry the network programs. The networks also own and operate some stations. It is an advantage to a station to be affiliated with a network because of the access to quality programming and, thus, larger audiences. This, in turn, makes the station attractive to advertisers, who can be charged higher rates.

Network television has traditionally meant ABC, CBS, and NBC. Fox, Warner Brothers (WB), and United Paramount Television (UPN) have begun to challenge this dominance by developing networks with independent stations. These new networks provide limited amounts of programming each week, unlike the Big Three networks, which offer programming for almost the entire day. Network television programming borrowed heavily from radio, trying to appeal to broad audiences through various program genres, such as game shows, variety shows, soap operas, dramas, comedies, and news. The networks, however, were not the only choices that viewers had. Independent stations offered over-the-air broadcasts. They have typically carried old movies and old network programs.

In addition to being challenged by the new networks, the traditional networks face competition from the cable industry. Cable television began as community antenna television: local televison operations designed to make it possible for people in small towns far away from media markets or those whose signals received interference from hills and mountains to receive television programming. More than 65 percent of American homes are now wired for cable, which provides alternative niche programming that has siphoned off the network audience (Folkerts & Lacy, 2001; Vivian, 2001). Viewers interested in sports, movies, old television programs, children's programs, music, the outdoors, adventure, news, comedy, and other specific genres can find channels catering to their tastes.

Although it caters mostly to commercial interests, cable television has helped to empower communities. The cable networks are required to make channels available to the communities they serve. These cable access channels have advanced democracy by empowering communities to document events from the perspective of the average person and, in general, to create programs that serve the needs of citizens in ways that commercial and public broadcasting do not. Cable access channels serve communities in individual cable districts rather than media markets, which consist of cities and surrounding suburbs and towns. Individuals can see themselves represented. One downside is that these productions often lack the sophistication of the professional stations; thus, viewership is often limited to individuals with a vested interest in the subject (e.g., members of a church or a civic organization). The cable industry has also helped to make U.S. democracy more transparent to its citizens. The Cable Satellite Programming Network (C-SPAN), which is funded by the industry, carries Congressional legislative sessions, as well as speeches and discussions by political leaders and government officials.

Cable television itself is being challenged by direct broadcast satellite services, such as DirecTV and SkyB, which deliver programming directly to homes through small satellite dishes, bypassing cable services. At present, they offer more channels of programming than cable.

Because of scarce resources and ideological preferences, some governments around the world have played active roles in the regulation and funding of television. American television, however, has developed in the tradition of the other media, which follow free-market principles. American television has been primarily operated by the private sector. However, the industry has to operate under the policies set by the FCC regarding engineering and licensing (e.g., the number of stations that can be owned by individuals or companies and the length of time for which licenses can be held).

Despite the mostly commercial nature of broadcasting in the United States, there has always been a noncommercial broadcasting sector. Noncommerical broadcasting began in the 1920s when universities started to use radio to provide education and instruction to broader audiences. By the 1940s, the FCC recognized the important role of noncommercial broadcasting in providing programming that commercial stations would not produce, and it allocated specific frequencies for educational broadcasting. This principle was carried over to the allocation of the spectrum for television.

An important milestone in the history of U.S. broadcasting is the Public Broadcasting Act of 1967, which created the Corporation for Public Broadcasting (CPB). This act broadened the concept of noncommercial television to include programming to serve the public interest. It also linked the existing noncommercial stations into a network, the Public Broadcasting Service (PBS). CPB disburses federal funds to stations and producers, while PBS distributes programs from independent producers and member stations. PBS has earned a reputation for providing quality children's, public affairs, and cultural programming that might not be profitable for a commercial station. For example, symphonies and documentaries are staples on PBS.

In recent years, however, PBS has often had to justify its existence as Congress weighs the benefits of appropriating funds for CPB. Some legislators have argued that PBS is no longer necessary because some of the new cable channels deliver the programs that were once the province of PBS. For example, Bravo and Encore offer musical and theatrical performances, while The Discovery Channel and The Learning Channel offer science and nature programming. However, the major difference between PBS and these channels is that PBS offers free over-the-air service, while cable services require subscribers to pay a monthly fee.

Because it has not been in the commercial sector, PBS has been able to take risks, often pointing the way to the future of broadcasting. PBS was the first to use satellites to relay programs. It has been among the first to offer closed captioning for the hearing impaired and Descriptive Video Service, which uses the separate audio program (the SAP feature on television sets) to offer descriptions of programs for the sight-impaired. PBS is demonstrating its leadership role in the new world of digital television. Rather than adopting the commercial networks' stance of slowly rolling out HDTV programs as they wait for a critical mass of consumers to buy HDTV sets, PBS introduced the first interactive program for children in 1999, and the network was also planning an all-digital twenty-four-hour channel for children that would receive the same digital signal as the PBS Kids Web site.

THE FUTURE OF TELEVISION

We are indeed standing on the verge of a technological revolution, much as our ancestors did a century ago. Digital technologies are about to become more sophisticated and change our lives just as the automobile, electricity, and radio and recording technology changed the world.

What will television look like in 2025? Of course, the screens will be flat. The bulky set using the cathode ray tube will be replaced by a plasma-display set. You will be able to hang your HDTV television set on the wall or take it around in your pocket. Television sets will look a bit different in another way. The aspect ratio of the screens will be 16 to 9 rather than 4 to 3, making the screen closer to the proportions of a movie theater screen. Large sixty-inch screens will be commonplace, especially because picture clarity will not be compromised in large sets. Children will look at photographs of our current television sets with the kind of curiosity at which we look at the gramophone.

More important, the distinction between the computer, the television, and the telephone will be gone. Telephones will browse the Web, televisions will double as personal computers, and devices will turn your home's electrical lines and outlets into communication and security networks. The television will be the core of a digital data center that will include computer, telephone, and camera functions (Drummond, 1999; O'Neill & Ginchereau, 1998). It will not only provide entertainment, but information. It will be the hub of the heating, lighting, and security systems in our homes. Thus, computing and television entertainment will have an equal place in the family room of 2025, and the personal digital assistant will allow you to enjoy your favorite programs and, at the same time, maintain your calendar or call a friend.

This PC–TV future has been envisioned by several communication companies. For example, WebTV allows the audience to receive many services: enhanced and interactive data services, Internet access, video on demand, e-mail, games, and electronic program guides. The new televisions will have picture-in-picture capability to allow viewers to access Web pages and download media content while watching TV shows (Tedesco, 1998). The separation of leisure from work in the home will no longer occur, as the entertainment center will accomplish what have been traditionally telephone, television, and computer activities. "Couch viewing" will be replaced by "desk viewing," as consumers consult data banks, engage in bank transactions, and view their favorite shows with the same device (Sartori, 1998). The current interactive program guides will be expanded to provide viewers with additional information beyond program descriptions. They will include information about the characters and other background information related to the programs viewers are watching. For example, RePlay Networks has unveiled its RePlay TV that, through a set-top box, can replay selected scenes from television broadcasts that can be recalled by program name or actor (Drummond, 1999).

Currently, you can watch television on your computer if you have the right software and hardware. Digital television will make this easier. Not only will you be able to choose the programs you want to watch, you will be able to choose when you want to watch them. Rather than depending on a set-top box, you will have the benefit of the interactive technologies being built into your communication center. You will be able to respond to program offers directly.

The remote control is about to undergo a transformation. The remote controls of 2025 will be more sophisticated than the current ones that allow you to use interactive program guides provided by the cable systems. The same device that operates the television function will operate the computer function. In addition, voice-recognition technology will be refined so that viewers will not have to learn how to use a bewildering array of buttons. Imagine being able to tell your television what to do! The blurring of the distinctions between television and the computer means that the distinction between Web and broadcast or cable programming will no longer exist. For example, there will be no difference between CNN and its Web site, CNN.com.

Already, the World Wide Web has become a medium that complements traditional broadcasting. CNN has been incorporating the Web into its programs. *Talkback Live* is shown on its Web site in real time. Viewers can participate in the show by calling in, sending faxes, or sending e-mail messages that are received and responded to as the program airs. President Clinton's impeachment trial was carried live by the news channels and also at their Web sites. Victoria's Secret found an innovative way to incorporate the Web into its advertising and publicity campaign when it launched its swimsuits in January 1999. An ad was shown during the Super Bowl as a teaser for the launch on Victoria Secret's Web site. This innovation became a newsworthy event, as network newscasts announced the impending Web launch.

Accessing the Internet will be much faster. Rather than accessing it through telephone modems, you will use the electric wires that deliver electricity to your home. In addition, improvements to the Internet will allow for video that is of the same quality as that of television and for CD-quality sound. Thus, the current video quality that is reminiscent of silent movies will be a thing of the past.

The VCR will also be a museum piece by 2025. Customers will be able to order and download movies through the Internet, with digital video and audio, surpassing the quality of the best VCRs. Currently, the technology exists to capture television images through a computer with the right hardware. The problem is that the compression technology has not developed to the point whereby one can efficiently store the images on a computer's hard drive. By 2025, this will not be an issue, because home communication centers will be connected to large servers that will facilitate the many functions customers will need.

Satellites will still play a major role in program delivery. Direct broadcast satellite services, rather than cable, will be the preferred mode of delivery. Such services are now being offered by companies such as DirecTV and PrimeStar. The receiving dishes for these services will be even smaller than they are now, and viewers will have access to the 500 channels they have been promised.

Satellite and computer technologies have made instantaneous communication around the globe possible, making it easier to manage large corporate empires that span continents. We have seen mergers in the banking, communication, entertainment, and other industries that are creating ever bigger corporate entities. This trend will continue in 2025, because the domination of mass communication by large corporate empires makes it difficult for small companies to compete. For example, the independent Ted Turner decided that CNN and its related companies had a brighter future as part of a larger corporation, Time Warner, Inc., which owns book publishing, movie studios, cable franchises, television programs, record labels, magazines, theme parks, sports teams, and other businesses. Broadcasters will continue to merge with companies that produce computer software and hardware. Microsoft has been investing in the television industry in the United States and Europe. MSNBC is just one example of these relationships. So, even if small companies develop new technologies, they will need to become parts of larger entities in order to survive. The large corporations also have an interest in buying these smaller companies in order to expand their markets and increase profits.

One feature of global capitalism is that it transcends national borders. Satellite technology will allow transnational communication corporations to continue to deliver programming simultaneously to societies around the world. Production will still be expensive because of the costs of hiring talent to produce programming with high production values. Thus, large companies will dominate and export their products around the world to get maximum returns on their investments, and programming from the United States will continue to dominate the global market. The development of generic entertainment software or programming with cultural shareability will therefore be important as producers try to make their products suitable for the largest audience possible (Goonasekera, 1997, p. 39).

Despite the continued presence of large communication corporations, there will still be a role for smaller entities that can cater to the cultural and linguistic needs of special-interest audiences more adequately than the large broadcasters. These services will most likely be funded by a combination of governments and the private sector. WETV, which is based in Canada, is such an example. It is a "partnership-based global network," financed by public-sector agencies and some advertising (Nostbakken & Morrow, 1998). Its programming is created by independent producers and production houses to save on the costs of owning and operating studios, and to encourage diverse programming. The shows are delivered to broadcasters in thirty nations via satellite and videotape. Other examples are Brazil, which has had success in exporting soap operas to Africa and Russia, and China and India, which have been distributing dramas in Southeast Asia. These services all fill a niche for programming that more closely reflects the cultures and values of particular ethnic groups and societies that are overlooked by the large global corporations.

The new technologies have the potential to unite peoples around the world, realizing Marshall McLuhan's dream of a global village. People of different cultures can share experiences simultaneously. Geography will not be a barrier to communication. People in remote locations will have access to the same information as those living in metropolitan areas. Many may recall how the world was united in collective grief as people everywhere watched Princess Diana's funeral in real time. However, the fact that television will still be dominated by a few Western conglomerates has implications for the cultural sovereignty of non-Western nations (Mowlana, 1998).

As mentioned before, television programming around the world is dominated by the United States. The U.S. broadcasting system has always been primarily commercial and almost fifty years of programming exists that was designed to appeal to wide audiences. Many countries are concerned about the political and moral values promoted by many of these programs. There is the possibility for the creation of media-created subcultures in developing countries that might be at odds with mainstream cultures in other societies

(Goonasekera, 1997, p. 29). These subcultures, because of their access to Western media, might adopt behaviors that go against their cultures, and this could lead to social upheavals. Some governments (e.g., Malaysia and Saudi Arabia), have sought to limit citizens' access to satellite dishes. Some, such as Singapore, have tried to filter the Internet through national servers. Other countries though, such as Japan and England, have allowed foreign satellite television in with few, if any, content restrictions.

The new technologies will alter societies as new relationships are forged among peoples. This is already happening, as cyberrelationships have been developing among some users of the Internet. As the media converge, "The medium, the message and the audience will not be discrete entities. They are interacting and merging to become parts of civil society—an intelligent community" (Goonasekera, 1997, p. 4). Audience members and producers will develop new ongoing relationships without necessarily having interpersonal contact.

Commercial television exists to bring audiences to advertisers. Stations and networks are successful to the degree that they are able to sell enough advertising time at good rates. Thus, U.S. programming tends to be entertaining to audiences, if not educational. The networks have already established a pattern of safe programming. Diversity in content suffers as producers use the tried and true in order to ensure profitability. If one network produces a successful program, the others tend to duplicate the idea. Although broadcasters have generated unique programming ideas over the years, according to Walker and Ferguson (1998),

Network television programming characteristically exhibits imitation, innovation, and stagnation. Programmers attempt to minimize risk by imitating the successful formulas and established talent, those that have generated high program ratings. Only when such imitation fails, or their resources are limited, do programmers pursue more innovative forms and new personnel. (p. 22)

Even the advent of twenty-four-hour news channels has not done much to widen coverage of events around the world; instead, there is more, often repetitive, coverage of the same few stories. The newscasts are produced with the audience and, hence, the advertisers in mind. The stories chosen are often those considered the most interesting to the audience. Events in the United States, Europe, and Asia (in terms of financial information) feature predominantly on CNN and Fox newscasts, for example. Events in South and Central America and Africa are covered in cases of natural disasters and sometimes war. The war in Sierra Leone in early 1998 received almost no mention. No doubt, news editors thought that U.S. audiences would have very little interest, if any, in a distant place that they had probably not heard of. The titillating saga of U.S. President Bill Clinton and Monica Lewinsky dominated coverage for thirteen months even when there was no new information. It is true that presidential wrongdoing is news; however, it was an easy story with sex and a somewhat dubious cast of characters that read like a soap opera and required little explanation. Everyone in the audience could understand it and form an opinion.

The new technologies offer the potential for everyone to be a communicator. With convergence blurring the distinctions among broadcasting, computing, and telecommunications, everyone who wants to say something will be able to say it. Right now, you could create your own Web site to speak to the world. Interactive television will offer more opportunities to do this. This democratization of the media could be healthy, as it takes some control of content from the large conglomerates and empowers citizens. The downside could be a deprofessionalization of the media, particularly the news media. Without the filters of professional reporters and editors, rumors could rule the day.

We have seen instances of rumors getting started on the Internet. Matt Drudge, editor of the *Drudge Report*, his own Web publication, became a media star based on his one-man crusade against U.S. President Bill Clinton and his breaking of the Monica Lewinsky story on his Web site. The stories on his Web site were not always accurate. They were sometimes based on rumors, but the fame that he gained from breaking the story made him a marketable commodity.

In addition to facilitating individual expression, the new technologies will offer opportunities for groups to communicate with and educate one another, thus increasing citizen involvement in democracies. Currently, each cable system is required to provide a channel for citizen expression, the public access channel. The poor quality of program content on some of these stations has caused these channels to be the butt of stand-up comedians' jokes, but public access provides a forum for members of a community to share their common experiences, educate one another, and preserve traditions.

It is true that there will be many more channels to choose from. Rather than offering one program at a time, broadcasters will be able to make available a menu of programs to audiences, who can choose what they want to watch at a given moment. However, television has operated on the parsimony principle; that is, exploiting each product to the fullest extent through repetition. If current business practices continue, much of the programming will be repetitive. For example, many cable outlets, such as The Learning Channel, Home & Garden Television, and The Discovery Channel, repeat their prime time (8 to 11 P.M.) lineup at 11 P.M. The movie channels show the same movies several times over a period of a few weeks. It is true that this allows more viewers more flexibility in accessing programs, but it also helps to keep production costs down. In addition, several channels carry off-network programs (i.e., reruns of network programs). Nickelodeon, TV Land, and WTBS are only a few examples. It is cheaper to air a program that is already made than to produce something new. Thus, the increased number of channels that we shall have access to in 2025 will mean more program choices, but not necessarily as many as we might have expected.

Interactivity has the potential to increase citizen participation, but the citizens must have access to the technology. The global capitalist economy does not result in an equitable distribution of resources, either among or within countries. Disparities in resources will create information gaps between the "haves" and "have-nots," the information rich and the information poor. The new digital technologies, although cheaper in 2025 than they are now, will not be free. Free over-the-air services will represent just a fraction of the available television content, thus shutting out those who cannot afford subscriber services. Information gaps will exist between wealthy and poor countries. The poorer countries have been trying to keep up; however, the pace of technological innovation makes this difficult. Thus, those with resources will be able to dominate, or even dictate, global debates.

The multiplicity of channels will increase the practice of narrowcasting, and interactive viewers will be able to choose what they want to consume and the manner in which they do so. In the United States, where many cable customers have access to sixty or seventy channels, many people watch only a few on a regular basis. CNN currently allows individuals to customize the news they want to receive from its Web site. Thus, individuals will be able to expose themselves to only those things that interest them. While providing convenience for the television viewer or media consumer, narrowcasting has the potential to fragment societies. This would be a result that reverses the traditional role that the mass media have played in uniting societies.

The increasing willingness of viewers to stay within a narrow focus may be related to information overload. Many feel that there is just too much information, much more than they can absorb. Gone are the days when the wealthy had a well-stocked library that contained "all the knowledge of the world." Information overload can lead to passivity, whereby people stop trying to take advantage of all the options they have access to and limit themselves to just a few tried and tested favorites.

Brand identity will become more important for broadcasters as they try to attract and hold the attention of more fragmented audiences. Viewers often do not know the names of the stations or channels they are watching. Broadcasters will continue to superimpose their logos on the screen to help viewers associate the programming they are viewing with the provider. Saari (1998) predicts "the media may become more like the service industry, having also to deal with such issues as consumer loyalty, satisfaction and retention" (p. 41). Saari also suggests that with the merging of the broadcast and cable media and the Internet, the individuals in the audience could consume the same media for various purposes. Although two individuals might be accessing the same content or program, one might be watching the actual program while the other might be focusing on ancillary activities or information that can be accessed through the program.

This increased narrowcasting and the ability of viewers to customize what they view will necessitate changes in audience measurement. The current problems associated with accurately measuring viewers who graze channels, zap commercials, and watch their VCRs will be compounded with the options presented with the digital technologies. The current people meters, which require viewers to punch in a code each time they enter and leave the room, will be inadequate to measure viewers. More invasive technologies will probably be developed because advertisers are interested not only in the number of people who consume television but demographic and psychographic information to aid them in targeting their commercial messages. The industry has been trying to develop devices that can recognize who is in the room without the individuals' having to remember to indicate when they enter or leave the room. Of course, there are ethical concerns regarding the degree to which individuals should be monitored while in the privacy of their own homes.

Finally, the new technologies raise new concerns about piracy for the industry. Neither the VCR nor the audio cassette recorder has the ability to reproduce studio-quality recordings. This weakness has not stopped piracy. With digital technologies, consumers will be able to produce studio-quality recordings (i.e., there will be no degradation between the original and the copy). Cable systems now offer satellite music services with CD-quality sound. Record companies are already concerned about customers' unlicenced downloading of music files as digital systems deliver music to PCs through Web networks. Soon broadcasters will share these concerns. Thus, national and international copyright laws will need to be revised. Because satellite delivery of programming has the possibility of spanning national borders, international agreements regarding copyright laws will have to be signed and, more important, enforced to protect intellectual property. Whether an international agreement can be enforced is debatable. Countries that are members of the World Trade Organization currently have an agreement on the protection of intellectual property rights; however, some of the individual countries do not have laws and regulations in place that facilitate enforcement.

CONCLUSION

We are living in an exciting period as we witness the dawn of digital television. As we project to 2025, it is clear that we can no longer think of television in isolation, but must see it as one component of a digital data center combining television, telephone, and computer technologies. In the age of media convergence, we shall be consumers interacting with content that we can tailor to meet our needs. Digital television and its related technologies have the possibility to be liberating forces in society, educating and enriching all if used ethically.

REFERENCES

Bagdikian, B. H. (1997). *The media monopoly* (5th ed.). Boston: Beacon Press.
Baran, S. J. (1999). *Introduction to mass communication: Media literacy and culture.* Mountain View, CA: Mayfield.

Bazalgette, S. (1998). Music choice and digital copyright: The arguments over audio licenses. *InterMedia, 26* (5), 9–11.

Drummond, M. (1999, January 19). Lines blurring at electronics show; Consumer gadgets going multipurpose. *San Diego Union-Tribune*, p. 4.

Folkerts, J., & Lacy, S. (2001). *The media in your life: An introduction to mass communication* (2d ed.). Boston: Allyn & Bacon.

Goonasekera, A. (1997). Cultural markets in the age of globalisation: Asian values and Western content. *InterMedia: Special Report, 25* (6), 2–43.

Head, S. W., Sterling, C. H., & Scholfield, L. B. (1994). *Broadcasting in America: A survey of electronic media* (7th ed.). Boston: Houghton Mifflin.

Hiebert, R. E., & Gibbons, S. J. (2000). *Exploring mass media for a changing world.* Mahwah, NJ: Lawrence Erlbaum.

Mowlana, H. (1998). Globalization of mass media: Opportunities and challenges for the South. *Cooperation South, 2,* 16–39.

Nostbakken, D., & Morrow, C. (1998). Investing in culture for development: The role of cultural expression through television. *InterMedia, 26* (5), 18–23.

O'Neill, L., & Ginchereau, W. (1998, October 26). I want my DTV! *InfoWorld*, p. 63.

Saari, T. (1998). Knowledge media and the new masters of the media: How the new technologically empowered consumer will challenge the traditional attitudes of mass media corporations. *InterMedia, 26* (5), 40–44.

A sampling of services and options. (1999, January 20). *USA Today*, p. 4D.

Sartori, C. (1998). Digital market and digital democracy: Can they live together? *InterMedia, 26* (5), 28–32.

Spigel, L. (1995). Making room for TV. In D. Crowley & P. Heyer (Eds.), *Communication in history: Technology, culture, society* (2d ed., pp. 272–280). White Plains, NY: Longman.

Tedesco, R. (1998, December 7). Microsoft demos Web TV platform. *Broadcasting & Cable*, p. 74.

Vivian, J. (2001). *The media of mass communication* (updated on-line ed.). Boston: Allyn & Bacon.

Walker, J., & Ferguson, D. (1998). *The broadcast television industry.* Needham Heights, MA: Allyn & Bacon.

Wilson, J. R., & Wilson, S. R. (2001). *Mass media mass culture: An introduction* (5th ed.). Boston: McGraw-Hill.

11

Politics

Robert M. Knight

It is January 2025. The president, who first gained public notice as an actor who pitched lower transmission rates on the Internet, has just completed her State of the Union address. The House speaker, a member of the party in opposition to that of the president, addresses the camera.

"The initiatives listed by the President may all be well and good, but first she has some explaining to do," he says. "At the top of the agenda is the passage of a joint resolution condemning her for a catty remark she made during a Camp David picnic last June, from which we have a complete video-tape and transcript."

Such is the substance of what is coming out of Washington. Taxation, the environment, foreign relations, defense, Social Security, the domestic and international economies, education, health care, public works—all are issues that affect the voters, but all are complex and none are very sexy, literally or figuratively. Apparently, what inquiring Americans want to know is, what is Congress going to do about that catty remark? It had something to do with a rock star, the chairman of the House Ways and Means Committee, a member of the British royal family, an aging O. J. Simpson, and an apparition of Elvis.

If media and political trends continue in the direction they appear to be going in the year 2000, U.S. politics of tomorrow will be most aptly described as frivolous. If, however, some seriousness should kick in as the result of a pendulum swing, American politics could go quite the opposite way—toward a form of totalitarianism, perhaps. Either way, the driving force will most likely not be the political process itself, but the public perception of the political process. In a democratic republic, politics often thrives without the benefit of substance, but it cannot survive an hour without a steady diet of perception. Assuming the First Amendment is still alive a quarter of a century from now, or even if it is not, U.S. politics will continue to rely, as it always has, on public perception.

The politics of 2025, then, will depend largely on what types of news media exist then, and who controls them. Chances are, the news media will have at their core an interactive technology, based on today's Internet, which will have had an additional quarter century to mature. The chances are very good that the filtering mechanism based on accepted standards of newsworthiness, today represented by the reporter and the editor, will no longer exist.

REVERSING DISTURBING TRENDS

That might not be bad, because in recent years we journalists have made a mess of the way we cover politics. We can be, and maybe we should be, replaced. By taking the documents, public statements, and personal reports from which reporters now extract news stories and giving them directly to the people on the receiving end of the Internet, we might abort three disturbing trends, trends that have distorted political coverage to the point that the author of the First Amendment, Thomas Jefferson, might wonder why he bothered to write it.

U.S. political coverage has been warped first by the trivialization of our news judgment; second, by our breathless pursuit of anything that a celebrity does. The third trend combines the other two. Now we must not fail to question the most intimate moments in the lives of our celebrities, and politicians are, by definition, celebrities. No longer can the voters be trusted to judge political candidates simply by what they have done or plan to do to help or hurt the nation's well-being.

This prediction is based on some pieces of recent history. Trivial news and celebrity news is easy to cover, and they have a ready audience. Significant news, the kind that can have a profound effect on voters' lives, is often too complex or too subtle to attract immediate audience response, especially on a visual medium like television. For example, during the past decade, fewer issues have been more significant to the voter, or less well-covered, than campaign financing.

As a result, about all many voters know about their Congressional candidates is what the candidates themselves have decided the voters should know. And that almost always takes the form of a broadcast commercial. Commercials are expensive. So, because a large fraction of the voters do not have the sophistication to distinguish between a commercial and a news report, the candidate with the most dollars—which came from who knows whom—has a distinct advantage.

Voters can be further confused by the difficulty in distinguishing responsible news media from the likes of supermarket tabloids, *The New York Post*, Howard Stern, Rush Limbaugh, G. Gordon Liddy, Geraldo Rivera, Montel Williams, or *Hard Copy*. Mainstream journalists would not deny the benefits of the First Amendment to any of them, but they find themselves wishing people would not get them mixed up with the legitimate news media.

None of what we have thus far described is new to those with some political sophistication. But it bears repeating, because without tighter campaign-finance laws and limits, the question of what U.S. politics will be like in 2025 will be easy enough to answer. Those whose power is fueled by big money will control politics.

All this assumes, of course, that the richest and most powerful country in the world will continue its dominance twenty-four years hence. Maintaining a republican democracy would be nearly impossible if our economic or military vehicles should break down.

Now, let us repeat that these predictions are based on recent history. The "historian" makes predictions realizing that few things are more perilous than writing history too soon and then making predictions based on that recent history.

THE PERILS OF PROGNOSTICATION

At a recent estate auction in south central Pennsylvania, an investment of seven dollars bought a set of five small books, monthly issues of *Current History*, printed by the New York Times Company between October 1931 and May 1932. Mispredictions pepper these little books and show what an oxymoron "current history" can be. For example, the October 1931 issue of *Current History* carries the opinion that Dr. Heinrich Brüning, who had been German chancellor for one and one-half years, "has steadily grown, that Brüning himself is irreplaceable" (Klein, 1931, p. 25). Fourteen months later, Adolph Hitler was elected chancellor.

An article in the January 1932 issue declares that "the American economy was and is 'fundamentally sound'" (Tugwell, 1932, p. 525). The Great Depression was to drag on for at least five more years.

In the April 1932 issue, Benito Mussolini is characterized as the Italian leader who transformed himself from "the greatest builder of armaments and the arch-imperialist of Europe" to "the most drastic advocate of disarmament and world peace" (Elliot, 1932, p. 15). Three-and-one-half years later, on October 2, 1935, Mussolini sent an invasion force to conquer Ethiopia, known then as Abyssinia, and wrecked what was left of the League of Nations.

Such are the perils of writing recent history. "Current history" is indeed an oxymoron. Unless, however, we ignore George Santayana's oft-quoted warning that those who cannot remember the past are condemned to repeat it, we must grab at any history that exists. And so little exists to guide us through the current communication revolution that we must, in this case, rely on recent history.

To protect oneself, the would-be historian and prognosticator tries to return to constants that don't go away whenever the currents of history change course. And one constant that remains with us is that the perception tail wags the political dog. There is little point in describing the politics of 2025 without determining first what is happening, or will happen, to the news media.

A QUESTION OF SUBSTANCE

Before we can determine the evolution of the news media, however, we must listen to a refrain we journalists hear more and more. Serious readers, listeners, and viewers complain that they're getting less substance for the time they invest in the news. And they are not getting much of the perspective that Jefferson, for one, considered vital to the survival of democracy.

Surprisingly, not even the old refrain of media bias is heard much anymore. It never did quite live up to its billing. Although critics are usually correct when they charge reporters with leaning toward the left in their personal politics, the publishers they work for most often lean toward the right. In the great majority of newspapers, the bias shows up only on the editorial pages anyway, and that's legitimate.

It is fair to say, however, that news magazines, especially *Time* and *U.S. News & World Report*, each week bend to a rightward bias. They have taken it upon themselves to interpret political news for their readers, and those interpretations still sometimes reflect the conservative views of their founders, Henry Luce and David Lawrence, respectively.

Television news, especially local TV news, is usually much too bland to offer anything so provocative as political bias. Slanted commentary does, however, appear with alarming frequency on radio talk shows, and it looks as if the flow of information on the Internet is following their example.

Regardless, those who complain that the news coverage they're getting is shallow and lacks perspective are not imagining things. The so-called dumbing down of newscasts and news columns has not happened by accident. In the best marketing traditions, newspapers, news magazines, radio news departments, and television news departments are giving the customers what they want.

Apparently, most do not want substance. One major reason they have decided they don't want to be informed is that much of the news media have decided that news must either be informed and dull or superficial and titillating. It cannot possibly be interesting and, at the same time, have any value.

'TWAS EVER THUS?

Certainly, there is nothing new about journalists who perceive that their first responsibility to the U.S. public is one of titillation. Sensationalism has ebbed and flowed like the tides, or swung like a pendulum.

The year 1833 brought with it the penny press and, with it, "the emphasis on emotion for its own sake," according to historian Edwin Emery (1962, p. 213). It was James Gordon Bennett's *New York Herald* that typified the genre. Readers of the penny press eventually matured to the point that Horace Greeley could find a market for his *New York Tribune* in 1841. Although it carried the taint of political partisanship, Greeley mixed his Whig beliefs with a whimsical combination of socialism and Manifest Destiny ("Go West, Young Man"). In the process, he returned sensationalism to its dormant stage for about fifty years.

Then came "yellow journalism," so named because the symbol of the era was a comic strip, "The Yellow Kid," which appeared in Joseph Pulitzer's *New York World*. According to Emery (1962), Pulitzer and his arch rival, William Randolph Hearst, pioneered the use of "bigger headlines, more readable stories, pictures, and blobs of color." Effectively used, these devices could be useful and desirable, but they could also be used "to emphasize sensationalism at the expense of news" (p. 415).

Hearst's use of yellow journalism had the more profound effect. He manipulated his readers into supporting a questionable Spanish–American War, beginning a relationship with right-wing dictators in Cuba that was to produce strong feelings of resentment toward the United States and, indirectly, stick us with Fidel Castro. When Hearst asked his front-page readers, "How do you like the *Journal's* war?" Pulitzer began to withdraw from the competition. By 1910, responding to a greater sophistication demonstrated by readers who had taken advantage of educational benefits unknown to their parents—many of them immigrants—most U.S. newspapers had begun to make more intelligent use of headlines, pictures, and printing.

Not for long, however. In 1917 the United States began its year-and-a-half participation in World War I, and a jaded and weary public was ready for a new wave of titillation. New ingredients now added to the old formulas of sex and crime: the tabloid format and photography.

JUST ANOTHER PENDULUM SWING?

It's tempting to view the latest tide of sensationalism as temporary, just as the penny press, yellow journalism, and jazz journalism were temporary. But in the past the pendulum has swung back to responsibility in reaction to a higher level of public education achieved by Americans who, after all, still had to be able to read. Now, however, the main culprit appears to be a medium that requires nothing of its audience except a desire to sit dumbly before an electronic picture machine. The quality-of-education trend no longer is up, so there is no new public incentive to swing the pendulum back by demanding responsible journalism.

What's sobering is that unsophisticated voters who do look for substance but who demand something a little lighter in tone than public television's *Nightly News*, the *New York Times*, or National Public Radio's *All Things Considered* are tempted to turn to some of the more strident homepages on the Internet for political news and views, just as they turn to more strident radio talk shows.

There is hope. Because the technology undoubtedly will be interactive, we are about to be weaned from a fifty-year vacation from having to use our brains. That vacation has been fostered by television. Because TV is addictive and demands nothing, many Americans have failed to develop one of the brain's basic organizers, the language that communicates and processes the data, knowledge, and information that the brain absorbs and disseminates. But now, if we are to use an interactive medium, we will be required not only to read, but, somehow, in some way, to write. And maybe the experience of writing will enrich our brains just enough that we will again begin to demand that the news media behave responsibly, and the pendulum will be forced to swing back.

If it doesn't, politics in the United States will devolve into a long series of silly scenarios like the one that began this chapter. The voters will be caught up in a swirl of breathless reports on what politicians ate for dinner and whom they went to bed with—not just now, but twenty or thirty years earlier. The news media, if interactive communication can be called that, will focus on the pool parties of public figures and the petty vindictiveness that transpires in such places.

Issues? If they get addressed at all by the candidates We the People have elected, the voters would not know much about them. The news media would not bother to cover them, and the politicians would not care, because issues would not be what they were elected to address. Republican democracy, that noble experiment that the United States did so much to develop, would die with the whimper that T. S. Eliot was so fond of writing poetry about.

There is, however, the small chance that the pendulum will indeed swing back. We can only hope that if that occurs, the pendulum will not go so far that if fosters some brand of McCarthyism, as often happens when the public and the news media perceive themselves as "responsible."

Of course, the pendulum will have no effect if the institutions of the United States fail to survive the next 25 years; if the great experiment that began 124 years before the millenium is not swept away by the weight of mass ignorance, the devastation of international belligerence, the crush of world poverty, or the final wheeze of a fragile economy. All are catastrophes that can be mitigated by responsible journalism.

But can we? And do we care?

REFERENCES

Bayley, E. R. (1981). *Joe McCarthy and the press*. Madison: University of Wisconsin Press.

Carey, J. (Ed.). (1990). *Eyewitness to history*. New York: Avon Books.

Elliott, Y. W. (1932). Mussolini turns to thoughts of peace. *Current History, 36* (1), 15.

Emery, E. (1962). *The press and America* (2d ed.). Englewood Cliffs, NJ: Prentice Hall.

Klein, F. (1931). Chancellor Brüning of Germany. *Current History, 35* (1), 25.

Tebbel, J., & Zuckerman, M. E. (1991). *The magazine in America*. Oxford: Oxford University Press.

Tugwell, R. (1932). Flaws in the Hoover economic plan. *Current History, 25* (4), 525.

12

Religion

Michael A. Longinow

Martin Marty (1984) has noted that those living in the United States have perhaps always been a people unsettled and searching—probing for something more, something beyond.[1] A certain religious impulse about the American vision for itself and its future has helped shape moments of uncertainty into spiritual pilgrimages of many kinds, each narrated by an accompanying media of religion rich with cultural life. Indeed, what sets American religion apart at the dawning of the twenty-first century is the enormous capacity, heightened by technological advances, of religious leaders and followers in this nation to make media part of their self-identity, their guide in the journey of faith. Study of the ways communication has shaped the development of American religious life and culture over time has been neglected too long (Sweet, 1993, pp. 1–3). This chapter helps fill that gap, suggesting insights into change within American religious media applicable to students of American culture, religion, and communication as they look toward upcoming decades.

Media examined in this chapter will be that range of communication tools, from newspapers and magazines, to television and radio, to feature films and Internet communication, that in the late 1990s had become a perplexing sea of images and stories. Perplexity notwithstanding, religious media have maintained a firm grip on the attention of those who care about faith and the pursuit of God. Recent research suggests that Americans want to believe as much as they ever did, at the same time craving a feeling of connectedness, to each other and to the source of their faith, on their own terms. Increasingly, those terms involve media. A Yankelovich study in 1996 indicated that twenty-something Americans often feel discontented and disillusioned with the ways traditional religion treats their mobile, fluid lifestyles (Sparkes, 1996, p. 43). Where media and religion connected creatively, younger Americans appeared to be taking notice (Waters, 1996, p. 41).

Linkage between growth in religion and media, of course, is not new. It can be argued that alongside the birth, dissolution, or debate over any organized religion in recorded world history, there has been an accompanying—perhaps a guiding—thrust of media. Preserved stories, narratives, and images of a shared experience of faith drew humans into shared systems of tradition that anchored them as individuals to a culture of belief (Tanner, 1997, pp. 31–33). Some, such as Michael Schudson (1992), note that such imaging within late twentieth-century American culture is fraught with a tendency toward inflated and embellished memory. "Human beings treat the past as a real, contemporary force," argues Schudson (p. 2), and use it as a cognitive tool, a way of "thinking out loud" to themselves (p. 14). If this is true of Americans dealing with the past, perhaps it could also be how they make sense of an uncertain future, including future thought about religion. Historian Averil Cameron (1991), backed by sociologists Roger Finke and Rodney Stark (1992), suggests that within American religious history the sharpest advances have come through those willing. Assuming the dawn of the twenty-first century can be expected to contain new variations of this trend, Judaism, Islam, and Christianity will take center stage in this study of it. Hinduism, Buddhism, Taoism, and Native American Shamanism will also be included, for in the late twentieth century these too have informed public religion in the United States in important ways.

REALITY CHECK? RELIGION STILL MATTERS IN AMERICAN MEDIA

Though myths abound regarding the religiosity of America's colonial founders, it cannot be denied that they lived in a world filled with faith practices. True enough, some braved the sea to escape British law or to capture wealth. But most also brought their own brand of Protestant or Catholic religion to the New World, shaped by at least tacit conviction—bred of a European sense of religion's sociopolitical centrality—that the church should influence, if not govern, in this new land. Naturally then, the Mayflower Compact contained references to God. Shipboard sermons clothed the continental venture in religious language (Boorstin, 1987, p. 5). New cities and local governors took their authority from the Crown, and from the Lord—seen in leadership of the local parish. And it must be noted that at least some of the first inklings of a free press and freedom of inquiry in America derived from writings of a Puritan, John Locke (LaTourette, 1975, p. 978). The First Amendment's language, as but one prominent example of this, sets forth a radical notion of religious nonestablishment in ways that hint at a high socio-cultural regard for religion (Buddenbaum, 1998, pp. 19–20). That debate about this clause still rocks the nation in socioreligious ways suggests a continuing priority in American society for both religion and communication practice.

Yet researchers in the latter twentieth century appear to have ignored the important ways that deeply religious commitment informs communication practices (Lulofs, 1993). Maybe it's a given (Buddenbaum, 1998, pp. xiii–xv), or maybe it is something we have never liked to admit, or, even if we did, lacked the energy or inclination to describe it in academic or popular media (Lulofs, 1993; Carpenter, 1984, p. 3). Or perhaps we've grown tired in the West of wrestling with makers of religious subcultures whose power over implicit and explicit communication about religion has been a centuries-old dynasty (Silk, 1998, pp. 3–11). Whether we are inclined to research it or not, change in religious communication is coming as surely as change in communication in other areas of American culture. As one researcher has noted, our grasp of this change is as important to our understanding of religion as it is to understanding ourselves within a communication-driven society (Hutchinson, 1963, p. 13).

NEXT CENTURY'S CHRISTIAN MEDIA: CULTURALLY ADAPTABLE?

Most visible in the next century, for a variety of reasons, will be changes to Christian print media, that vast variety of written pieces ranging from pocket tracts to slick magazines to glossy hardbound books. Christianity in America, due in part to its Western European origins, has roots in the printed word tracing to Gutenberg and the Reformation impulse to grasp knowledge of God and the created order with an individualistic wrestling of mind with heart (Purves, 1998, p. 7). Americans carefully guard their religious texts. Most carefully protected among them, from Christianity to Judaism to Islam, have been reprinted sacred pieces written in antiquity. Whether it is a pocket New Testament or an ornamented copy of the Koran, no amount of revisionist religious fiction or popular religious media (and these have become a study unto themselves) has been able to replace the socioreligious power of these original documents. Indeed, technology has been devised to make the un-tainted text of these writings available across the globe by means of audio-tape, compact disc, and, in the waning twentieth century, Internet sites (Purves, 1998, pp. 11, 17–19).

For a variety of reasons, the impulse toward Christian media cannot be separated from the impulse toward education—formal and informal—in reli-gious thought within American communities of faith (Wallace, 1991, pp. 3–4; Longinow, 1996, p. 53). Given this teaching function of media—acknowledged more by some media than others—some types of religious print media in decades to come can be expected to resemble print media of centuries past. Where such media begins to lose popularity, the reason, rather than a waning interest in religion itself, could be that Americans for the most part have come to read and learn differently. Such has been the trend in the 1990s, tracing to the beginning of the century. Thomas Leonard (1995, pp. 220–222), noting newspaper readership, observed that the United States, by the end of the twentieth century, had made the shift from a nation of communal readers to one of isolated skimmers. Christian publications ranging from the more mature *Christianity Today* to Christian teen magazines and *Cornerstone* (a publication of Jesus People, USA) have responded to the phenomenon by tailoring their products to the browsing audience.

A related challenge facing Christian media in American life of the next century will be its struggle for audience in a postliterate society. And it will be no small struggle. While it was the printed page, ranging from broadsides to broadsheet newspapers, that spread popular Christianity in the United States through the end of the nineteenth century and early decades of the twentieth, the mid- to late 1900s became a time of diminishing popular interest in reading. Not that words did not matter (Roof, 1994, p. 77); rather, alongside reading sprang up a fascination with images: audio images by radio, filmed images on celluloid, or, later, videotape, and still photographic images alongside text and graphics. It has been argued that the implications of new media will challenge previous assumptions about "the rational, autonomous individual" and could promote new ways of seeing the self within society—one constantly changing, driven by multiple identities being shaped by performative language (Poster, 1995, pp. 58–59).

An ironic twist of media characteristics in the next century could be the priority on a new orality (Purves, 1998, pp. 28–31). What goes around comes around. And American Christianity, having moved from the spoken word to the written word over some 200 years, has during the 1990s responded to a devalued literacy by rediscovering the sociocultural potential of recorded oralities in television, radio, film, and the lyrics of recorded music (Ong, 1988, pp. 174–179). Such media innovations have perhaps the strongest precedent within American Protestantism, which traces to the very Reformation itself a drive to speak and sing its doctrines. Hence, evangelical Christians in the mid-1990s could be seen pushing their way into mainstream recorded music by the pounding, swinging rhythms of such solo artists as Amy Grant and Michael W. Smith and by groups with such Biblically connected names as "Jars of Clay." Evangelical Christian toddlers chortled at the video antics of animated vegetables acting out Biblical values in daily-life dramas (Miller, 1998, p. B1), and older children heard action stories aimed at Christian teens and preteens on such nationally distributed radio programs as *Adventures in Odyssey* (Gerson & Garrett, 1998, p. 23). Growth of the "electronic church" phenomenon—ranging from televangelism to televised worship—despite scandals that in the 1980s and early 1990s seemed to taint all but the most circum-spect Christian broadcasters, can be expected to continue drawing the atten-tion of both cable subscribers and network viewers across the United States, as long as they are willing to pay for it (Elvy, 1987).

Of course, such innovation not only made socioreligious sense; it was sim-ply good business. Christian young people—along with their moms and dads and grandparents—didn't just go to the mall more often in the 1990s; they went to Christian bookstores, places packed mainly with Protestant materials and glistening with marketing genius. Such outlets have become a prominent sociocultural and socioreligious niche within the American economy in the late twentieth century. As such they can expect serious questions in the twenty-first century—from mainstream news media if not the Christian press—about the uses of Mammon in pursuit of the evangelical Christian Kingdom of God (Wuthnow, 1998).

Catholic publications and media, with an equally storied past in the United States, have grown up through immigrant roots, postimmigrant stages, and into a late twentieth-century fragmentation touching much of American cul-ture (Deedy, 1963, pp. 68–69). Despite clear persecution at the hands of Prot-estant denominational leaders in the nineteenth century, Catholic media and education, having firmly affixed themselves on American socioreligious cul-ture, can be expected to maintain this presence in the twenty-first century. The Catholic presence in American political life over social issues can be expected to continue and grow—the abortion controversy being one promi-nent example (Reichley, 1985, p. 293)—and will likely continue in tandem with political involvements across denominations and socioreligious bound-aries. Catholic clergy as characters in modern film have a storied past in American communication history of the mid- to late twentieth century (Keyser & Keyser, 1984). It is an unfinished story likely to take on new twists as American cinema, along with television, continues its fascination with estab-lished denominationalism—particularly the liturgical—in American life.

In ways mirroring Protestant efforts in the 1990s, American Catholic church leaders and varieties of publishers, scholarly and otherwise, are reaching out to local communities with media ranging from parish newsletters to book series to stalwart denominational newspapers and magazines to Web sites. In Chicago, a favorite on-line stop is www.holynamecathedral.org, a site living out the city's cathedral parish motto, "Celebrating the Past, Creating the Future."

Indeed, nowhere in American Christian media, Catholic or Protestant, will there be more blending in the next century of spoken, musically accompa-nied, and visually illustrated media than in the array of Christian sites on the World Wide Web. Here, followers of religion can expect to find faith-oriented text juxtaposed with still or motion pictures, audio images, music, or com-posites of them all. Synthetic or not, this new media will create, as it has already, a heady impression that no distance is so great that an American believer cannot make the connection, be it with the thought and culture of a new prophet or aliens on a passing spacecraft behind a comet. Rocket science? Not really. In fact, it's stuff we all know quite well. One scholar notes that the rules in this new world of hypertext will come from "a melding of the conventions used by advertisers, illustrators, comic book artists, writers, and programmers" (Purves, 1998, p. 60).

MEDIA, FUNDAMENTALISM, AND SOCIAL ACTION: THE VOLATILE LINK

Some have argued that radical religious groups in the United States, from both the left and right, and in all religions, pose one of the greatest threats to the democratic dialogue within American culture in the next century (Diamond, 1989, pp. 231–236). Media of these groups, acting as a catalyst to cohesion among scattered believers, can be expected to gain momentum technologically and in target marketing. Such media, ranging from followers of Jerry Falwell to supporters of advancing Israeli interests, will likely continue to be readily available by means of both paper-and-ink publishing and Internet sites. At the same time, emerging case law regarding the control of religious printed material, broadcast speech, and Internet publications can be expected to bring further curbs on what types of communication are allowed (Jackson, 1981). Yet as surely as judicial tests of religious media power can be expected in the next century, so too can greater diversities of that media. This should not be surprising, for the history of Western media has been one in which the greater the ease of media access has become, the wider has become the diversity of media language, with these languages growing up as a kind of insulation around sociopolitical and sociocultural systems (Altschull, 1984, p. 4).

The challenge, then, will be the ways media adapt themselves to fundamentalisms within American religions of all kinds, or how fundamentalists create and distribute media. It is a challenge that was inevitable, and related in part to the very public nature of fundamentalism at the end of the twentieth century. Much depends, of course, on how one defines fundamentalism. If it can be seen as any religious group's orthodoxy wrestling with modernity (Pinnock, 1990, p. 43), then, by reason of late twentieth-century American news values, fundamentalism will likely become, as one scholar put it, "a blue-chip stock in that massive industry of symbol production known as journalism" (Lawrence, 1989, p. 3). Accordingly, as the new century dawns we can expect to see media images of extremists blasting abortion clinics or hurling condoms into church aisles. They're likely to be seen on both the evening news and on newspaper front pages as long as gatekeepers of news make these actions points of high-profile coverage. It can also be expected in the religious media of fundamentalist groups whose theology laces destruction and bloodshed into their pursuit of social action, as seen in some strains of early twentieth-century Christian fundamentalism (Marsden, 1980, pp. 210–211), Islam (Lawrence, 1989, p. 217), and Zionism (Cuddihy, 1987, p. 34).

Christian journalists, caught between the impulse to inform believers and the desire to pursue evangelical purposes, could be caught in the middle of fights over ideology that come up in their coverage, as has been the case with Pat Robertson's Christian Broadcasting Network (CBN) (Rose & Schultze, 1993, pp. 415–416). Also in danger of cross-fire damage are college journalism programs seeking to prepare Christian journalists for both religious and secular media careers, a phenomenon noted by Schultze (1993, pp. 524–529) in comments about fundamentalist higher education generally. A key example of the phenomenon is the first-of-its-kind Regent University, founded in 1978 by Pat Robertson as CBN University, a graduate school in Virginia that includes a growing college of communications (pp. 513–519).

Can we look for moral courage in the pursuit of religious media? Perhaps. And if it appears, the democratic experiment could be the better for it. Though some might believe, along with Greenspahn (1987), that Americans "do not regard religion as important enough to fight for" (p. ix), it could, on the other hand, be expected that Americans will seek out media and practice that explores the distinctiveness of their faith within their sociopolitical culture—and be willing, at least in some cases, to sacrifice to do it. As this happens, tensions visible at the end of the twentieth century between religious groups, Jews against Christians, Muslims against Jews, and the like, can be expected to continue.

Where these tensions diminish, it will be as groups find ways of culturally blending their faith into the vast sea of American media expression. In this sense, assimilation, lamented by researchers of ethnic-minority media (Riggins, 1992, pp. 279–285), can be seen as part of a needed synergy within the democratic experiment (Moore, 1994, pp. 264–265). Those American believers fed up with the tensions of established religion and its rhetoric—in any context—can be expected to craft an ideology of their own, built on one of the thousands of media strands available in new media locations. Such could prove a challenge to traditional belief. Bellah (1987, pp. 217–222) cautions that perhaps the greatest threat American religion faces in the next century is that of radical privatization of religion—so much so that its collective aspects disappear.

JUDAISM

Jewish media in the United States, viewed from within Judaism, has been either nearly invisible or highly prominent within the American media landscape. This split image can be expected to continue into the next century as Judaism continues to redefine itself amid changing religious culture in the United States. Were it possible to describe Jewish media in one word (and to do so is risky), that word might be "fragmented" (Jais & Dobie, 1994, p. 174). Though Christian media warrant a similar descriptor, fragmentation of Jewish media stems from the unique variations in ways that American Jewish culture has either assimilated itself or stood apart from surrounding communities (Handlin, 1979, pp. 276–277).

Some of the ambivalence within conservative Jewish thought toward the place of media within Judaism has stemmed from whether popular media in the American sense is necessary to the pursuit of traditional Jewish faith. Silverman (1963, pp. 128–129) notes that media such as newspapers were not considered a cultural priority within conservative Jewish media until the Enlightenment, when the notion of Jewish commentary on current events and culture within and outside Jewish communities began to grow, and even then, quite slowly. Like American Christian media over the last century, much of the more mainstream orthodoxy within Jewish media emanated from the pens or under editorial approval of religious educational institutions, whether colleges, universities, or seminaries. This was still the case in the 1990s, with some of the more accessible and user-friendly Jewish Web sites connected with educational institutions.

It can be argued that framers of the U.S. Constitution's establishment clause protecting American religion had at least a side thought toward beliefs of those other than Christians. Jews were first granted religious toleration in 1740, in Philadelphia (Copeland, 1997, p. 27), and a marginal but persistent attention to media—tied to or paralleling attention to Jewish education—was growing through the next decades in cities as far flung as New York, Chicago, and Cincinnati. Jewish culture spreading across the continent tended, at least in some cases, to build bridges rather than walls amid socioreligious culture surrounding it. But it was rarely easy. Part of the story of Jewish faith practice in the United States is an unfortunate tendency among Christians to vilify Jews—too often in media—and urge their immersion into Christian cultural practice. Korelitz (1997, p. 75) argues that Jewish newspapers aimed at fighting both assimiliation and anti-Semitism as Judaism advanced into uncharted Western territories.

After 1914, a peak year in the growth of the foreign-language press, about 1,300 newspapers and periodicals were being published. Of that group, about 1,000 could be classified as newspapers, and about 140 were dailies, about one-third of them in German. Jewish newspapers in Yiddish comprised a well-read subset of this foreign-language press. Among these was the labor press, especially available in large cities. The New York *Vorwarts* or *Jewish Daily Forward* was established in 1897 by the Jewish Socialist Press Foundation. Yiddish newspapers, though prominent in the period between 1920 and 1960, were steadily replaced by English-language Jewish periodicals through the post–World War II era (Mott, 1947, p. 731).

Thus, by the 1990s media such as the *Chicago Jewish News* were among a host of Jewish publications across the nation serving not only subscribing and newsstand readers, but an increasing number of Internet followers (www.chijewishnews.com). *Chicago Jewish News,* a tabloid-format publication, looks like any of a number of religious weeklies, with feature articles, community announcements, obituaries, and classified advertising. What makes it distinctly Jewish is its cultural fare, such as Jerusalem travel tips, and its window on how Jewish communities view popular American culture. In mid-December 1998 the *Chicago Jewish News*'s cover story was a four-page review of Steven Spielberg's film, *Prince of Egypt* (Aaron & Shira, 1998). The review, titled "Moses at the Movies," touts the animated work as an important one, telling "the story of our slavery in and exodus from Egypt" (p. 18). The write-up includes seven still frames from the film, along with mug shots of Dreamworks cofounder Jeffrey Katzenberg and the film's director, Brenda Chapman. "Let my people go see this movie," admonishes the reviewer (p.21). A sidebar article to the lengthy film review showcases Jewish characters in American films through 1998 (Pfefferman, 1998, p. 19).

Such contemporary interactions between Judaism and contemporary culture mark an attempt—suggested with some controversy by thinkers such as Martin Buber—that to counter alienation within Jewish life in America there must come a more culturally inclusive discourse based in existential beliefs within Judaism (Silberstein, 1989, pp. 72–74). Will we see animated kosher vegetables acting out Biblical stories for toddler audiences or Jewish-flavor music videos aimed at drawing teens into the religious fold? Not likely, say Jewish scholars, who argue that the agitators for better communications within Judaism—and likely the most visible outside Judaism—are known as restorationists, those who care deeply about preserving tradition within Judaism. This is not to say Judaism eschews all innovation. Jewish believers, bottom line, await the Messiah, and "the interim is very long." Cultural refinement of religious practice, including uses of media, is part of that interim (Heilman, 1987, pp. 117, 130).

ISLAM

Muslims, as communicators in the United States, can be seen as those seeking cultural "space," but, as was the case with Judaism, as having done so, through the 1990s, swimming upstream in an increasingly diverse media marketplace. Nonetheless, thanks to increasing dexterity with a globalized media and an increased willingness to make Islam "portable," Muslims in the United States have been able to create an increasingly firm sense of identity for themselves (Metcalf, 1996, p. 6). For the most part, American Muslims at the end of the twentieth century are professionals tied, in one way or another, into a global network of loyalties to religion, business, and family. These linkages, albeit firmly rooted in traditions of ritual (Abdul-Rauf, 1983, pp. 272–273), are far from fixed, and have tended to ebb and flow based on factors as varied as fluctuations in the economy to events in Muslim homelands (Metcalf, 1996, pp. 1–2).

Though followers of Islam in the United States at least attempted to build bridges with mainstream American culture in the late twentieth century, the exception—an outspoken one—has been the African-American population. Many of these believers, including those in prisons, have taken on an Arab identity in both language and custom in pursuit of Islam. An interesting phenomenon in the late twentieth century has been the rediscovery among some black Muslims of the life and example of Malcolm X, the media-prominent follower of Elijah Muhammed. Since the 1960s, black Muslims have enjoyed more media presence, ranging from coverage of Louis Farrakhan (Singh, 1997) to news-feature coverage of new mosques being built in various U.S. cities. Yet it can be argued that not all media coverage has been helpful. One observer noted in early 1999 that "as an American Jew, I see how the media often ill-treats the concerns of Muslim Americans, generally through basic misunderstanding of their culture" (Ravnitzky, e-mail, 1999). The comment, made by a law student familiar with American media practice, including investigative journalism, counseled journalists to better educate themselves in both Islam and Judaism. (He also urged Jews and Muslims to enter the field of journalism to add cultural insight to coverage of American religion.)

Muslims in America have suffered some of the same media vilification as Jews, most recently in the wake of tensions in the Persian Gulf (Mernissi, 1992, pp. 1–8). Yet American Muslims have been able nonetheless to create a media base from which to build cultural foundations for their faith communities. So much so that, mirroring cultural effects seen in Spielberg's popular films, Islamic films are now available that portray the purity of Muslim lifestyles in juxtaposition with intruding foreign culture.

Just as Judaism can be expected to seek a sense of relevance for the pursuit of religious media in the United States in the next century, so too will Islam. Though there is a sense in which Muslims have sought a purity of cultural tradition linked with Asian and African regional practices, relevance has been a function of at least portions of their media. Young Muslims are "fluent in the popular culture of North America," observes one researcher (Schubel, 1996, p. 195). Prominent, albeit controversial examples are the works of Salman Rushdie and editors of such trendy Muslim publications as *MuslimWise* and *Trend.* The latter, by playing with language in the difficult transliteration problem of Arabic to American English, have invited readers to experience Islam amid currents of competing popular culture. Some editors have even dispensed with the traditional Allah reference in favor of references to God, a more universally accepted term. The exception, since the 1970s, has been media of both traditional and African-American Muslims, who, as noted earlier, adamantly prefer Arabic names and terms in media language (Metcalf, 1996, pp. xvi–xvii).

HINDUISM, BUDDHISM, AND TAOISM

Hinduism, Buddhism, and Taoism have grown in America as immigrant populations have brought their faiths to this country, and as Americans—in the searching mode noted earlier—reach for elements of transcendent meaning deemed absent from traditional Christian faith practices. Alan Watts's spiritual pilgrimages into Buddhism, Zen, and Taoism can be seen as a prototype of this approach (Ballantyne, 1989, pp. 437–440). Shamanic pursuit of spirituality—the pursuit of trancelike ecstasy, a magic moment, separating soul from body—is likely to gain popularity amid the increasingly hectic pace of urban life as Americans lose touch with reality in a haze of visual and audio images that rival or surpass their daily realities (Albanese, 1993, pp. 337, 353–354).

It can be argued that as coming generations of Americans continue searching for strands of faith personal to their experiences, particularly as ethical questions persist regarding limits of materialism in Western culture, the questions about material existence raised in Hinduism, Buddhism, and Taoism about material reality will continue to draw inquirers. That American pop musicians and celebrities ranging from film stars to basketball coaches have pursued these religions suggests that a following for them not only has persisted but can be expected to continue. Any such continued pursuit of them, moreover, can be expected to be influenced by media technology as much as the more heavily populated religious movements in the United States, evidenced by the growing universe of religious Web sites and stubbornly constant varieties of published religious materials available in bookstores and libraries.

CONCLUSION

Religion and communication, inseparably linked by the presuppositions each make about audiences, meaning, and community, can be expected to be part of the future of American sociocultural change in the next century. What is less certain is what this intertwining will look and sound like in an age when communication faces perplexingly rapid change. The religious communication that will be the most enduring can be expected to be aimed at persons rather than institutions, and at transcendent meaning rather than the passing whims of media gatekeepers, regardless of the medium or technology used to craft the message.

NOTE

1. This study's foundations lie in theories of culture since the 1920s, dominant as a paradigm within anthropology, following the teachings of Franz Boas and Claude Levi-Strauss and symbolic or interpretative anthropologists. It is a perspective that has come under criticism by post-Geertzian anthropologists and poststructuralist cultural critics (see Geertz, 1973; Turner, 1967).

REFERENCES

Aaron, J., & Shira, G. (1998, December 8–24). Moses at the movies. *Chicago Jewish News*, pp. 18–21.

Abdul-Rauf, M. (1983). The future of the Islamic tradition in North America. In E. H. Waugh, Abu-Laban, A. Baha, & R. B. Qureshi (Eds.), *The Muslim community in North America* (pp. 272–273). Edmonton: University of Alberta Press.

Albanese, C. H. (1993). From new thought to new vision: The shamanic paradigm in contemporary spirituality. In L. I. Sweet (Ed.), *Communication and change in American religious history* (pp. 337, 353–354). Grand Rapids, MI: William B. Eerdmans.

Altschull, J. H. (1984). *Agents of power: The role of the news media in human affairs* (p. 4). New York: Longman.

Ballantyne, E. C. (1989). Alan Watts. In C. H. Lippy (Ed.), *Twentieth-century shapers of American popular religion* (pp. 437–440). Westport, CT: Greenwood Press.

Bellah, R. N. (1987). Competing visions of the role of religion in American society. In R. N. Bellah & F. E. Greenspahn (Eds.), *Uncivil religion: Interreligious hostility in America* (pp. 217–222). New York: Crossroad.

Boorstin, D. J. (1987). *The image: A guide to pseudo-events in America* (p. 5). New York: Atheneum/Macmillan.

Buddenbaum, J. M. (1998). *Reporting news about religion: An introduction for journalists* (pp. 19–20). Ames: Iowa State University Press.

Cameron, A. (1991). *Christianity and the rhetoric of empire: The development of Christian discourse.* Berkeley and Los Angeles: University of California Press.

Carpenter, J. A. (1984). From fundamentalism to the new evangelical coalition. In G. Marsden (Ed.), *Evangelicalism and modern America* (p. 3). Grand Rapids, MI: William B. Eerdmans.

Copeland, D. A. (1997). *Colonial American newspapers: Character and content* (p. 27). Newark: University of Delaware Press.

Cuddihy, J. M. (1987). The elephant and the angels; or, the incivil irritatingness of Jewish theodicy. In R. N. Bellah & F. E. Greenspahn (Eds.), *Uncivil religion: Interreligious hostility in America* (p. 34). New York: Crossroad.

Deedy, J. (1963). The Catholic press: The why and the wherefore. In M. Marty (Ed.), *Religious press in America* (1st ed., pp. 68–69). New York: Holt, Rinehart and Winston.

Diamond, S. (1989). *Spiritual warfare: The politics of the Christian right* (pp. 231–236). Boston: South End Press.

Elvy, P. (1987). *Buying time: The foundations of the electronic church.* Mystic, CT: Twenty-Third Publications.

Finke, R., & Stark, R. (1992). *The churching of America, 1776–1990: Winners and losers in our religious economy.* New Brunswick, NJ: Rutgers University Press.

Geertz, C. (1973). *The interpretation of cultures.* New York: Basic Books.

Gerson, M. J., & Garrett, M. (1998, May 4). A righteous indignation: James Dobson—psychologist, radio host, family values crusader—is set to topple the political establishment. *U.S. News & World Report, 124* (17), 20–26.

Greenspahn, F. E. (1987). Introduction. In R. N. Bellah & F. E. Greenspahn (Eds), *Uncivil religion: Interreligious hostility in America* (p. ix). New York: Crossroad.

Handlin, O. (1979). American Jewry. In E. Kedourie (Ed.), *The Jewish world: History and culture of the Jewish people* (pp. 276–277). New York: H. N. Abrams.

Heilman, S. C. (1987). Orthodox Jews: An open or closed group? *Uncivil Religion: Interreligious hostility in America* (pp. 117, 130). New York: Crossroad.

Hutchinson, J. A. (1963). *Language and faith: Studies in sign, symbol and meaning.* Philadelphia: Westminster Press.

Jackson, G. (1981, August 8–11). Electronic religion and the separation of church and state. Paper presented at the annual meeting of the Association for Education in Journalism, East Lansing, MI.

Jais, M., & Dobie, M. (1994). Report on Jewish culture. *Yale French Studies, 85*, 174–180.

Keyser, L., & Keyser, B. (1984). *Hollywood and the Catholic church: The image of Roman Catholicism in American movies*. Chicago: Loyola University Press.

Korelitz, S. (1997). The menorah idea: From religion to culture, from race to ethnicity. *American Jewish History, 85*, 75–100.

LaTourette, K. S. (1975). *A history of Christianity: Reformation to the present* (Vol. 2, rev. ed.). San Francisco: HarperCollins.

Lawrence, B. B. (1989). *Defenders of God: The fundamentalist revolt against the modern age*. Columbia: University of South Carolina Press.

Leonard, T. C. (1995). *News for all: America's coming of age with the press*. New York: Oxford University Press.

Longinow, M. A. (1996). *Mysterious and spontaneous power: Shaping of an evangelical social culture for revivalist higher education in Henry Clay Morrison's Pentecostal Herald, 1911–1942*. Unpublished doctoral dissertation, University of Kentucky.

Lulofs, R. S. (1993, April 19–23). *The culture of disbelief: Religious commitment as a neglected variable in social science research*. Paper presented at the annual meeting of the Central States Communication Association, Indianapolis, IN.

Marsden, G. M. (1980). *Fundamentalism and American culture: The shaping of twentieth century evangelicalism, 1870–1925*. New York: Oxford University Press.

Marty, M. E. (1984). *Pilgrims in their own land: 500 years of religion in America*. New York: Penguin Books.

Mernissi, F. (1992). *Islam and democracy: Fear of the modern world* (M. J. Lakeland, trans.). Reading, MA: Addison-Wesley.

Metcalf, B. D. (1996). Toward Islamic English: A note on transliteration. In B. D. Metcalf (Ed.), *Making Muslim space: North America and Europe* (pp. 1–2, 6). Berkeley and Los Angeles: University of California Press.

Miller, L. (1998, September 1). Ripe for stardom: Christian videos of cartoon cukes. *The Wall Street Journal*, p. B1.

Moore, R. L. (1994). *Selling God: American religion in the marketplace of culture*. New York: Oxford University Press.

Mott, F. L. (1947). *American journalism: A history of newspapers in the United States through 250 Years, 1690–1940*. New York: Macmillan.

Ong, W. J. (1988). *Orality and literacy: The technologizing of the word*. London: Routledge.

Pfefferman, N. (1998). In film: Jewish characters this year go beyond the usual movie image. Reprint from the *Los Angeles Jewish Journal* in the *Chicago Jewish News*, p. 19.

Pinnock, C. H. (1990). Defining American fundamentalism: A response. In N. J. Cohen (Ed.), *The fundamentalist phenomenon: A view from within, a response from without* (p. 43). Grand Rapids, MI: William B. Eerdmans.

Poster, M. (1995). *The second media age* (pp. 58–59). Cambridge: Polity Press.

Purves, A. C. (1998). *The web of text and the web of God: An essay on the third information transformation*. New York: Guilford Press.

Ravnitzky, M. (1999, February 5). Posting to listserv of the Investigative Reporters and Editors, Inc. [On-line]. Available: ire-l@lists.missouri.edu. Used by permission.

Reichley, A. J. (1985). *Religion in American public life* (pp. 4–8). Washington, DC: The Brookings Institution.

Riggins, S. H. (1992). *Ethnic minority media: An international perspective*. Newbury Park, CA: Sage.

Roof, W. C. (1994). *A generation of seekers: The spiritual journeys of the baby boom generation*. San Francisco: HarperCollins.

Rose, S., & Schultze, Q. (1993). The evangelical awakening in Guatemala: Fundamentalist impact on education and media. In *Fundamentalisms and society: Reclaiming the sciences, the family, and education* (pp. 415–416). Chicago: University of Chicago Press.

Schubel, V. J. (1996). Karbala as sacred space among North American Shi'a. In B. D. Metcalf (Ed.), *Making Muslim space: In North America and Europe* (p. 195). Berkeley and Los Angeles: University of California Press.

Schudson, M. (1992). *Watergate in American memory: How we remember, forget and reconstruct the past*. New York: Basic Books.

Schultze, Q. (1993). The two faces of fundamentalist higher education. In M. E. Marty & R. S. Appleby (Eds.), *Fundamentalisms and society: Reclaiming the sciences, the family and education* (pp. 524–529). Chicago: University of Chicago Press.

Silberstein, L. J. (1989). *Martin Buber's social and religious thought: Alienation and the quest for meaning*. New York: New York University Press.

Silk, M. (1998). *Unsecular media: Making news of religion in America*. Urbana: University of Illinois Press.

Silverman. D. W. (1963). The Jewish press: A quadrilingual phenomenon. In M. E. Marty (Ed.), *The religious press in America* (pp. 128–129). New York: Holt, Rinehart & Winston.

Singh, R. (1997). *The Farrakahn phenomenon*. Washington, DC: Georgetown University Press.

Sparkes, T. (1996). Generation Xers on morality and religion. In T. Gallagher (Ed.), *What's important to generation X* (p. 43). Reston, VA: Future of Newspapers Committee, American Society of Newspaper Editors.

Sweet, L. I. (1993). *Communication and change in American religious history* (pp. 1–3). Grand Rapids: William B. Eerdmans.

Tanner, K. (1997). *Theories of culture: A new agenda for theology*. Minneapolis: Fortress Press.

Turner, V. (1967). *The forest of symbols*. Ithaca, NY: Cornell University Press.

Wallace, J. M. (1991). *Liberal journalism and American education, 1914–1941*. New Brunswick, NJ: Rutgers University Press.

Waters, P. (1996). Gen Xers and community involvement. In T. Gallagher (Ed.), *What's important to Generation X* (p. 41). Reston, VA: Future of Newspapers Committee, American Society of Newspaper Editors.

Wuthnow, R. (1998). *The crisis in the churches: Spiritual malaise, fiscal woe*. New York: Oxford University Press.

13

Women

Carolyn M. Byerly

Talking about women and media means also talking about politics, economics, work, and other social institutions where matters of gender have surfaced over the years. Women and media questions are entertwined with women's broader daily experiences, their efforts to get their fair share and take part in their communities, and the barriers they have encountered in the process.

If public speech is the first criterion for democracy, then mass communication in general and the news media in particular must be understood as major variables in women's ability to assume meaningful roles in their societies. Conversely, inhibition to public speech through the news and other media, where the most serious agendas for social debate and public policy are set, must be understood as an underlying cause of women's secondary status. In examining women's relationship to the news media in the next quarter of a century, this chapter recognizes that women spent the last quarter of a century laying important theoretical, political, and practical groundwork to democratize media systems, to gain a public voice and presence, and thereby to advance in status and potential as public actors in their societies.

The work is not complete, of course. The media have changed in some respects, but in many others they remain stubborn and forbidding. Therefore, in taking stock of women's relationship to the news media today, we must also outline the obvious (and perhaps less obvious) directions that women might take to better utilize those media. "Utilize" may be translated to mean gain greater power and control, both within and over news organizations, so these will better serve women. While the major emphasis here is on women's relationship to the mainstream news media, alternative news sources, which give women maximum control over their own message making and increasingly serve to bridge feminist and mainstream audiences, will also be considered.

The discussion will necessarily be international in scope, even though I will give primary emphasis to women and news media issues and events in the United States, the intended geographic focus for this text.

Questions about women's right to communicate, and the corresponding concern of women's access to media, arose through feminist movements and forums over the last three decades, both in the United States and around the world. Therefore, "feminism" should be understood here in its broadest sense: the often loosely aligned, organized efforts by women to end gender-based oppression by redefining laws, policies, beliefs, and practices in order to bring greater value for femaleness and more power and status for women as a biological class. Although individual women and some groups still chafe at the term feminist, it has become so widely appropriated and embellished in its meaning by women around the world over the last quarter century that there is no more appropriate word to draw together the threads of women and media developments. Issues related to gender and communication are on the public and academic agendas today only because feminist women's movements put them there.

RESEARCH DEFINES GENDER PROBLEMS

Women's Right to Communicate

Research is indispensable to understanding women's evolving relationship to the media. Women have long understood that their advancement depended on being able to communicate, both among each other and with wider audiences. This has been demonstrated in women's establishment of their own media for around 250 years (Steiner 1992, p.121), as well as their various efforts to get their views and accomplishments into other news and literary media of their day.

The theoretical developments related to women's right to communicate have emerged more recently within the context of modern feminism, both in the popular realm and in the academy. Popular feminist writers and leaders in the 1960s, like Betty Friedan, decried the tendency of American television programs, magazines, and news of all kinds to either ignore women altogether or to represent them solely in traditional stereotypic roles of sex symbols and caretakers (e.g., wives and mothers).

When the National Organization for Women (NOW) formed in 1966, with Friedan as its first president, the group vowed to "protest and change the false image of women now prevalent in the mass media and in the texts, ceremonies, laws and practices of our major social institutions" (Beasley & Gibbons, 1993, p. 7). One of NOW's first activities was to challenge sex-segregated want ads in newspapers, but the organization went on to demonstrate its understanding that it would have to set news agendas if modern women's concerns were to surface. By the early 1970s, NOW succeeded in moving feminist activities into mainstream news with a well-orchestrated public-relations campaign for its state-by-state legislative program to reform rape, abortion, and other laws (Byerly, 1999, p. 389). Other feminist groups followed suit.

At the international level, women from diverse nations spoke through programs for action adopted in the general assemblies of three conferences during the U.N. Decade for Women, 1975 to 1985. Those documents, crafted by delegates in Mexico City (1975), Copenhagen (1980), and Nairobi (1985), contained sections on communication, which recognized that the mass media held the potential to both inhibit and promote women's status, depending on the extent of news and whether news actually reflected women's analyses, concerns, and political agendas (Byerly, 1995). The U.N. Decade for Women, which will be referred to periodically throughout this chapter, served as the springboard for research, training, and projects aimed at increasing women's participation in news and other media industries.

Patterns of Misrepresentation

U.S. academics presented their foundational critique of women's marginalization and misrepresentation in the mass media in a volume of collected essays and empirical studies edited by Tuchman, Daniels, and Benet in 1978. In her introductory essay to *Hearth and Home: Images of Women in the Mass Media*, Tuchman called women's absence from serious news and broadcast programming a form of "symbolic annihilation," a concept that has resonated in decades since, as women still strive to get coverage of their political and social-change activities, their ideas, and their individual achievements.

Tuchman (1978) went on to examine in more depth the reasons that news organizations systematically omitted women and feminist activities as one part of her definitive study of newsmaking, *Making News*. She found that traditional news criteria served to exclude most feminist groups and members from the news, because feminism and the issues associated with it had not emerged through public newsworthy events, but rather through consciousness raising and other small-scale meetings at which women talked without set agendas.

In addition, prototype feminist groups were also often leaderless (and therefore spokespersonless)—on purpose, in order to avoid replicating male-identified top-down structures. Moreover, early feminist groups were unaware of news-gathering processes and deadlines, and they often distrusted the occasional reporters who sought them out, wondering why reporters had so long ignored the things that represented and affected their daily lives. The reasons for the news media's failure to cover feminism, according to Tuchman's (1978) study, were complex.

Sexism in the Industries

Whereas Tuchman focused on explanations created through professional routines, others dismantled the news media's deeply sexist tendencies. The U.N. Decade for Women produced several important policy documents and subsequent United Nations Economic, Scientific, and Cultural Organization (UNESCO)–funded cross-cultural studies that revealed for the first time the universal nature of women's exclusion and sex-role stereotyping in the news, broadcast programming, and advertising. Ceulemans and Fauconnier (1979) conducted their comparative review of women's images in the media in every region of the world. The authors concluded that mass media industries were male-dominated, male-oriented, and male-biased structures that had perpetu-ated female stereotypes in every nation of the world at that time, except for the Scandinavian nations, where women enjoyed a greater degree of equality.

In that same time frame, Gallagher's (1981) *Unequal Opportunities: The Case of Women and the Media* contributed to the theoretical analysis of women's relationships to media by questioning the socioeconomic context within which women remained subordinated, and within which the media enterprises operated. The media, Gallagher said, help to extend women's lower status by limiting their visibility and voice, hiring fewer women as profes-sionals, and paying their female professionals less than male professionals. Gallagher conceptualized these problems as ones of resource distribution and access to media channels. She and other researchers of the time (see Mattelart, 1976, 1978) thus established the critical framework of gender and political economy of the media.

A more recent UNESCO (1987) study, *Women in Media Decision-Making: The Invisible Barriers*, documented patterns in women's media employment in the nations of India, Ecuador, Nigeria, Egypt, and Canada. The nations differed in geography, culture, history, and degree of development; still, the study revealed, women in their media were viewed with similar suspicion and less respect than men received within the same enterprises. In some cases, misogynist attitudes were held by both men and women, ingrained over time by the larger society and manifested in specific ways (i.e., both policies and behavior) on the job. Women's barriers to advancement remain largely invis-ible, even though they are measurable and effective in their discrimination against women, the study concluded.

Overarching Fact of Male Ownership

All the problems discussed so far occur within news industries that are nearly all commercially supported, profit-oriented enterprises that are increas-ingly transnational and conglomerate in their structures, and almost entirely male and Western in their ownership. The economic arrangements within the commercial media, of course, parallel those in the rest of U.S. society, which for half a century has been the dominant nation economically and politically. The capitalist system, with the United States its most powerful player, has become ever global in its reach since the 1970s. Communication industries of all kinds have been a central factor in U.S. (and other Western nations') success and staying power.

The United Nations Conference on Trade and Development (1995) reported that the global information revolution expanded the market for communication technology from $745 billion in 1985 to $2 trillion in 1995. In that same decade the companies that controlled the media technology—and the information and images that it transmitted—had also gone through an upheaval by way of mergers and buyouts that led to a dramatic concentration of ownership. Today, there are some half-dozen giant companies—nearly all of them based in Europe or North America—that control publishing houses, film production, recorded music, telecommunications, newspapers, and other mass media.

The conglomeration and globalization of the communication media have served to consolidate the wealth and power of white, male, and mostly Western men. This is not to say that there are not smaller, locally owned media companies, and a plethora of alternative print and electronic media. These do exist and, in many cases, are the sites at which women and other marginalized groups have made the most progress. However, women's ability to gain real power in terms of resources and control over policy will remain very limited until they find ways of making major interventions into what remains a male monopoly. Therefore, women have a stake in ferreting out the gender issues inherent in the media industries that hold sway over so much of the public discourse.

These are the downsides to women's relationship with the news media through the 1990s. What have been the upsides?

WOMEN'S PROGRESS IN MEDIA

While keeping a questioning, skeptical eye on the politics and economics of the media industries and those media's treatment of women through the years, we must also survey important gains. As Rapping (1994) argues so convincingly, we are not at the same place that we were in the 1960s, when feminism initially targeted the news and entertainment media for both neglecting and stereotyping women and women's organizations sought to end workplace discrimination in the media and elsewhere. Today, we can see advancement in employment, in the inclusion of feminist points of view in news content, and in the amount of coverage that women receive.

Within the Media Workforce

Progress within the United States can be seen in several areas, thanks largely to the hundreds of sex discrimination suits filed by female journalists in the

1970s. Congress passed Title VII of the Civil Rights Act of 1964 in 1972, extending discrimination in employment to cover sex. The law created the basis for lawsuits by women over hiring, pay, and promotion issues in the next few years, and generally put employers on notice that they had to open their ranks to female journalists. Seeing the proverbial handwriting on the wall, newsrooms gradually adopted employment policies that gave female professionals greater workplace equity.

For this reason, women were able to advance slowly through the next two decades. Women made up only about 20 percent of the journalistic workforce in 1971; two decades later, that figure had increased to somewhere between 39 and 45 percent, depending on the source (Lafky, 1993). While few of those women hold decision-making positions, there is both anecdotal and empirical evidence to suggest that the feminist presence has generally helped to bring progressive thinking into newsroom policies and the content of news. In their survey of male and female journalists at eighteen top-circulating U.S. newspapers, Byerly and Warren (1996) found that the majority of their respondents considered themselves "feminists" and said they had worked for policy changes, news assignments, and storylines that reflected feminist principles, in some cases since the 1970s.

Female journalists also told the researchers of remobilizing flagging women's groups in many newsrooms over their outrage at the way their male editors had trivialized women's experiences in high-profile stories like those involving law professor Anita Hill's questioning by male members of Congress in 1991 over her allegations that she had been sexually harassed years earlier by her then-supervisor, Supreme Court nominee Clarence Thomas. Their goals included changing the content of news stories and editorials to better explain the effect of discrimination on women's lives.

In these same years there were also hopeful signs in the mainstream media elsewhere. For instance, in their comprehensive survey of approximately 3,500 Canadian male and female journalists, Robinson and Saint-Jean (1997) found that females represent 28 percent of those employed in newspapers and 37 percent of those employed in television news today. A majority (53%) of the female respondents said they hoped to hold a management position eventually, compared to only 37 percent of the men. Gallagher's (1995) comparison of females working in media professions at 239 print and broadcast media in forty-three nations showed that employment has risen unevenly for women, in spite of nearly three decades of global feminism.

Only two nations—Lithuania and Estonia—showed female media professionals on a fifty–fifty par with men. The nation reporting the lowest female employment was Pakistan at 3 percent, but also in the single digits were India at 4 percent, Bangladesh at 5 percent, and Japan at 8 percent. In other areas, women have advanced slightly through the years of feminism. In six Latin American nations, female media professionals averaged 25 percent; in Central and Eastern Europe, 45 percent; in the Nordic States, 41 percent; in Western Europe, 35 percent; and in the United States, 33 percent.

Gallagher (1995, p. 10) emphasizes that many of these jobs are part-time and insecure. Even more significant was her finding that women averaged only 12 percent of the decision-making roles in the media, a fact that underscores how little real control women have over the messages and images produced and disseminated. Advancing into supervisory gatekeeping posts must become a goal for women in future years.

Improved News Coverage

A successful feminist political and cultural movement in the larger U.S. society—one that managed to remain intact even through the conservative years of the 1980s—has helped to move women's experiences from the margin into the mainstream of news coverage. For example, most newsrooms today cover the issues and events associated with feminism—abortion debates, pay inequity, day care, access to health care, sexual harassment, battering, rape, incest—routinely and, in many cases, using a "feminist frame"; that is, the questions, perspectives, language, and sources that have emerged through the women's movement.

The amount and feminist orientation of such news varies from one newsroom to another, and women who are poor and nonwhite receive much less attention for some of their problems than middle-class white women, to be sure (see Marian Meyers's [1996] excellent study on news of wife battering in the Atlanta area for examples of how women of color and poor women are routinely ignored and misrepresented by major mainstream news media). Still, two decades of a noisy, effective feminist antiviolence movement has generally brought both more news and better news about sexual assault and domestic violence into print and broadcast news. Most news media today do not identify the victims of those assaults, who are primarily female. In addition, there is a greater likelihood that articles will contain more background about the nature and causes of battering, rape, stalking, and other forms of sexual and domestic violence and what police and other systems are doing to address it.

For example, in 1995, major daily newspapers, including *The Washington Post, Los Angeles Times*, and *Nashville Tennessean*, gave extensive coverage to the on- and off-the-field violence of football players, and the counseling programs that the National Football League (NFL) and National College Athletic Association (NCAA) developed to counsel male athletes who had been arrested or convicted for battering and sexually assaulting females. Questions about and programs to address football players' violent behavior followed O. J. Simpson's acquittal of charges that he had murdered his ex-wife Nicole Brown and her friend Ronald Goldman that same year. Brubaker's (1995a, 1995b, 1995c) companion pieces in *The Washington Post* presented a feminist perspective by emphasizing the players' responsibility for the violence and harm to victims; using victim, psychologist, and advocate interviews to help tell the story; and letting the data on players' arrest and conviction rates show the long-term patterns of violent behavior.

Many reporters today, both male and female, do a credible job of covering a wide range of discrimination and other gender issues raised by feminism. Though still uneven in both quantity and quality, stories featuring gender issues today are more likely than in previous years to occur within a feminist frame. Such a frame is accomplished, as in the Brubaker stories on football players' violence, by using feminist sources and the language and perspectives of feminism to develop the story. Date rape, domestic violence, sexual harassment, and a woman's right to choose abortion are feminist-created terms that reconceptualized gender relations and, in the process, became imbedded in our daily vocabularies (for a fuller discussion of feminism's enduring impact on news and popular culture, see Byerly 1999).

There is both anecdotal and empirical evidence that women's stronger presence in the media has helped to place these terms and the new social analyses they represented in greater circulation. U.S. journalists Mills (1997), Sanders and Rock (1988), and Gilliam (quoted in Mills, 1988) recount their own experiences getting coverage for women in the 1970s by pursuing storylines and sources suggested by the women's movement. Mills (1997) asserts, "Sometimes just having a woman strategically placed at the news hierarchy determines whether an entire set of stories is done and, once completed, prominently displayed" (p. 47). Such was the case when then-senior editor Patricia Gaston of the *Dallas Morning News* conceived and orchestrated what became a Pulitzer Prize–winning series on violence against women at her paper in 1993.

The stories, published in the weeks leading up to International Women's Day on March 8, examined battering, rape, wife burning, genital mutilation, and other forms of violence against women in nations around the world (*Dallas Morning News*, 1993). The international series raised questions about gender discrimination and oppression that feminists had formulated over two decades. Stories emphasized not just the problems but also ways that women in various nations were addressing them. Moreover, stories provided important background on the current global feminist campaign to make such acts violations of human rights laws.

Feminist presence in the newsroom has had its effect everywhere, particularly over time. Indian researchers Joseph and Sharma (1994) analyzed news from several Indian dailies over a ten-year period from 1979 to 1988 and found that the increase of women in newsrooms was accompanied by a decrease in what they called "sexist writing." By this they meant less emphasis on the sensational events involving women, such as dowry-related killings, and more on a wider range of issues raised by Indian feminists. They also noticed an increase in editorials explaining and supporting women's rights in these years, reflecting the number of women advancing into senior editorial-writing positions.

Innovations in Women's Alternative News Sources

Where mainstream news media carry feminist messages to wide, diverse audiences, women's own news and information sources help to connect smaller, more cohesive groups. At the end of the 1990s there were dozens—perhaps even hundreds—of feminist-oriented magazines published in diverse languages. U.S. audiences are familiar with the liberal feminist *Ms.* magazine that journalist Gloria Steinem founded in the early 1970s and that has gone through several transformations, including its present no-advertising format, as well as the more radical tabloid *off our backs*. Feminist news periodicals have also proliferated for a quarter of a century all over the world. The women's collective Isis, headquartered in Rome, began publishing its quarterly, *Isis-International*, in 1974. Today, the organization publishes a monthly newsletter, *Women Envision*, and another quarterly magazine, *Women in Action*. The Fempress organization, headquartered in Santiago, Chile, publishes its monthly news magazine, *Fempress/Mujer*, in Spanish for distribution throughout Latin America. Fempress also produces a weekly radio program of women's news, available on cassette. Across the world in Katmandu, Nepal, *Asimita* news magazine has been publishing women's news since 1988. Its two feminist editors recently initiated a second bimonthly publication, *Sachari*, for neoliterate and semiliterate rural women (Byerly, 2001).

In addition, the now well-established feminist news agency Women's Feature Service (WFS), headquartered in New Delhi, India, distributes hundreds of feature stories, editorials, and other information to mainstream and specialized print and broadcast media over the Internet and in regular mail each year. WFS began in 1978 with funding from UNESCO to increase the amount of news defined, gathered, and written by progressive women. Today WFS remains an important informational bridge, not only between feminist and mainstream publics, but also between audiences of developing and industrial nations. The agency's stories are written in the development-journalism format, which emphasizes issues and events within historical, political, and economic contexts. Women's issues are thereby set within a big picture (Byerly, 2001).

The 1990s witnessed a virtual explosion of women's on-line news sources. Most of the news magazines already mentioned have Web sites, making samples of their publications available to anyone with access to the World Wide Web. These can be located through Web sites like "Magazines and Newsletters on the Web" (www.library.wisc.edu/libraries/WomensStudies/mag), available through the University of Wisconsin Library system. The site provides links to *Agenda*, a South African feminist journal; *Analize*, a Romanian journal of feminist studies; *Ariadne Newsletter*, a women's studies resource from the Austrian National Library; *Adantis*, a women's studies journal from Nova Scotia, Canada; and *AVIVA*, an international monthly Web zine. The Women in Development Network (WIDNET, located at www.focusintl.com/rlaafriq.htm) provides links to news and information about women's progress in Africa. The San Francisco–based Institute for Global Communication's "Womensnet" page (www.igc.org/igc/issues/women/index.html) is a vast resource of links to feminist organizations and publications around the world on subjects like women and technology, violence, economics, activism, health, and women's studies.

FACING THE FUTURE

Signs of advancement must be read as only the partial truth they are and serve to inspire women to begin the next stage of activism rather than slow their efforts through self-congratulation. The years ahead hold enormous challenges for women if the mass media are to serve their communicative needs. Those who are educated and middle class in socioeconomic status, whether employed in the newsroom or the academy, can easily lose touch with masses of women at the bottom of our own and other societies who are still struggling to eat, feed their children, and otherwise survive. How can we help them, as well as ourselves, to speak publicly and articulate real problems, analyses, and solutions?

Understanding Women's Human Rights

Let's turn the last part of this discussion to areas where women might focus their attention and efforts in the years ahead if they are to find a better relationship to the media. The basic entitlements to speak publicly and to participate in one's society are set forth in the Universal Declaration of Human Rights, adopted by the United Nations General Assembly on December 10, 1948. Therefore, women's goals to improve their communication options in the years to come should logically revolve around this concept of democratic participation: the ability to have a bigger voice and meaningful roles in their communities and nations.

The following broadly stated goals suggest areas in which women working in small or large groups can develop achievable strategies toward these ends. However, the importance of working together in an organized effort cannot be stressed strongly enough. If the present situation is to improve at a greater pace than it has in the last twenty-five years, women will have to strengthen their present social-change organizations, develop new ones, and learn to work in coalitions with already established groups that may be willing to support their communication agendas.

Ways of Increasing Women's Media Power

Intervening in Male Ownership of Media Industries

How can women begin to challenge male economic power, particularly in the Western industrial nations where these media conglomerates are headquartered? Strategies might include (1) leveraging the resources to begin acquiring enough financial interest to gain a voice at the stockholders' tables, and (2) developing legislative agendas to dismantle the conglomerate industries into smaller enterprises. The strategy in both cases would be to increase women's power at the top of mainstream media organizations in order to oversee the development of policies and practices that would benefit women. Neither will be easy or quick in coming. The starting point, therefore, is a broader discussion of economic issues among women in their own periodicals and Web pages. Strategies must emerge from increased numbers of individual women taking stock of the gendered nature of economic structures and developing both small- and large-scale activities toward change.

Advancing Further Within Mainstream Industries

Sex discrimination is more difficult to fight these days in that it is practiced more subtly. Employers are more careful to put a clean legal face forward, to guard their public comments, and to document fairness in hiring and promotion decisions. But the data speak for themselves: Women are grossly underrepresented at decision-making levels of the news and other media industries. Feminist organizing in the newsroom, which has often included the active participation of progressive male allies, can create a climate in which much can be accomplished in advancing women into better news assignments and positions of responsibility. Appealing to unions to give higher priority to sex-discrimination issues is another approach to increase women's power in newsrooms. Though expensive, time consuming, and often frustrating, civil suits are also sometimes needed to get employers to respond to sexist practices. The victors in any formal challenge, however, must commit themselves to working for other women's advancement or they simply become part of the machinery of discrimination.

Increasing the Role of Women-Owned Alternative Media

All the signs point to an endless expansion of news sources for, about, and by women on the World Wide Web. Though these resources are available mainly to literate, middle-class women, they can serve as one important way to create both national and international dialogues, disseminate much-needed radical analyses of political and economic systems, and mobilize action campaigns like letter writing or public demonstrations. As we have seen, women in various nations are also turning their energies toward publications and audiovisual information sources for women of limited literacy as a way of making progressive, feminist ideas available to the widest range of socioeconomic and ethnic audiences. All such efforts, through women's own management, are needed in the years to come.

In addition, women's news organizations can forge important working relationships with both government and nongovernment women's organizations toward setting news agendas. One model for this can be found in the three-day invitational workshop on improving news coverage of women and religion convened by Women's Feature Service outside Amsterdam in September 1998. The all-women meeting included mainstream and alternative journalists; representatives from Christian, Jewish, Muslim, Bahai, and other faiths; and academics concerned with women and news. Participants had come from several African and European nations, the United States, and India.[1] The event served to raise problems of stereotypes in covering religious women (e.g., the icon of the shrouded Muslim woman), produced a number of informal agreements among participants to inform each other of their activities, and set the stage for several news projects by the journalists in attendance.

Using Women's Organizations to Set News Agendas

Special-purpose women's organizations hold the key to setting progressive news agendas on a regular basis. Just as the National Organization for Women used well-orchestrated public-relations campaigns to place feminist ideas into mainstream news in the 1970s, women's groups today can continue articulating women's concerns and analyses in the new millennium. There are many ways to accomplish this. Periodic news releases can place factual information about a group's members and issues before reporters. Press conferences featuring celebrity guests who are primed to make cogent statements on women's behalf can serve as news events. Establishing working relationships with savvy reporters who are open to being kept informed of issues, group plans, and events can lead to more regular coverage of women's groups.

Improving Journalism Education to Include
Gender, Race, and Class as Essential Components

News reporters get their first messages about what defines news and how controversial issues should be covered in their college journalism classes. Therefore, journalism-education programs should adopt multicultural curricula that incorporate gender, race, and class information as regular parts of their courses. This means that news-reporting courses would include how to question whether the criminal justice system is treating all citizens equally, whether women and men (and, by extension, those of varied races and socioeconomic status) experience health-care services the same way, why females are the usual victims of male violence, why and how women come to experience poverty at higher rates than male citizens, and so forth. Students should also be encouraged to balance their stories with female sources, including feminist leaders in local organizations, when appropriate. Both male and female journalism students should be equipped to do responsible, credible reporting on gender issues by the time they graduate.

CONCLUSION

The foregoing discussion has been part historical, part cookbook for action in its reflections on women's relationship to the media. The message to emerge is that the new millennium should hold few surprises for anyone in terms of gender issues in media industries. With persistence, women in the United States and other parts of the world where progress has been made could continue to make small gains in media employment and news stories told from progressive (feminist) perspectives. There is even greater hope in the promise of ever-expanding women-made news and information media, particularly those on the World Wide Web. But the challenges will also persist, defined by political and economic structures that drastically marginalize women, particularly in many developing nations.

The mainstream media industries—increasingly conglomerated in the hands of a few rich, Western white men—will probably never fully guarantee women's right to communicate on the public stage until women have more power over and within those industries. That probability suggests the need for intensive discussions, strategy formation, and mobilization for structural change among women of developed and developing nations through women's organizations and women-managed media. In the next millennium, then, women's democratic communicative activities must include helping women (and men who support them) to understand the larger political and economic environment within which the mainstream news and other media operate and thrive.

NOTE

1. WFS intended to convene a second, similar meeting in India at a later date for women in Asia and Latin America. This author attended as a facilitator in sessions for journalists and NGO leaders.

REFERENCES

Beasley, M. (1997). How can media coverage of women be improved? In P. Norris (Ed.), *Women, media and politics* (pp. 235–244). New York: Oxford University Press.

Beasley, M. H., & Gibbons, S. J. (1993). *Taking their place: A documentary history of women and journalism*. Washington, DC: American University Press, in cooperation with the Women's Institute for Freedom of the Press.

Brubaker, B. (1995a, November 13). NCAA intensifying educational effort. *The Washington Post*, p. A25.

Brubaker, B. (1995b, November 13). NFL teams support Perry despite past. *The Washington Post*, p. A24.

Brubaker, B. (1995c, November 13). Violence follows some in football off field. *The Washington Post*, pp. A1, A24.

Byerly, C. M. (1995). News, consciousness and social participation: The role of women's feature service in world news. In A. N. Valdivia (Ed.), *Feminism, multiculturalism, and the media: Global diversities* (pp. 105–122). Thousand Oaks, CA: Sage.

Byerly, C. M. (1999). News, feminism and the dialectics of gender relations. In M. Meyers (Ed.), *Mediated women: Representations in popular culture* (pp. 383–403). Cresskill, NJ: Hampton Press.

Byerly, C. M. (2000). Women's feature service, 1978 to present. In E. Burt (Ed.), *Historical dictionary of women's press organizations* (pp. 265–272). Westport, CT: Greenwood.

Byerly, C. M. (2001). Press: Feminist alternatives. In C. Kramarae & D. Spender (Eds.), *The Routledge international encyclopedia of women's studies.* New York: Routledge.

Byerly, C. M., & Warren, C. A. (1996). From margin to center: Organized protest in the newsroom. *Critical Studies in Mass Communication, 13* (1), 1–23.

Ceulemans, M., & Fauconnier, G. (1979). *Mass media: The image, role and social conditions of women* (Reports and Papers on Mass Communication, no. 84). Paris: UNESCO.

Dallas Morning News. (March 7–June 14, 1993). Violence against women: A question of human rights (series).

Flanders, L. (1997). *Real majority, media minority: The cost of sidelining women in reporting.* Monroe, ME: Common Courage Press.

Gallagher, M. (1981). *Unequal opportunities: The case of women and the media.* Paris: UNESCO.

Gallagher, M. (1995). *An unfinished story: Gender patterns in media employment* (Reports and Papers on Mass Communication, no. 110). Paris: UNESCO.

Joseph, A., & Sharma, K. (Eds.). (1994). *Whose news? The media and women's issues.* New Delhi, India: Sage.

Kielbowicz, R. B., & Scherer, C. (1986). The role of the press in the dynamics of social movements. *Social Movements, Conflicts and Change, 9,* 71–96.

Lafky, S. (1993). The progress of women and people of color in the U.S. journalistic workforce: A long, slow journey. In P. J. Creedon (Ed.), *Women and mass communication* (2d ed., pp. 87–103). Thousand Oaks, CA: Sage.

Mattelart, M. (1976). Chile: The feminine version of the coup d'etat. In J. Nash & S. I. Safa (Eds.), *Sex and class in Latin America.* New York: Praeger.

Mattelart, M. (1978). Reflections on modernity: A way of reading women's magazines. *Two Worlds, 1* (3), 5–13.

McChesney, R. W. (1999). The U.S. left and media politics. *Monthly Review, 50* (9), 32–41.

Meyers, M. (1996). *News coverage of violence against women: Engendering blame.* Thousand Oaks, CA: Sage.

Meyers, M. (1999). *Mediated women: Representations in popular culture.* Cresskill, NJ: Hampton Press.

Mills, K. (1988). *A place in the news: From the women's pages to the front pages.* New York: Columbia Journalism Press.

Mills, K. (1997). What difference do women journalists make? In P. Norris (Ed.), *Women, media and politics* (pp. 41–53). New York: Oxford University Press.

Norris, P. (Ed.). (1997). *Women, media and politics.* New York: Oxford University Press.

Rapping, E. (1994). *Media-tions: Forays into the culture and gender wars.* Boston: South End Press.

Robinson, G. J., & Saint-Jean, A. (1997, May). *Women's participation in the Canadian news media: Progress since the 1970s, summary of findings* (Report). Montreal, Quebec: McGill University; Sherbrooke, Quebec: Universite de Sherbrooke.

Sanders, M., & Rock, M. (1988). *Waiting for prime time: The women of television news*. New York: Harper & Row.

Steiner, L. (1992). The history and structure of women's alternative media. In L. Rakow (Ed.), *Women making meaning: New feminist directions in communication* (pp. 121–143). New York: Routledge.

Tuchman, G. (1978). *Making news: A study in the construction of reality*. New York: The Free Press.

Tuchman, G., Daniels, A., & Benet, K. (1978). *Hearth and home: Images of women in the mass media*. New York: Oxford University Press.

UNESCO. (1987). *Women in media decision-making: The invisible barriers*. Paris: UNESCO.

United Nations. (1995). *United Nations and the advancement of women, 1945–1995*. New York: United Nations.

United Nations Department for Policy Coordination and Sustainable Development (UNCTAD). (1995). *Women in a changing global economy: 1994 world survey on the role of women in development*. New York: UNCTAD.

Valdivia, A. N. (1995). Feminist media studies in a global setting: Beyond binary contradictions and into multicultural spectrums. In A. N. Valdivia (Ed.), *Feminism, multiculturalism and the media: Global diversities* (pp. 7–29). Thousand Oaks, CA: Sage.

14

Developing Nations

Bala A. Musa and Emeka J. Okoli

As the international community enters the twenty-first century, there is a general apprehension regarding the future of civilization. Prophetic voices of all shades have emerged to forecast their version of what the next millennium holds for humanity. Few people doubt the fact that society is going to experience a major paradigm shift in social, economic, and political systems. What is not certain is the nature of the change. However, some critical structures on the landscape of the new era are beginning to emerge. The purpose of this chapter is not to pontificate with absolute certitude the details of what the new holds. Instead, the goal is to use data currently available to create solid navigational tools for those concerned with the future of mass communication in the developing countries. Such information will be relevant to individuals and corporate planning in areas such as financial investment, public policy, diplomacy, and defense.

The focus of this analysis is the perceived state and role of the mass media in developing nations (also referred to as Third World) in the first quarter of the twenty-first century. To clarify the key terms, the "mass media" as used here means the system of information dissemination for reaching a large, diversified, anonymous, and widely scattered audience (Wilson, 1995). Although advancement in mass-communication science has significantly redefined the perceived characteristics of the audience, many of the traditional elements associated with the notion of the audience as a mass still hold true, especially in developing countries. The critical word is "media," which implies the channel or instrument of communication. Therefore, the term "mass media" as used in this discourse includes newspapers, magazines, books, radio, television, multimedia, the Internet, films, billboards, compact discs, and audio and video tapes.

Developing countries are the nonindustrialized countries of the Southern Hemisphere whose political economies are characterized by dictatorship, poverty, disease, illiteracy, and low standards of living. Most of these countries are in Africa, Asia, and Latin America. The developed countries, on the other hand, are mostly industrialized, democratic, modern societies whose citizens enjoy a high standard of living. Until lately, the primary distinguishing factor between developed and developing countries was per capita income.

Research has shown that the two-thirds of the world's population who live in the regions referred to as developing countries enjoy only 15 percent of the world's income (Melkote, 1991; Van Soet, 1978). This means that of the estimated 6 billion people on Earth, about 2 billion consume over 80 percent of the world's goods. The remaining 4 billion share less than 20 percent of goods and services. This imbalance in resource distribution is also reflected in the distribution of information technology, access to and control of information, and quality and direction of communication flow. This imbalance in global infrastructure defined the state of the mass media and other institutions in developing countries throughout the nineteenth century. It also has great implications for the future of the media in those parts of the world.

THIRD WORLD MEDIA SYSTEMS: PAST, PRESENT, AND FUTURE

Past Experiences

To some it may appear presumptuous, even preposterous, to attempt an analysis of the next quarter century when the features appear but faintly in the horizon. Sufficient tools and techniques abound in the research community that make such an exercise tenable. This chapter uses a historical-cultural approach to analyze trends in global media development and its implication for Third World media in the new century. Proper projections regarding the future must of necessity rest on known facts. Previous patterns do not always repeat themselves, but are reliable sources of information regarding the properties and behavior of the subject of study.

As Toffler (1980) suggests, the Western world is entering a "third wave" of civilization that is regarded as the Information Age. The characteristics of this era are different from the previous cultural waves, referred to as the agricultural and the industrial revolutions. Historically, the agricultural revolution lasted from 1000 B.C. to the 1800s. The period from the 1800s to the

1950s represents the heyday of the Industrial Revolution, while the information revolution marks the era from the 1960s onward. In each of these epochs in human civilization, wealth and power were defined differently. In the agricultural era, landownership was the source of wealth and influence. During the industrial revolution, money made the difference between the elite and the masses. In this newest age, access to and control of information is what distinguishes the haves and the have-nots (Mowlana, 1997; Castells, 1996).

In any of these eras, possession and control of these economic commodities gave individuals, nations, and groups power and influence over others. Changes from one form of economy to another were also reflected in the instruments of labor (technology) and labor relations (nature of work and compensation for work). The reality of some countries being developed and some underdeveloped (Rodney, 1980) underscores the point that the clock of cultural change ticks differently for different regions. The differentiation of regions into First World (North America and Western Europe), Second World (Eastern Europe and Southeast Asia), and Third World (Africa, Asia, Latin America, and the Caribbean) is an index of where those regions stand on the progress continuum.

The view of development that emerged after World War II was framed narrowly in terms of modernization. Capitalism and urbanization were the principal criteria for measuring progress. However, the traditional approach whereby national development was measured purely in terms of physical or economic growth has become obsolete (Casmir, 1991). Nevertheless, there are certain characteristics that distinguish the mass media in the developing world from those in other parts of the world. An appreciation of these characteristics is essential to a proper analysis of the future status and role of the media in Third World countries.

The media in any country reflect the sociopolitical and economic environment in which they exist (Siebert, Peterson, & Schramm, 1956; Schramm, 1964). Developed countries with an abundance of modern technology and resources are able to afford high-level technical equipment that gives their media the edge in a competitive environment. This is a function of the industrial revolution that separated Western cultures from the rest of the world. The mass media that consist of modern technology emerged from and promoted industrialization. Therefore, the developed countries have been better endowed with mass-media technology. The capacity of the people in the developed world to acquire, access, and utilize the media also accounts for the disparity in the availability and use of the mass media between the developed and the developing worlds. Speaking of information technology penetration in the society, Melody (1991) observed that over 80 percent of British households had access to a personal telephone, while the average for Third World countries ranged between 1 and 10 percent.

The disparity is even more acute when one looks at the distribution of the mass media. At the turn of the last decade in the twentieth century, the United

Nations noted that sub-Saharan Africa (which arguably is the least developed of the underdeveloped world), had fewer newspapers, magazines, radios, and television receiving sets, and new communication technologies than any other major groupings of nations (Boafo, 1991). According to these findings, sub-Saharan Africa, which is inhabited by 11 percent of the world's population, enjoys only 0.6 percent of the world's television receivers, 1.6 percent of the global circulation of daily newspapers, and 3.4 percent of radio receivers. The picture from the rest of the developing world is by no means significantly different.

This situation underscores the structural dimension of Third World economies. The Centre d'Etudes Prospectives et d'Information Internationales estimates that today the regional distribution of the world's production of goods and services is as follows (Castells, 1996, p. 110):

North America	23.4 percent
Western Europe	27.3 percent
Developed Asia	22.1 percent
Eastern Europe	17.6 percent
Other Asian Countries	4.9 percent
Latin America	3.0 percent
Africa and Middle East	1.7 percent

In other words, the developing countries will continue to produce less than 10 percent of the world's goods and services. The implication of this situation for mass-media distribution is that it highlights what others have termed "the heritage of dependency" (Oliveira, 1991, p. 200) or "dependent development" (Boafo, 1991, p. 103) in the manufacturing and consumption of information technology. This dependency occurs at various levels in the global communication system. At the level of hardware, Third World countries have generally relied on the industrialized nations for the supply of communication hardware.

While communication technologies developed in the industrialized world as part of their cultural and economic revolution, they were imported into Africa, Asia, Eastern Europe, Latin America, and the Caribbean Islands in the hope they would promote development. In other words, while the technology evolved as part of the industrial culture in the West, they were seen as agents of industrialization in the developing world (Katz & Weddell, 1978; Musa, 1997). Third World countries spend huge amounts of money in importing new communication technology from countries like the United States, Britain, Germany, and Japan. Many countries have incurred high foreign debts in the bid to acquire the latest communication technology. Mody and Borrego (1991) have attributed some of the inducement for Third World countries to import foreign communication technology to "pressure from domestic elite seeking newest technology to put them on a par with their New York counterparts, 'nationalist' interest groups pushing for disassociation from the world business system, foreign universities and philanthropic foundations urging the use of new technologies for education and development, and superpower propaganda agencies" (p. 152).

Usually, such technology seems to hold promise for advancement in education, economic growth, and other forms of social change. Many Third World leaders eager to bring about change in the standard of living for their people think that the new technologies hold the solutions to their problems. While there is no doubting the fact that communication technology brings about social change, there is great disparity in the kinds of change and influence these foreign technologies introduce. According to Boafo (1991), some apparent impacts of the importation of foreign technology on many Third World countries are increased debt and more dependency on developed nations.

Another characteristic of Third World media in the last century has been the inflow of software. Developing countries not only rely on industrialized nations for hardware, but also for media content. The developing countries rely heavily on the West (in particular North America) for the supply of news and entertainment programs, films, music, and videos, as well as books. The leading news agencies of the world are American or Western European. The near total dependence of the Caribbean media on North American cultural products is described by Lent (1991) as follows:

The dependency in technology and the resultant cultural domination not only persist, they have greatly magnified, to the extent that indigenous cultural forms are not acceptable to the region unless they have been North Americanized. In fact, foreign domination has reached a crisis point, with most efforts to avert the problem being too halting, too unsure and too minor in scope to seriously challenge the "tentacles" which CNN, cable TV, video, radio, film, coca-cola [sic] designer jeans and musical fads have wrapped around our cultures. (p. 66)

This graphic portrait of the domination of Caribbean media by U.S. cultural products is not limited to the islands. The picture fits all other parts of the developing world, with the probable exception of the Arab world, where foreign media content has been more strictly regulated. The one-way flow of information from the North (developed countries) to the South (developing countries) is a natural fallout of the imbalance in the concentration of information-production hardware between the two worlds. It is much cheaper to produce information and entertainment programs in the media-rich industrialized countries of the Northern Hemisphere and distribute them to the rest of the world than to produce them locally. Third World countries find the cost of producing programs locally prohibitive. Even when programs are produced locally, they do not compete favorably with imported ones (Lent, 1991).

In the 1970s, leaders of Third World nations mounted stiff protests against what they considered the qualitative and quantitative imbalance in the flow of communication between the developed North and the underdeveloped South. The interest groups, government and nongovernment, stated their cases on the platform of UNESCO. Their main slogan was a call for a New World Information and Communication Order (NWICO). Advocates of the new order criticized the industrialized nations for fostering a structural imbalance in the flow of international communication. They lamented the cultural domination of Third World countries by developed countries.

The call for a New World Information and Communication Order centered on the need to dismantle what was perceived as the yoke of cultural imperialism imposed on Third World countries. Critics of the existing international communication system blamed the industrialized nations for dumping Western media products on the developing world (Mowlana, 1997). The direction and quality of news flow was a central point of dispute in this debate. Third World countries complained that the Western media, which dominated the global news market, always portrayed the developing world in a negative light. They objected to the situation where news from Third World nations consisted only of coups, earthquakes, and wars.

In the effort to redress this distorted image of Third World countries in the global media, alternative regional and national news agencies were established to counterbalance the "negative" news about developing countries with "positive" news. Several agencies were born in this era, including the Non-Aligned News Agency (NANA), the Pan African News Agency (PANA), the Middle East News Agency (MENA), and hundreds of national news agencies (Merrill, 1995). Despite these bold attempts to break away from the hegemony of the big media, Third World countries have continued to depend on metropolitan nations for supply of information and information technology.

The other effect that economic deprivation had on mass-media development in Third World countries was low audience penetration. Several factors conspired to prevent the growth of true mass communication in the Third World. The print media required literacy and the electronic media were capital intensive. In regions with very low per capita income, the people could not afford newspapers and magazines. Television remained out of the reach of peasants. As Fortner (1995) states, while the elite basked in the wealth of excess information, the masses were being excommunicated from the information revolution. The low consumption capacity of Third World audiences has contributed to the underdevelopment of their media.

Other dimensions of Third World media during the twentieth century were the ownership and control patterns. While capitalist democracies favored private ownership and freedom of the press, the media in the developing world generally reflected the authoritarian philosophies of their governments. Until recently, the broadcast media in Africa were exclusively owned and controlled by the government. Media practitioners functioned as civil servants, and had to be loyal to the government. Freedom of expression and the view of the press as the "Fourth Estate" of the political realm were alien to them. The dominant philosophy of the press was the development-media theory. This view holds that the media exist to promote the government agenda of nation building. The media, therefore, must see themselves as allies of the government in the promotion of guided social change.

This meant that Third World media were not only constrained by lack of infrastructure, they were hampered by a hostile political atmosphere. Retrogressive laws and policies were employed to arrest, detain, and jail journalists who expressed opinions considered unfavorable toward the government. Time and again, media organizations were shut down and publications were banned from circulation or withdrawn from the newsstand. The Third World media functioned in an infertile environment where growth and progress were nearly impossible.

If the preceding picture leaves the reader with the impression that the introduction of the mass media into developing countries was a total failure, then only half the story has been told. While the media have not been as successful in developing countries as their counterparts in the developed nations, they have by no means been a total failure. Despite the limiting circumstances already highlighted, Third World media have made significant strides that deserve fair credit. The relative successes are discussed in the next section to set the tone for what the future might hold for the media in the first quarter of the twenty-first century.

Current Experience

Seers (1977) opines that in order to know whether a country is developing, one needs simply to pose questions as to what has been happening to unemployment, illiteracy, injustice, and poverty. Have they been rising or declining? While it is beyond the scope of this chapter to examine all these and other indices of development in Third World nations, a look at recent trends in their media industry can shed some light on what to expect of Third World media in 2025.

Privatization

The media in Third World countries are fast changing from predominantly public to private ownership patterns. This is a reflection of general economic and political trends. In the last decade of the twentieth century, many countries that were once ruled by military or civilian dictators embraced democratic forms of government. Critical in this direction have been the collapse of the Soviet Union and the spread of democracy and market economies throughout Eastern Europe. In Africa, Asia, and Latin America, elected governments are likewise fast replacing despotic regimes.

Privately owned media are becoming the norm in most societies. Individuals and organizations willing to establish their own media are given permission to do so. This was not the case just a few years ago. With the opening of the playing field to private investors and interests has come an avalanche of new participants. Local and foreign capital has been attracted into the media markets of developing countries.

Proliferation

The democratization of communication in many Third World countries has given rise to competition. Whereas in the past the monopoly mentality of government media stifled creativity on the part of journalists, competition has brought about a change of attitude. The availability of options has helped to improve the quality of media products, as well as increased access. The commercialization and privatization of the electronic media in particular have significantly increased the number of radio and television stations in many countries.

Professionalization

An attendant effect of media proliferation has been a trend toward higher professional standards. For decades, Third World media practitioners have been trained in the West or by experts from the West (Katz & Weddell, 1978). However, the political and cultural climate prevented the development of real professionalism among media practitioners. The most articulate, brilliant, and independent-minded of them were often persecuted in order to protect the ruling class from criticism. Regarding the Indian press, Rampal (1984) said that journalists expended much effort protecting their freedom to the detriment of primary journalistic functions. The wider latitude of freedom enjoyed by the media and the need to compete effectively in the new environment have forced the professional standards of journalists in Third World countries upward.

Participation

Trends in audience characteristics also reveal significant changes. There has been a gradual move toward audience demassification. This means the breaking up of social and cultural groups into smaller niches that are catered to by small rather than big media. Toffler (1980) describes demassification as a fundamental dimension of the information economy. McLuhan (1965) describes it as the process of retribalization created by the emergence of secondary "orality" (electronic communication).

For Third World audiences, the phenomenon of retribalization is very real. Occasioned by the global changes in post–Cold War international politics, many cultural groups are seeking identity in a form of ethnonationalism that is "parochial and centrifugal" (Tehranian, 1993, p. 194; Fortner, 1995; Musa, 1998). This has found expression in religious fundamentalism, xenophobia, ethnic wars, and racial tensions. Different kinds of "small media" have emerged to serve different interest groups. Sreberny-Mohammadi and Mohammadi (1997) state that "small media has [*sic*] become a popular rubric for various kinds of mediated alternatives to state-run broadcasting systems" (p. 221). They come in the form of community radio as found in Bolivia and Chile (Huesca, 1995), or the rebel radio in Bosnia, Burundi, and Rwanda. These are ways through which the media exclude as well as include various segments of the society.

Pirating

The metaphor of pirating is used here in a positive sense. It describes the situation whereby Third World countries are quickly jumping unto the bandwagon of new technologies without having to go through the rudimentary stages in the invention and use of those technologies. Examples include the use of satellite communication, cellular telephones, and multimedia technology. Just as in river piracy, Third World countries whose technologies lag far behind those of the industrialized world have the benefit of adopting these technologies no later than they are introduced in the information societies of North America and Western Europe. Many countries of Eastern Asia, such as Malaysia, Singapore, Hong Kong, and Taiwan, have capitalized on this advantage and leap-frogged into the information age to become competitive information economies. Will other Third World countries also experience this dramatic economic transformation, or will they delink into oblivion? This is the multi-billion-dollar question concerning Third World media in the twenty-first century.

Future Expectations

Between the present struggling state of Third World media industry and the promised land of twenty-first-century information society is the chasm of infrastructural (industrial) deprivation. Yet the new millennium holds out the promise of a global culture where the gap between the haves and the have-nots will be eliminated. Some see this as a real possibility; others think that only the information-rich countries of the West will survive the future. A look at the evidence for both sides will provide a balanced perspective.

The dawn of cybercommunication offers the opportunity for the creation of the global village. Former U.S. Vice President Al Gore, a champion for the information superhighway, argued that the system holds the solution to the disparity between rich and poor nations (Fortner, 1995). He propounded the theory that the Internet will bring communities to the same level of access to information in the information age. Many Third World countries are already taking advantage of this. Multinational corporations are able to conduct business via the Internet with partners in different parts of the world.

Third World media organizations are enjoying competitive access to the global database, thanks to the World Wide Web. This is certainly narrowing the gap between the information-rich and -poor nations in terms of access.

Another impact that modern communication technology is having on the flow of information in the developing world is that it has eliminated the stranglehold that governments had on the exchange of information. However, as in the case of Singapore and Malaysia, experience has also shown that technological advancement does not necessarily lead to social or political emancipation. While there is a proliferation of technology in these societies, cultural change in the direction of government deregulation and free exchange has been slow in coming.

Third World media currently stand at a crucial crossroads. They could immediately alight onto the train of technological innovation and be carried along, not caring whether they reach the desired destination, or they could make selective choices that will respond to their needs more readily than the demands of international businesses.

It seems that Third World media in the era of globalization stand to benefit from shared resources. The media in the developing world will be able to use the new resources in gathering information and disseminating it (Harper, 1998). People now have the opportunity to choose which media they patronize. Newspapers and magazines from the developing world now enjoy a global audience, as do the big media, thanks to the information superhighway.

The euphoria regarding the dawn of the information age, however, needs to be tempered by the lessons of the past. Just as some societies were left behind during the industrial wave, so also is the likelihood that not all groups and cultures will be prepared for the new dispensation. Gunkel and Gunkel (1997) caution,

The cyberspatial researchers who forecast and celebrate a utopian community that is "raceless, genderless, and classless" do so at the expense of those others who are already excluded from participating in this magnificent technocracy precisely because of their gender, race, and class [and, if we may add, nationality]. Far from resolving the crisis of the multicultural society, cyberspace could perpetuate and reinforce current systems of domination. (p. 131)

Research has shown that rather than reducing the gap between the information haves and have-nots, new communication technologies are widening it (Sinclair, Jacka, & Cunningham, 1996). Ndegwa (1989) observes that while the industrialized countries have continued to grow economically, many Third World countries have been experiencing economic stagnation if not decline. He sees the possibility of an "involuntary delinking" (p. 11) between the countries that will ride the spaceship into the heavenly realm of cyberexistence and the technological laggers of the Third World that will be glued to the reality of preindustrial technology.

Voluntarily or not, it is obvious that some people will be excluded from the information fare of the twenty-first century, Third World countries and third-class citizens of the First World alike. Fortner (1995) suggests, "Some people will be excluded by location or economic capability, some by the confusion of claim and counterclaim, or by the complexity of systems, and some because they choose not to partake of such technological marvels" (p. 149).

For instance, the introduction of HDTV poses a dilemma to developing countries that are struggling with rudimentary technology under the present system. Many of them cannot afford the cost of changing from the linear to the digital system. However, if they fail to change over to the new system, they stand the risk of delinking involuntarily. The option being offered to developing countries is to open their economies and communication industries to foreign investors. That is very tempting in that it offers the hope of enjoying a free ride in the new space technology.

The other area that Third World media will have to adapt to in the next millennium is the media-consumption habits of the audience. The traditional audience allegiance that most media enjoyed in the past is fast being eroded by globalization. The media, including Third World media, have to repackage their products to reach a new audience that is bred on a multimedia–interactive–visual communication system as opposed to a passive audience. They have to know that their audience, though local in a physical sense, function and think globally. Technology is not neutral. Changes in the mode of communication will certainly affect cultures and relationships. The interface between local and global culture will pose a challenge for Third World media practitioners. However, technological innovation must be sensitive to the pace of cultural change among the audience. Failure to do so will excommunicate the majority of the public.

CONCLUSION

The cultural reality of the twenty-first century is going to be different from that of the previous era. While technology is helping to create a global village, the life views of the different peoples are further fragmenting. The media in the Third World are faced with internal cultural and technological lag on one hand and international competition on the other. Many developing countries lack the resources to acquire and support the latest communication technology. However, economic necessity and popular taste compel them to invest in modern foreign hardware and software.

In the Information Age, the media in developing countries are faced with numerous possibilities and challenges. Many countries are taking advantage of new communication technologies that enable them to gain visibility and improve the quality of their products. For the media to survive in the era of globalization, they have to respond to the needs of their audience. They cannot afford to be independent. To do so will lead to delinking from the World

Wide Web that technology has woven around the globe. They must not remain dependent either. Such a posture will not serve the needs and national interests of their people. They have to seek interdependence regionally and internationally. The media and other institutions that want to survive in the new era will have to think globally and act locally. That is going to be the pattern of media consumption in the twenty-first century.

REFERENCES

Boafo, S.T.K. (1991). Communication technology and dependent development in sub-Saharan Africa. In G. Sussman & J. A. Lent (Eds.), *Transnational communications: Wiring the Third World* (pp. 103–124). Newbury Park, CA: Sage.

Casmir, F. L. (1991). *Communication in development.* Norwood, NJ: Ablex.

Castells, M. (1996). *The rise of the network society.* Malden, MA: Blackwell.

Fortner, R. S. (1995). Excommunication in the information society. *Critical Studies in Mass Communication, 12,* 133–154.

Gunkel, D. J., & Gunkel, A. H. (1997). Virtual geographies: The new worlds of cyberspace. *Critical Studies in Mass Communication, 14,* 123–137.

Harper, C. (1998). The emerging world of online journalism. In C. Harper & the Indiana Media Group (Eds.), *Journalism 2001* (pp. 227–233). Boulder, CO: CourseWise.

Huesca, R. (1995). A procedural view of participatory communication: Lessons from Bolivian tin miners' radio. *Media, Culture and Society, 17,* 101–119.

Katz, E., & Weddell, G. (1978). *Broadcasting in the Third World: Promise and performance.* New York: Macmillan.

Lent, J. A. (1991). The North American wave: Communication technology in the Caribbean. In G. Sussman & J. A. Lent (Eds.), *Transnational communications: Wiring the Third World* (pp. 66–102). Newbury Park, CA: Sage.

McLuhan, M. (1965). *Understanding media: The extensions of man.* New York: Signet Press.

Melkote, S. R. (1991). *Communication for development in the Third World: Theory and practice.* Newbury Park, CA: Sage.

Melody, W. H. (1991). The information society: The transnational economic context and its implications. In G. Sussman & J. A. Lent (Eds.), *Transnational communications: Wiring the Third World* (pp. 27–41). Newbury Park, CA: Sage.

Merrill, J. C. (Ed.). (1995). *Global journalism* (3d ed.). White Plains, NY: Longman.

Mody, B., & Borrego, J. (1991). Mexico's morelos satellite: Reacing for autonomy? In G. Sussman & J. A. Lent (Eds.), *Transnational communications: Wiring the Third World* (pp. 150–164). Newbury Park, CA: Sage.

Mowlana, H. (1997). *Global information and world communication* (2d ed.). Thousand Oaks, CA: Sage.

Musa, B. A. (1997). Uses and abuses of development media theory in sub-Saharan Africa: Critique of a quasi-descriptive/prescriptive theory. *Ecquid Novi: Journal for Journalism in Southern Africa, 18* (1), 132–147.

Musa, B. A. (1998). *Retribalization and conflict management in the new world disorder: The media, diplomacy and the framing of domestic implosions in Bosnia and Rwanda.* Unpublished doctoral dissertation, Regent University, Virginia Beach.

Ndegwa, P. (1989). National policies for balanced and sustainable development in the poor countries: How to avoid involuntary delinking. *Development: Journal of SID, 1*, 11–18.

Oliveira, O. S. (1991). Mass media, culture, and communication in Brazil: The heritage of dependency. In G. Sussman & J. A. Lent (Eds.), *Transnational communications: Wiring the Third World* (pp. 200–213). Newbury Park, CA: Sage.

Rampal, K. R. (1984). Adversary versus developmental journalism: Indian mass media at crossroads. *Gazette, 34*, 3–20.

Rodney, W. (1980). *How Europe underdeveloped Africa*. Washington, DC: Howard University Press.

Schramm, W. (1956). *Mass media and national development*. Stanford, CA: Stanford University Press.

Schramm, W. (1964). *Mass media and national development*. Stanford, CA: Stanford University Press.

Seers, D. (1977). The new meaning of development. *International Development Review, 19* (3), 2–7.

Siebert, F. S., Peterson, T., & Schramm, W. (1956). *Four theories of the press*. Urbana: University of Illinois Press.

Sinclair, J. (1996). Mexico, Brazil, and the Latin World. In J. Sinclair, E. Jacka, & S. Cunningham (Eds.), *New patterns in global television* (pp. 33–66). New York: Oxford University Press.

Sinclair, J., Jacka, E., & Cunningham, S. (Eds.). (1996). *New patterns in global television*. New York: Oxford University Press.

Sreberny-Mohammadi, A., & Mohammadi, A. (1997). Small media and revolutionary change: A new model. In A. Sreberny-Mohammadi, D. Winseck, J. McKenna, & O. Boyd-Barrett (Eds.), *Media in global context: A reader* (pp. 220–235). New York: Arnold.

Tehranian, M. (1992). Restructuring for peace: A global perspective. In K. Tehranian & M. Tehranian (Eds.), *Restructuring for world peace: On the threshold of the twenty-first century* (pp. 1–22). Creskill, NJ: Hampton Press.

Tehranian, M. (1993). Ethnic discourse and the new world dysorder: A communitarian perspective. In C. Roach (Ed.), *Communication and culture in war and peace* (pp. 192–215). Newbury Park, CA: Sage.

Toffler, A. (1980). *The third wave*. New York: Bantam.

Van Soet, J. (1978). *The start of international development cooperation in the United Nations 1945–1952*. Assen, The Netherlands: Van Gorcum Press.

Wilson, S. L. (1995). *Mass media/Mass culture* (3d ed.). New York: McGraw-Hill.

15

Developed Nations

Leara D. Rhodes

Black-and-white movies of the 1950s that portrayed the future for humans did so with monorails connecting cities, hovercrafts moving people, buildings made of chrome and glass, people wearing science-fiction uniforms, and technology as abundant and as easy to produce as the cardboard backdrops used in the films. This was the future according to Hollywood. The future was projected as an era ruled by technology; but the people, the events, the problems of the society were the same problems that existed in the 1950s. Problems driving the plot of the 1950 movies included overcrowded cities, crime, and medical crises. In the early movies people played with technology and had it solve their problems. Medical advances saved lives. Space stations provided homes for people on the overcrowded Earth. Criminals were hunted down and destroyed with ray guns. Early filmmakers' visions of the future started with the premise that the future begins in the present. Not much has changed. The future of mass communication begins now, in the present.

In forecasting how media may be in 2025, one needs only to look at the problems affecting humans in 1950. These same problems are affecting people in 1999. What is unique about today is that although the future is somewhat set in stone, with policies already in effect, people have three choices as to how they will embrace the future. People can allow technology to drive the future. They can rebel and be Luddites. Or they can reinvent the future and find creative ways to solve societal problems. The pause caused by the furor of the turning of the millennium allows these choices.

DEVELOPED NATIONS DEFINED

To examine the present state of the media and to determine the transitional period linking today's media with media of the year 2025, the discussion will be limited to developed nations and specifically to the United States. In fact, the term "developed" will be used only to place the United States in a world context. This limitation is necessary because of the tremendous differences in media systems, media infrastructures, and media advances among countries. The advances and policies of the other industrialized nations deserve their own chapters.

The term "developed" is used here to indicate a division of the world. The world can be divided by languages, religions, philosophies, economics, climate, water availability, and even politics. However, this discussion uses an economic determinant paired with philosophy to divide the world. Thus, developed means having the economic ability to create a highly industrialized society supported by a market-driven philosophy. Other terms associated with developed countries include GNP, education, and trade levels. Market-driven societies include the richest countries in the world: the United States, Japan, the United Kingdom, Canada, France, Italy, and Germany. These countries use media and media products to promote a capitalist market. These are the developed nations. Other countries are assigned the terms "less developed" and "developing." Whereas these terms imply that countries so designated have less-developed economic structures, the term also implies less-developed media infrastructures.

During the 1970s and 1980s, tensions escalated between those countries with developed media structures and those without. Debates on one-way flow, two-way flow, and free flow of information entered U.N. conferences. The New World Information and Communication Order (NWICO) debate culminated in the MacBride Report and the formation of the nonaligned countries. The problem, as articulated by the countries that did not want to be aligned with the developed nations' philosophies, was that information was dominated by the developed countries in a one-way flow, a North-to-South flow, a biased flow. The less-developed and developing countries wanted changes toward equality of information flows.

The question remains as to how much progress the less-developed and developing countries have made in creating parity with the developed countries in communication industries and media usage. The argument exists that the developed countries have had the ability to create communication infrastructures and industries without the inclusion of the less-developed countries, so why should the developed countries worry about less-developed and developing countries in relation to communication? The answer is buried under policies, trade agreements, and new technology and could be linked to the mature American market, which requires exportation in order to maintain itself, much less to grow.

PRESENT STATE OF THE MASS MEDIA

American media are a pervasive element of the global society. Through technology and lifestyle choices, media have exploded to fill the lives of people who can afford them and be desired by people who cannot. Mass communication is by design aimed at majorities or large minorities (Pierce, 1968, p. 197); this places mass communication in a position to be easily moved by box-office sales—the whim of the market.

In the 1990s, the market is huge. Communication industries control three-fourths of the world's trade. The market is global. CNN covers the world news. Reruns of the television show *Dallas* circle the globe. American-produced movies, CDs, and computer software are bootleg enterprises in China and Trinidad. The market is also limited in ownership. Moguls are buying media companies, thereby limiting ownership to seven or eight men. Transnational corporations are replacing the mom-and-pop media outlets of the 1980s. In addition, the new market technology, the Internet, and on-line publications are changing how people get information.

Developed nations use this huge, global, limited ownership with new technology markets to increase their economic advantage and maintain their market-driven philosophy. These developed nations view media as a commodity. However, as changes in our society take place, these changes directly influence media. Therefore, a way of looking at the changes that may be affecting the communication industry is to use Daniel Bell's futurist structure, outlined in his book *Toward the Year 2000* (1968b) and his much touted *The Coming of Post-Industrial Society* (1973). In these books, Bell suggests ways to look at the future through the sources of change in a society. Bell (1968a, p. 4) suggests that there are four sources of change in society: (1) technology, (2) diffusion of existing goods and privileges in society, (3) structural developments in society, and (4) the relationship of the United States with the rest of the world.

Without question, communication technology has been a source of change in our society. Each new invention creates other products and services. Before television, living rooms were designed for conversation and for reading. Since the introduction of television, living rooms have become arranged with the best view of the television set in mind. Technology now defines how humans organize work, play, and other life experiences. Many homes in developed nations have more than one television, VCR, music center, and radio. Technology changes have made it possible to listen to books and jog, to check the weather across the country from computers, and to telephone Singapore from automobiles in New York City traffic jams. Satellite hookups allowed veteran reporter Joseph Albright to file stories for Cox Newspapers while in war-torn Russia.

Advances in technology changed how frequently people received information, beginning with the telegraph and penny press. Radio and television made news delivery even faster and changed political debate, news, public opinion, and how wars were covered, starting with the war in Vietnam and then the Gulf War. The computer adds to these changes how fast people get information: hourly or instantly (Postman, 1992, p. 8). The summer Olympics in Australia had American newscasters complaining that with the results already on the Internet, the races lost their impact when broadcast.

Communication is dependent on technology to provide information faster, in larger quantities, and with more visual impact. Bell (1968a) suggests that technology opens up many possibilities of mastering nature and transforming resources, time, and space (p. 4). Bell predicts that intellectual technology such as simulations, model construction, linear programming, and research will be linked to computers and will become the new tools of decision making (p. 5). These advances in technology have developed and have become new tools for decision making, but they come with a cost. Mosco (1998) suggests that the commodification of labor has shifted the balance of power in conceptualization from labor to "managerially controlled technological systems" as it disemploys media workers as a part of its rationalizing design (p. 15). People have been replaced in the workforce with robots and automated systems. Twenty-four-hour radio shows are using phone services to answer call-in requests. The callers' questions and responses are dubbed onto tapes of a disc jockey who may be hundreds of miles away. The caller may have talked with a woman, but a male voice is heard on the air.

Technology has made communication easier with better technology. In 1999 there was a worldwide surplus of 850 million workers (Sussman & Lent, 1998, p. 1). The value placed on choosing technology over humans in the workplace stems from what is more efficient and what will garner the largest profits for the organization. Mass communication depends on the capitalist model of market-driven profits to dictate choices of labor: humans, technology, or both. Labor is also being moved outside the developed nation's boundaries. Communication technology has moved labor to developing countries. Computer, telecommunications, and electronic components for developed nation's markets are built in Hong Kong. Cartoon images for U.S. animation studios are produced in East Asia. Data entries for airlines, banks, and insurance companies are processed in the Caribbean (Sussman & Lent, 1998, p. 1).

A second source of change according to Bell (1968a), is "the diffusion of existing goods and privileges in society, whether they be tangible goods or social claims on the community" (p. 5). He suggests that this is the manifestation of Tocqueville's summation of American democracy: What the few has today, the many will demand tomorrow. Applying this change to communication, the field is crowding human lives. There are hundreds of new songs played daily on the radio. There are more and more channels being added to television programming. There are thousands of magazines being published for every niche imagined. There are hundreds of thousands of books being published. There are millions of users of the Internet. There is information, information, information.

With the abundance of information, I suggest that communication overload is increasing. Future shock is with us. Along with this increased overload is the potential for irrational outbursts in society. Violence on television and in the movies is often used by media critics as the reason kids are killing. Protests and political statements staged for the media to arouse public sympathy are standard operating procedures. People react differently when the cameras are rolling and when they are not. Televising the Gulf War and making it a media event led to reporters being nominated for television awards and not news awards.

Whereas diffusion may be viewed as a trickle-down effect, the gap is widening between the information rich and the information poor. People who can afford technology own VCRs, televisions, music centers, CD players, and computers. These owners have access to information technology and the power associated with it. The disparity between the information rich and the information poor is not limited to developing countries. Allowing for inflation, U.S. wages have fallen more than 20 percent in the last twenty-two years. Of eighteen- to twenty-four-year-old U.S. workers, 47 percent held full-time jobs that paid less than a poverty income in 1996. Income disparity is evident when the top 20 percent of all households earn 55 percent of all the money and the bottom 80 percent split the remaining 45 percent (Snyder, 1996, p. 8). Not to be pessimistic, history shows that another revolution, the Industrial Revolution, created high-value jobs and made the United States prosperous. However, this revolution took more than a century and resulted in terrible social costs.

Bell (1968a) then suggests that a third structural development in society offers a source of change. He suggests that a subtle structural change has been the transformation of the economy into a "postindustrial" society. The shift from a product to a service society has materialized in developed nations. American society is shifting into the information society. The dilemma is how the social order is defining itself. Frank (1968) proposed that "a social order that cannot reaffirm its aspirations, goals, values and also revise and reconstruct its institutions must succumb to increasing disorder and conflict or decline as the torch of human advance is taken over by new nations" (p. 184).

Structural developments in society in the 1990s include transnationalization of production as well as a new political geography. Imperialism by Britain, France, Belgium, and The Netherlands ended between 1950 and 1980. As a result of the independence of some countries and conflicts and alliances among others, new nation-states have been established. Along with this new geography is a movement of the people of the world into urban centers. These urban centers provide work, services, and entertainment. More than half the world's population lived in urban areas in 1990. Movement to the city is increasing so fast that while it took eight millennia for half the world's population to become urban, it will take less than eighty years for this process to be completed (Clark, 1998, p. 85). Urbanization is taking place as an indirect consequence of the impact of transnational corporate capitalism upon the economies of developing countries. The transnationalization of production involves the manufacture of global products with global brand names, which are assembled across the world from components made in a number of countries (Dicken, 1999; Dunning, 1992). The transnationalization of media industries includes data transfers over national borders and cultural imperialism through exportation of television programming, films, and music. The information society based in developed nations uses English in computer software development.

The fourth source of change in structural developments in society, according to Bell (1968a), is the relationship of the United States to the rest of the world. The United States has been referred to as the leader of the industrialized countries. This places the United States in a position of specifying how mass media should function. The American philosophy has been that freedom of the press is a necessity for democracies. Knowledge is considered a condition for public dialogue, debate, and adjudication. People need to be informed about socially relevant affairs. This knowledge, and its transmission by the mass media, is a fundamental public "institution" of democracy. The institution of a free press is one of the key institutions of a political society and is linked inextricably to the continuous maintenance of such a polity (Mickunas & Pilotta, 1998, pp. 168–169).

Besides advocating freedom of the press, the United States promotes a capitalist approach to media. American products and services are promoted globally. Denim jeans are the pants of choice. American movies, television, and music permeate other societies. The United States epitomizes the one-world concept or the Westernizing process. Dissemination of Western ideas, such as equality, human rights, democracy, freedom of expression, individual autonomy, and free enterprise, is part of what developed countries do (Hachten, 1992, p. 191). Modernization of the world through global dissemination of technical, scientific, economic, and social information and practices emanates from Western society.

In journalism, non-Western nations have adopted the equipment, practices, norms, ethical standards, and ideology of the Western press. Western mass media also have conditioned the world to use the media for entertainment and leisure. Western dominance guides decisions concerning spectrum and satellite orbit allocation as well as broadcast-program flows. These Western decisions preempt any autonomous cultural development. The United States produces 98 percent of its television programming and imports only 2 percent. Other countries are limiting American products. The United Kingdom limits imports of American programs to 14 percent. Developing countries use 80 to 90 percent American programming (Hachten, 1992). According to Bailie and Winseck (1997), "Mass communication fused with global capitalist ambition reintegrated Third World societies within an informal American empire" (p. ix).

Bell's (1968a) four sources of change in society as applied to communication place media in the present. Technology has changed the ways media are used and marketed. Diffusion of existing goods and privileges in society have increased the gap between the information rich and the information poor. Those who can afford computers have access to the communication superhighway and those who cannot afford computers do not have easy access. Structural developments in society can be illustrated through the major debates in the news about American jobs being lost as a result of outsourcing labor to developing countries. Yet Americans accept the fact that 98 percent of American programming is American based and export programming without recognizing the friction being created between U.S. exports and other countries, thus straining the relationship of the United States with the rest of world. These examples offer a view of media in the present and may offer predictions for the future.

TRANSITIONAL PERIOD: DOES IT EXIST?

Communication technology for the next twenty-five years will continue to change and grow. The digital revolution will enter homes and tie televisions to computers, telephones, alarms, lights, music systems, and offices. The Internet will provide linkages with data through new search engines. Diffusion of existing goods and privileges in society will mean that even fewer people may have communication products and services due to the widening of the information gap between the rich and the poor. Structural developments in society indicate the movement toward urbanization will continue.

The relationship of the United States to the rest of the world means more U.S. products and more tension between the United States and other nations concerning trade of communication products, information flows, and intellectual property rights. These topics will grow out of the continued need for the mature market system of the United States to seek outside markets if it wants to continue to grow. This growth is likely to continue, particularly in communication industries, since competition and profit margins are still the deciding features of a market-driven communication system and since world communication policy often originates in the United States.

Policies are in place that will determine the direction of media for the next twenty-five years. There is already in place a singular, integrated, telecommunications-linked world economic system in the developed world. Power relationships have not changed since the end of the Cold War. The developed nations were in power in 1967; they are in power in 1999. Transnational inequality between the developed nations and the developing nations is still a factor. Exploitation or cultural imperialism by the developed countries of the developing countries is still a debate. Issues in 2000 include regulatory reform, privatization, economic development, and democratization of communication.

There are worldwide debates on the status of the communication industry. The Global Information Infrastructure Project (GII) was created during the Clinton administration to discuss communication policy (Hamelink, 1996, p. 47). Japan and the European Union have also set up commissions to discuss communication policy. These developed countries, including the United States, expressed concerns over universal access to the information superhighway, protection of intellectual property rights, privacy issues, impact of the information society on jobs, social isolation caused by communication technology, and deregulation of telecommunication markets.

MASS MEDIA IN 2025

The future of mass communication begins in the present. If the communication policies in place do not change, and if transnational business and political elites continue in control, Hamelink (1983) will be correct: It will be business as usual. There will be few surprises or changes. However, the discussion should not end here. The three choices offered at the beginning of the discussion were (1) allowing technology to drive the future, (2) rebelling and becoming Luddites, or (3) reinventing the future by reconceptualizing technology to find creative ways to solve societal problems.

Can societal problems be solved based on technology? Can policies already in place be continued to protect the market-driven society? Is the care of sick people compatible with the profit motive? Is the replacement of workers to enable technology to produce higher profits a way to solve unemployment and urbanization issues? Dunkerley (1999) warns that it is a problem to "limit our vision and look at everything through the eyes of money—economic justification" (p. 131).

Technology (like science) is so often defined in opposition to "society." Can technology be reconceptualized to provoke a reappraisal of the concept of "social" (Grint & Woolgar, 1997, p. 4)? Prophets of the information age have asserted that to realize the economic benefits of the computer revolution it will be necessary for essentially all citizens to subject themselves to even greater external discipline in the form of rigorous academic skills, technical competencies, and flexible, collaborative workstyles (Snyder, 1996). According to the experts, it takes one to two generations (fifty to seventy years) to fully mature and assimilate the productive potential of a new technology. Snyder predicts that by 2010 to 2015 the United States will become a mature information-intensive economy and surpass the levels of general prosperity and upward mobility experienced during the 1950s and 1960s (p. 12). He suggests that Americans are in a recurring historic cycle:

We in America are reinventing our corporations, reinventing government, reinventing labor relations, reinventing health care and public education. We are reinventing all of our great institutions, and when we are all done, we will have reinvented America. The other industrial nations are beginning to reinvent themselves as well. Eventually, the whole world will be reinvented. (p. 13)

If the future of mass communication begins now, the time may be right to reinvent the future. There is enough of a pause with the beginning of the new millennium to ponder the choices between allowing technology to drive changes or adopting a bunker mentality.

REFERENCES

Bailie, M., & Winseck, D. (1997). *Democratizing communication? Comparative perspectives on information and power*. Cresskill, NJ: Hampton Press.

Bell, D. (1968a). The year 2000—The trajectory of an idea. In D. Bell (Ed.), *Toward the year 2000* (pp. 1–13). Boston: Houghton Mifflin.

Bell, D. (1968b). *Toward the year 2000*. Boston: Houghton Mifflin.

Bell, D. (1973). *The coming of post-industrial society: A venture in social forecasting*. New York: Basic Books.

Clark, D. (1998). Interdependent urbanization in an urban world: An historical overview. *Geographical Journal, 164* (1), 85–95.

Dicken, P. (1999). *Global shift: The internationalisation of economic activity*. London: Paul Chapman.

Dunkerley, M. (1999). *The jobless economy? Computer technology in the world of work*. Cambridge, UK: Polity Press.

Dunning, J. H. (1992). *Multinational enterprises and the global economy*. Reading, MA: Addison-Wesley.

Frank, L. K. (1968). The need for a new political theory. In D. Bell (Ed.), *Toward the year 2000* (pp. 177–184). Boston: Houghton Mifflin.

Grint, K., & Woolgar, S. (1997). *The machine at work: Technology, work and organization*. Cambridge, UK: Polity Press.

Hachten, W. A. (1992). *The world news prism: Changing media of international communication* (3d ed.). Ames: Iowa State University Press.

Hamelink, C. J. (1983). *Cultural autonomy in global communication: Planning national information policy*. New York: Longman.

Hamelink, C. J. (1996). *World communication: Disempowerment & self-empowerment*. Atlantic Highlands, NJ: Zed Books.

Mickunas, A., & Pilotta, J. J. (1998). *Technocracy vs. democracy: Issues on the politics of communication*. Cresskill, NJ: Hampton Press.

Mosco, V. (1998). Political economy, communication, and labor. In G. Sussman & J. A. Lent (Eds.), *Global productions: Labor in the making of the "information society"* (pp. 13–38). Cresskill, NJ: Hampton Press.

Pierce, J. R. (1968). Communication. In D. Bell (Ed.), *Toward the year 2000* (pp. 297–309). Boston: Houghton Mifflin.

Postman, N. (1992). *Technopoly: The surrender of culture to technology.* New York: Alfred A. Knopf.

Snyder, D. P. (1996). The revolution in the workplace: What's happening to our jobs? *Futurist, 30* (2), 8–13.

Sussman, G., & Lent, J. A. (1998). Global productions. In G. Sussman & J. A. Lent (Eds.), *Global productions: Labor in the making of the "information society"* (pp. 1–12). Cresskill, NJ: Hampton Press.

Selected Bibliography

Abrahamson, D. (1996). *Magazine-made America: The cultural transformation of the postwar periodical*. Creskill, NJ: Hampton Press.

Alten, S. R. (1996). *Audio in media/The recording studio*. Belmont, CA: Wadsworth.

Altschull, J. H. (1984). *Agents of power: The role of the news media in human affairs*. New York: Longman.

Bagdikian, B. H. (1997). *The media monopoly* (5th ed.). Boston: Beacon Press.

Bailie, M., & Winseck, D. (1997). *Democratizing communication? Comparative perspectives on information and power*. Creskill, NJ: Hampton Press.

Baran, S. J. (1999). *Introduction to mass communication: Media literacy and culture*. Mountain View, CA: Mayfield.

Barnouw, E. (1990). *Tube of plenty: The evolution of American television* (2d rev. ed.). New York: Oxford University Press.

Bartee, T. C. (Ed.). (1986). *Digital communication*. Indianapolis, IN: Howard W. Sams.

Bayley, E. R. (1981). *Joe McCarthy and the press*. Madison: University of Wisconsin Press.

Bell, D. (Ed.). (1968). *Toward the year 2000*. Boston: Houghton Mifflin.

Brack, R. K., & Kummerfeld, D. (1999). *Magazines*. New York: Magazine Publishers of America.

Buddenbaum, J. M. (1998). *Reporting news about religion: An introduction for journalists*. Ames: Iowa State University Press.

Cameron, A. (1991). *Christianity and the rhetoric of empire: The development of Christian discourse*. Berkeley and Los Angeles: University of California Press.

Casmir, F. L. (1991). *Communication in development*. Norwood, NJ: Ablex.

Click, J. W., & Baird, R. N. (1990). *The magazine industry: Magazine editing and production* (5th ed.). Dubuque, IA: Wm. C. Brown.

Creedon, P. J. (Ed.). (1993). *Women and mass communication* (2d ed.). Thousand Oaks, CA: Sage.

Crowley, D., & Heyer, P. (Eds.). (1995). *Communication in history: Technology, culture, society* (2d ed.). White Plains, NY: Longman.

Czitrom, D. (1982). *Media and the American mind: From Morse to McLuhan*. Chapel Hill: University of North Carolina Press.

Diamond, S. (1989). *Spiritual warfare: The politics of the Christian right*. Boston: South End Press.

Dicken, P. (1999). *Global shift: The internationalisation of economic activity*. London: Paul Chapman.

Dunkerley, M. (1999). *The jobless economy? Computer technology in the world of work*. Cambridge, UK: Polity Press.

Dunning, J. H. (1992). *Multinational enterprises and the global economy*. Reading, MA: Addison-Wesley.

Foerstel, H. N. (1998). *Banned in the media: A reference guide to censorship in the press, motion pictures, broadcasting, and the Internet*. Westport, CT: Greenwood Press.

Gates, W. H., III. (1996). *The road ahead*. New York: Penguin Books.

Gelatt, R. (1971). *The fabulous phonograph: From Edison to stereo*. New York: Appleton-Century.

Grant, A. E., & Meadows, J. H. (Eds.). (1998). *Communication technology update* (6th ed.). Boston: Focal Press.

Griffiths, S. (Ed.). (1999). *Predictions*. Oxford: Oxford University Press.

Grint, K., & Woolgar, S. (1997). *The machine at work: Technology, work and organization*. Cambridge, UK: Polity Press.

Hachten, W. A. (1992). *The world news prism: Changing media of international communication* (3d ed.). Ames: Iowa State University Press.

Hamelink, C. J. (1983). *Cultural autonomy in global communication: Planning national information policy*. New York: Longman.

Hamill, P. (1998). *News is a verb*. New York: Deirdre Enterprises.

Head, S., & Sterling, C. (1998). *Broadcasting in America: A survey of electronic media* (8th ed.). Boston: Houghton Mifflin.

Hertsgaard, M. (1988). *On bended knee: The press and the Reagan presidency*. New York: Farrar, Strauss, Giroux.

Huber, D., & Runstem, R. (1990). *Modern recording techniques*. Carmel, IN: Howard W. Sams.

Illich, I., & Sanders, B. (1989). *The alphabetization of the popular mind*. New York: Vintage Books.

Joseph, A., & Sharma, K. (Eds.). (1994). *Whose news? The media and women's issues*. New Delhi, India: Sage.

Katz, E., & Weddell, G. (1978). *Broadcasting in the Third World: Promise and performance*. New York: Macmillan.

Keating, A. B., & Hargitai, J. (1999). *The wired professor*. New York: New York University Press.

Knoke, W. (1996). *Bold new world*. New York: Kodansha America.

Lehmann-Haupt, H. (1951). *The book in America: A history of the making and selling of books in the United States* (2d ed.). New York: R. R. Bowker.

Lewis, P. (1961). *Educational television guidebook*. New York: McGraw-Hill.

Library of Congress. (1984). *Books in our future*. Washington, DC: Joint Committee on the Library, Congress of the United States.

Lyle, J., & McLeod, D. (1993). *Communication, media and change*. Mountain Field, CA: Mayfield.

Malone, J. (1997). *Predicting the future: From Jules Verne to Bill Gates*. New York: M. Evans and Company.

McLuhan, M. (1996). *Understanding media*. Cambridge: MIT Press.

Melkote, S. R. (1991). *Communication for development in the Third World: Theory and practice*. Newbury Park, CA: Sage.

Merrill, J. C. (Ed.). (1995). *Global journalism* (3d ed.). White Plains, NY: Longman.

Meyers, M. (1996). *News coverage of violence against women: Endangering blame*. Thousand Oaks, CA: Sage.

Meyers, M. (1999). *Mediated women: Representations in popular culture*. Cresskill, NJ: Hampton Press.

Meyrowitz, J. (1985). *No sense of place*. New York: Oxford University Press.

Mickunas, A., & Pilotta, J. J. (1998). *Technocracy vs. democracy: Issues on the politics of communication*. Cresskill, NJ: Hampton Press.

Miller, M. J., Vucetic, B., & Berry, L. (1993). *Satellite communication: Mobile and fixed services*. Norwell, MA: Kluwer Academic Publishers.

Mills, K. (1988). *A place in the news: From the women's pages to the front pages*. New York: Columbia Journalism Press.

Mott, F. L. (1938). *A history of American magazines* (Vols. 1–5). Cambridge: Harvard University Press.

Mott, F. L. (1947). *American journalism: A history of newspapers in the United States through 250 years, 1690–1940*. New York: Macmillan.

Mowlana, H. (1997). *Global information and world communication* (2d ed.). Thousand Oaks, CA: Sage.

Negroponte, N. (1995). *Being digital*. New York: Vintage Books.

Norris, P. (Ed.). (1997). *Women, media and politics*. New York: Oxford University Press.

Palloff, R. M., & Pratt, K. (1999). *Building learning communities in cyberspace*. San Francisco: Jossey-Bass.

Parsons, P. R., & Friedman, R. M. (1998). *The cable and satellite television industries*. Boston: Allyn & Bacon.

Peterson, T. (1964). *Magazines in the twentieth century*. Urbana: University of Illinois Press.

Postman, N. (1992). *Technopoly: The surrender of culture to technology*. New York: Alfred A. Knopf.

Rakow, L. (Ed.). *Women making meaning: New feminist directions in communication*. New York: Routledge.

Rapping, E. (1994). *Media-tions: Forays into the culture and gender wars*. Boston: South End Press.

Riggins, S. H. (1992). *Ethnic minority media: An international perspective*. Newbury Park, CA: Sage.

Schramm, W. (1956). *Mass media and national development*. Stanford, CA: Stanford University Press.

Schwartz, R. E. (1996). *Wireless communications in developing countries*. Boston: Artech House.

Seitel, F. (1998). *The practice of public relations* (7th ed.). Upper Saddle River, NJ: Prentice Hall.

Siebert, F. S., Peterson, T., & Schramm, W. (1956). *Four theories of the press*. Urbana: University of Illinois Press.

Silk, M. (1998). *Unsecular media: Making news of religion in America*. Urbana: University of Illinois Press.

Sinclair, J., Jacka, E., & Cunningham, S. (Eds.). (1996). *New patterns in global television*. New York: Oxford University Press.

Sussman, G., & Lent, J. A. (Eds.). (1998). *Global productions: Labor in the making of the "information society."* Cresskill, NJ: Hampton Press.

Tanner, K. (1997). *Theories of culture: A new agenda for theology*. Minneapolis: Fortress Press.

Tebbel, J. (1969). *The American magazine: A compact history*. New York: Hawthorne.

Tebbel, J. (1975–1981). *A history of book publishing in the United States* (Vols. 2–4). New York: R. R. Bowker.

Tebbel, J. (1987). *Between covers: The rise and transformation of book publishing in America*. New York: Oxford University Press.

Tebbel, J., & Zuckerman, M. E. (1991). *The magazine in America*. Oxford: Oxford University Press.

Thomas, E. K., & Carpenter, B. H. (1994). *Handbook on mass media in the United States*. Westport, CT: Greenwood Press.

Toffler, A. (1980). *The third wave*. New York: Bantam.

Valdivia, A. N. (Ed.). (1995). *Feminism, multiculturalism and the media: Global diversities*. Thousand Oaks, CA: Sage.

Vivian, J. (1997). *The media of mass communication* (4th ed.). Boston: Allyn & Bacon.

Von Braun, W., & Ordway, F. L. (1975). *History of rocketry & space travel* (3d rev. ed.). New York: Thomas Y. Crowell.

Walker, J., & Ferguson, D. (1998). *The broadcast television industry*. Needham Heights, MA: Allyn & Bacon.

Watkinson, J. (1994). *An introduction to digital audio*. London: Focal Press.

Wilcox, D., Ault, P., & Agee, W. (1995). *Public relations strategies and tactics*. New York: HarperCollins.

Willis, E. E., & Aldridge, H. B. (1992). *Television, cable, and radio: A communications approach*. Englewood Cliffs, NJ: Prentice Hall.

Willis, J. (1990). *Journalism: State of the art*. New York: Praeger.

Wilson, S. L. (1995). *Mass media/Mass culture* (3d ed.). New York: McGraw-Hill.

Wolseley, R. E. (1969). *Understanding magazines*. Ames: Iowa State University Press.

Wolseley, R. E. (1973). *The changing magazine: Trends in readership and management*. New York: Hastings House.

Wuthnow, R. (1998). *The crisis in the churches: Spiritual malaise, fiscal woe*. New York: Oxford University Press.

Index

About the Editors
and Contributors

Paula Briggs has been involved in a variety of media courses as an assistant professor at Norfolk State University. She has taught radio broadcasting for six years; her students constitute much of the staff of the campus FM station. Briggs has worked as a radio announcer in Missouri and Virginia.

Carolyn M. Byerly is an assistant professor of journalism and international communications at the Park School of Communication, Ithaca College. She is also active in community organizations involving democracy, human rights, and domestic violence.

O. Patricia Cambridge is an assistant professor at the E. W. Scripps School of Journalism at Ohio University, where she teaches public relations and mass-communication theory. She previously served as public information coordinator for Ohio University's public broadcasting service. In addition, she has served as music director for the Ministry of Education in Georgetown, Guyana.

Brown H. Carpenter has been a reporter and staff editor for the daily newspapers in Norfolk, Virginia, since 1966, and is currently the layout and wire editor for the business section of the *Virginian-Pilot*. In 1999 he served on the staff of the newspaper's prize-winning year-long millennium project. He is the coeditor of *Handbook on Mass Media in the United States* (Greenwood, 1994).

Steven J. Dick, who worked in broadcast television for eight years, is an assistant professor of radio–television at Southern Illinois University at Carbondale. He teaches a variety of media technology and policy courses and is the author of numerous articles.

Julie K. Henderson is currently an assistant professor at the University of Wisconsin–Oshkosh in the department of journalism. Prior to this she taught at North Dakota State University. In 1998 she was named an American Society of Newspapers Editors fellow, and in 1999 a Wisconsin state teaching fellow. She has earned nearly 100 awards for her writing and editing from the North Dakota Press Women, Wisconsin Press Women, and the National Federation of Press Women. In 1995 Henderson was accredited in public relations by the Public Relations Society of America.

Curtis R. Holsopple is an assistant professor of mass media arts at Hampton University, teaching courses in radio, television, and desktop publishing and managing the school's computer labs. Previously, Holsopple was director of communications at Eastern Mennonite University in Harrisonburg, Virginia. He has written several articles and two books on electronic communication and has extensive experience in broadcast engineering.

Robert M. Knight teaches journalism and English at Gettysburg College. As a freelance journalist, he has been a frequent contributor to *The Chicago Tribune* and its Sunday magazine, *The Christian Science Monitor*, Reuters, and *The Washington Post*. Knight taught journalism part time for thirteen years at Northwestern University's College and spent three years as an associate editor at the City News Bureau of Chicago. Knight is a former president of the Chicago Headline Club chapter of the Society of Professional Journalists and the author of *A Journalistic Approach to Good Writing: The Craft of Clarity*.

Michael Lescelius has worked as a freelance engineer at a wide variety of Chicago broadcast and audio facilities. He designed, built, and operates MisunderStudio, a professional multitrack recording studio in Murphysboro, Illinois. He teaches audio production in the radio–television and music department of Southern Illinois University in Carbondale.

Michael A. Longinow is associate professor and journalism program coordinator in the department of communication arts at Asbury College. He has been teaching since 1989, when he left daily newspaper reporting in Illinois and Georgia. Longinow advises an award-winning weekly newspaper and is active with the Associated Collegiate Press and College Media Advisers. He is the national vice president of the Association of Christian Collegiate Media. Longinow has been a teaching fellow with the Poynter Institute for Media Studies and a fellow with the American Society of Newspaper Editors' Institute for Journalism Excellence. He has written numerous magazine articles and has contributed to books on the Promisekeepers and on American journalism in the eighteenth and nineteenth centuries.

Randy E. Miller is an associate professor at the University of South Florida, where he works as head of the news-editorial sequence. Miller has been a sportswriter and columnist as well as a copy editor at several newspapers, including the *Waco Tribune Herald* and the *Tampa Tribune*. He has been an ASNE fellow, working as a copy editor at *Newsday*, and has been a Gannett Teaching fellow as well. Miller has also served as head of the Newspaper Division of AEJMC. He has published several short stories and is a member of the Science Fiction and Fantasy Writers Association and the Horror Writers Association.

Bala A. Musa is an assistant professor of communication at Northwestern College. He has taught in several universities in the United States and Nigeria. He has published several articles on communication and national development; media, diplomacy, and conflict management; religious communication; and managing Third World media.

Emeka J. Okoli is an associate professor in the department of mass communications and journalism at Norfolk State University. Okoli's research interests include mass media, transcultural leadership, development, and organizational dynamics.

Leara D. Rhodes, an assistant professor at the College of Journalism and Mass Communication at the University of Georgia in Athens, specializes in magazines and international communications. In 1990 Rhodes won a Fulbright Scholarship to Haiti. Her publications include research on magazine issues.

Randall Scott Sumpter is an assistant professor of journalism at Texas A&M University, where he teaches media history and newspaper editing. Sumpter has worked for several newspapers and magazines as both an editor and reporter. His research interest is the professional routines of late nineteenth-century reporters.

Erwin K. Thomas is a professor and coordinator of the graduate program in the department of mass communications and journalism at Norfolk State University. He has authored *Make Better Videos with Your Camcorder* and is the coeditor of *Handbook on Mass Media in the United States* (Greenwood, 1994). His research interests include audiences, social issues, and mass media's future.

George Thottam chairs the department of mass communication at Iona College. He spent five years as a newspaper reporter and has been a columnist for fifteen years. He is the author of four books. Thottam's research interests include the application of new media technologies to journalism.

Edward Turner is the station manager of WNSB-FM, a National Public Radio affiliate. Turner recently attended the African-American Public Radio Summit in Airie, Virginia, and the Broadcast Education/National Association of Broadcasters' convention in Las Vegas.